Praise for *Marriage from the Heart*

"Lois Kellerman is a true guru when it comes to matters of the heart. She's wise, practical, compassionate and also unafraid to talk about the tough and sometimes impossible side of marriage. In *Marriage from the Heart*, she and Nelly Bly have created an inspiring guide to making your marriage more interesting and healthy, your home a warmer place, your heart more open and forgiving. The book deals with serious issues without ever losing sight of our need for joyfulness and hope. No book has ever made me want to be a 'good wife' as badly as this one." —Lois Smith Brady, wedding reporter for
The New York Times Vows column

"This book is wonderful, direct, and absolutely grounded. Required reading for all couples before the marriage ceremony and an inspiring resource for the years that follow."
—Janet Luhrs, founder of the *Simple Living Journal* and author of *Simple Loving*

"A magnificent, groundbreaking book. It will appeal to both those wanting timely advice and those seeking timeless wisdom on intimate relationships and lifelong commitment. It will help not just individual couples but also a broad array of helping professionals who are looking for compassionate, values-based approaches to building partnership in the context of larger circles of care."
—Reverend Pat Hoertdoerfer, Unitarian Universalist minister and religious educator

"An original and potent set of tools for cultivating a flourishing union in unstable times. The authors take a refreshing spiritual and ethical perspective, bringing high ideals down to earth and recommend that readers 'pray with their feet.' A commitment to this process can strengthen a marriage as profoundly as any grand insights into the legacy of our own upbringing."
—Wendy Mogel, Ph.D., therapist and author of
The Blessing of a Skinned Knee

ABOUT THE AUTHORS

Lois Kellerman is a Leader in the Ethical Culture Society, a religious and educational organization dedicated to improving the quality of human relationships for over a century, and has counseled hundreds of couples. She now lives in Half Moon Bay, California.

Nelly Bly graduated with distinction in English, magna cum laude from Yale University. A former book reviewer for *Publishers Weekly*, Nelly is a freelance writer and editor. She lives in New York.

Marriage
from the
Heart

❧

Eight Commitments
of a Spiritually Fulfilling
Life Together

❧

Lois Kellerman
and Nelly Bly

❧

Penguin Compass

PENGUIN COMPASS
Published by the Penguin Group
Penguin Putnam Inc., 375 Hudson Street,
New York, New York 10014, U.S.A.
Penguin Books Ltd, 80 Strand, London WC2R 0RL, England
Penguin Books Australia Ltd, 250 Camberwell Road,
Camberwell, Victoria 3124, Australia
Penguin Books Canada Ltd, 10 Alcorn Avenue, Toronto,
Ontario, Canada M4V 3B2
Penguin Books India (P) Ltd, 11 Community Centre,
Panchsheel Park, New Delhi – 110 017, India
Penguin Books (N.Z.) Ltd, Cnr Rosedale and Airborne Roads,
Albany, Auckland, New Zealand
Penguin Books (South Africa) (Pty) Ltd, 24 Sturdee Avenue,
Rosebank, Johannesburg 2196, South Africa

Penguin Books Ltd, Registered Offices:
Harmondsworth, Middlesex, England

First published in the United States of America by Viking Compass,
a member of Penguin Putnam Inc. 2002
Published in Penguin Compass 2003

1 3 5 7 9 10 8 6 4 2

ISBN 0-670-03118-6 (hc.)
ISBN 0 14 21.9621 5 (pbk.)
CIP data available

Printed in the United States of America
Designed by Nancy Resnick   Set in Adobe Garamond

For Hal and Mike

Spirituality is consciousness of infinite interrelatedness.
—FELIX ADLER, FOUNDER OF ETHICAL CULTURE, 1908

Contents

Eight Commitments of
a Spiritually Fulfilling Life Together · *xi*

Introduction: Home in Each Other's Arms · *xiii*

Eight Commitments of
a Spiritually Fulfilling Life Together

❧

FIRST COMMITMENT
Centering: I will create a warm, loving home life and place
my marriage at its center.

SECOND COMMITMENT
Choosing: I will cultivate the discipline of choosing wisely.

THIRD COMMITMENT
Honoring: I will have reverence for my partner and myself.

FOURTH COMMITMENT
Caring: I will be a source of loving care for my partner,
setting my heart upon what matters most.

FIFTH COMMITMENT
Abiding: I will have faith, patiently persisting
through life's many changes.

SIXTH COMMITMENT
Repairing: I will work to mend what is broken
in my partner and myself.

SEVENTH COMMITMENT
Listening: I will stay open to new insight,
however unlikely the source.

EIGHTH COMMITMENT
Celebrating: I will celebrate spiritual values
with my partner and others.

It is not for the love of a husband that a husband is dear; but for love of
    the Soul in the husband that a husband is dear.
It is not for the love of a wife that a wife is dear; but for love of the Soul
    in the wife that a wife is dear.
It is not for the love of a child that a child is dear; but for love of the Soul
    in the child that a child is dear.
It is not for the love of all that all is dear; but for love of the Soul in all
    that all is dear.

—FROM THE BRIHAD-ARANYAKA UPANISHAD, C. 800–400 B.C.E.

Introduction

Home in Each Other's Arms

❦

Seeking the Soul in Each Other

Sometime ago Sarah and Jeff met me for counseling at the founding Ethical Culture Society building, a magnificent white stone landmark on New York's Central Park. Sarah explained to me how her relationship with Jeff had recently slackened. Now five years into their marriage, Sarah had experienced a stroke of doubt that had changed the way she looked at her husband: Though she had married a man she respected and loved, and who loved her as well, she feared she had not married her *soul* mate.

A conversation ensued that inspired me to write this book. In our talk Sarah said that although she had come from a loving home, her parents had too often taken cause with one another. She had always imagined that the household she made with Jeff would be a "new and improved" version of the one she'd grown up in. Somehow, though, the choices she'd made in recent years had led her astray from that dream. While she had a beautiful house and economic security, she felt she lacked something—laughter, sensuality, trust—the joyful spark that makes a marriage last.

Poor Jeff sat listening to all this. I looked into his and Sarah's eyes and saw what I see in too many couples that have come to me in recent years. There was a deep regret reflected there, a sense of great loss. In that moment I knew at once that they needed this book. And they were not alone.

That afternoon I told Sarah and Jeff that true love is a lot like ruby slippers and golden grails: If, at the end of the day, we find what we've been questing for, we usually have what's deep inside us to thank for it. In fact, our dearest dreams—and that includes passionate, lasting love—are not "somewhere out there," at the end of a rainbow. They're right inside us, just waiting to be found—in ourselves and in each other.

Sarah's willingness to come to counseling told me that she cared, and Jeff's love for her was as plain as the pain on his face. And so, though Sarah feared she had not found her soul mate, I knew better. I knew she could find the soul *in* her mate. It was only a matter of seeking it out.

Coming Home

I recently counseled a divorcing couple who—if only they'd come to me earlier—might have had a chance. Another couple fighting over custody could have avoided some real suffering. Except in the most dire of circumstances, working toward spiritual fulfillment in a marriage can help couples get through innumerable difficulties—miscommunication, mistrust, depression, infidelity, in-law conflicts, sexual dysfunction. Even if your problems are more difficult to pin down, enhancing the spiritual dimensions of your partnership can bring relief from that vague and debilitating sense that

Sarah felt, as though some indefinite but vital element were lacking in her marriage.

Because pastoral counseling is by design short term, it can be a challenge for me to convey in such a condensed forum the substantial understandings I've gleaned over the years. Many a time I've wished I had thirty hours instead of three with a couple I was counseling, so that I could provide them with a significant grounding instead of dealing ad hoc with their issues. I've wished there were one approachable resource I could offer them, one they could use as a place to start, a place to return, and a place to aim for—wherever they were at in their marriage. *Marriage from the Heart: Eight Commitments of a Spiritually Fulfilling Life Together* is that resource. I've been writing it in my heart for many years.

As an Ethical Culture Leader, I serve a group with an especially universal outlook. I've presided over hundreds of wedding ceremonies and have worked with couples at every stage of married life. What I find most striking is that regardless of their beliefs or backgrounds, all partners tend to want the same thing: to feel that they are safe, that they belong, in the arms of their beloved. One bride perhaps said it best when she told me, "When I met my fiancé, it felt like coming home—only to a better home than I'd ever known before."

What is a spiritually fulfilling marriage, exactly? For this bride it was a sense of homecoming. But the specific answer to this question is different for everyone. Its contours emerge from the testing fires of a life together that range from betrayal to "dry spells" to fiscal hard times. In a spiritually fulfilling marriage a couple's love relationship is at once deeply grounded and open-ended—a partnership in which growth and transformation, resiliency and healing, trust and joyful play are all not only possible but also features of daily life. In these relationships love and concern are the primary motivators, as opposed to convenience, social pressures, or emotional insecurity.

How can we tell if our union is a "marriage from the heart"? To be sure, there are signs—just-because gifts, jokes told through eye contact, or a quiet touch at exactly the right moment. In the end, when we have achieved a soulful, robust marriage—a spiritually fulfilling marriage—we just know it. It feels right, deep down. Partners in this healthy mode seem tenderly amazed by one another. They have an immense respect for one another and an instinctual sense of kindness. They are physically and emotionally intimate, trusting, and comfortable. And in some way they practice—consciously or unconsciously—the Eight Commitments of spiritual intimacy offered in this book every day of their lives.

What's good in your marriage comes from the promises that you've already kept—promises to honor each other, to laugh together, to stand by each other in good times and bad. The Eight Commitments of this book are intentional choices that will give your marriage further grounding, connection, and resiliency. In this book I will take you on an adventure in which you will discover that you are already doing many things right in your marriage. You will learn to depend upon the bedrock of each other's commitments—little and big, daily and lifelong. *Marriage from the Heart* is a guide to a place of warmth and unconditional love. It is a book about coming home.

My Community and Me

By the time I was fifteen, I had fallen out of my own childhood faith community. (I was raised a nice Protestant girl). When I grew up, I married the "enemy" (Hal was raised a nice Jewish boy). By then both of us had spiritually moved to "someplace else" we couldn't quite define. We worried that we would have to walk solo, religiously speaking. Then I came across this incredible group of people who based their faith on the human capacity and longing for goodness and shaped their evolving spiritual practices around the exploration of ethical conduct. In discovering this resource for my family, I stumbled across my life's work as well.

After some time I was invited to enter an intensive training program to become a professional Ethical Culture Leader, which is the equivalent of an ordained minister, rabbi, or priest. Ethical Culture has so far been one of the world's best-kept secrets. Founded during the free religious movement of the late 1800s, it is rooted in American Transcendentalism and in the profound ethical inquiry borne of Judaism. Ethical Culture draws strength from philosophy and from diverse world religions in pursuing the "golden thread of ethics" wherever it leads.

For more than twenty years now, I have served this high-spirited organization. This book is an outgrowth not just of my experiences working with couples and families but also of a fourteen-year action research project I led and managed. The project sought to identify the core commitments that had undergirded Ethical Culture's work from its founding in 1876 to today. With the help of lay and professional leadership at all levels of Ethical Society life, I developed a general version of the Eight Commitments that Nelly Bly and I later modified for this book. Since 1994 these Commitments have been integrated into the spiritual life of our organization. And as I have seen again and again, they have a special potency for love relationships.

"God Is What Happens Between People"

Traditional religious communities have their own rich languages to describe a fruitful marriage. These days, however, I find that couples are increasingly wary of the word "religion." Gary and Elise, whom I counseled several years ago, expressed a surprisingly common attitude toward faith. One day, while planning a baby-welcoming ceremony for their second child, Gary explained, "You know, we're not particularly religious."

To which Elise immediately added, "But we're very spiritual."

I have mused for some time about what Gary and Elise—and many others like them—conveyed to me with their express distinction between religion and spirituality. For increasing numbers of people, the prescriptive, culture-specific laws of established religions are no longer in tune with their inner sense of what they think of as the divine. In contrast, the word "spiritual" speaks to a flexible experience they can directly access. For such people, spirituality is a verb. It is what they lovingly *do* with their lives together.

An early Ethical Culture Leader, John Lovejoy Elliott, used to say something like this: "I've known good people who believe in God and good people who don't, but I've never known good people who didn't believe in people." This is just another way of looking at the fullest goodness we can imagine—whether we conceptualize that goodness as God or Spirit or chi or dharma or an Ethical Manifold or the social contract, or in any other way. Some of you may feel that God is a single personality, deity, or supernatural power; others may hold that God dwells deep within each of us or is a mysterious and pervasive ground of being. Still others may believe that the term "God" represents an outdated concept that in the wrong hands can actually do harm. Whatever your thoughts, they will have come out of your very specific experience. Honor them and listen respectfully to the differing beliefs of others. This very human conversation has been going on for a long time and will continue for a long while more.

Helping Gary and Elise to pin down a working definition for themselves, I remembered the one my son thought up when he was five: "God is what happens when we hug each other." Even children can understand the profundity of love in our lives. Not unlike my (now grown-up) son, Gary and Elise told me they thought "God" is what happens between people. This idea of a larger goodness, intrinsically linked to how we relate to one another, allows couples from quite different backgrounds to build a spiritually fulfilling life together—interacting with respect, affection, and the best of intentions.

Spirituality is a very personal thing. It can be a subtle hunch or a straightforward practice. It may be tucked up within another area of life, such as your political involvement, your artistic expression, or your family's togetherness. But whether you attend mass daily or have never once uttered what you would call a prayer, spirituality is *there* in you—a key animating element of your personality. Your spiritual life is a critical part of you, and nurturing it (whatever form it takes) promotes personal growth and allows you to become more fully yourself. In a meaningful, happy marriage we find fulfillment by supportively accompanying each other on that journey.

It goes without saying that romance is a personal thing, too. As life partners, married couples are uniquely suited to each other—one vibrant personality complementing another. If this is true, then no matter how seemingly different your two senses of spirituality may be, they should be compatible. An atheist and a devout

Catholic I know found love in a runner's club: Powering their bodies along miles of road, they shared a feeling of rightness and flow, and they didn't need words to describe this feeling to each other. Look to experiences like this that have affected both you and your partner deeply. They are the first clues in finding the treasure of your shared spiritual life.

Using This Book

The Eight Commitments described in this book—Centering, Choosing, Honoring, Caring, Abiding, Repairing, Listening, and Celebrating—are all equally valuable for the spiritual health of a marriage. Together they are tools you can begin to use today (this very day!), and you can keep enjoying their effects as your marriage evolves over time. I've seen the Commitments work in many ways: for deep healing, for inspiration during adversity, for day-to-day problem solving, or for regaining romance. The Commitments will work for many different temperaments, unique partnerships, individual circumstances, and phases of life. What's more, with the ideas of this book in hand you will be in a position to change the world around you even as you celebrate your own "marriage from the heart."

I won't tell you the Commitments are quick fixes, but I will tell you that *they will work for you.* This is so in part because you began mastering the art of commitment making a very long time ago. In this book you will explore how to tap in to a rich resource that you have always had—a lasting, shared desire for deeper connection.

Marriage
from the
Heart

Centering

❦

I will create a warm, loving home life and place
my marriage at its center.

It had been a perfect evening at home. The way Laura Larsen described it to me months later in my office, Erik, her husband of thirty-four years, had just sprawled out on the sofa next to her. She recalled how Mister, the mutt with one albino-blue eye, had circled around and around feline style before settling his old bones at her feet. Mister's silky fur warmed her bare toes as Laura bent down to rub his back.

Laura watched her husband reach over to the ceramic candy dish full of Tums on the side table. Enacting their nightly ritual, Erik took out two chalky tablets—one for his heartburn and one for her bones. He popped a tablet into his mouth and fed her the other himself. As Laura chewed, she put her hand on Erik's knee and took a deep, contented breath. The fire crackled in the fireplace as she watched Erik reach over to pull a volume of poetry off the nearby bookshelves. Feeling calm and centered, Laura was savoring this moment of delicious everyday harmony when the phone rang.

She rose from the sofa to pick it up. After several "uh-huhs" she hung up, crossed the room, and flopped down by a painted box. Its sloping black top featured golden fruits in a Grecian-style bowl with borders of intertwined flowers.

"It's getting cold over here without you," Erik complained.

"I'll be right back," Laura replied as she lifted the cover. When Laura and Erik had first seen the box in the back corner of a flea market, it had been empty save for the torn brown paper lining on the bottom and inner sides. And it was the emptiness that had drawn them most—the mystery of it. What had been in this box before they bought it? A worker's coveralls? A wedding dress? Tonight it was filled with treasured keepsakes, which Laura removed one by one, pulling off newspaper coverings and wadding up a few into balls for Mister to chase.

"Whenever you say 'I'll be right back,' I'm sure to be waiting at least an hour," Erik complained. "Who was that on the phone?" He added with a hint of disappointment, "I just found our poem for tonight."

"Oh, that was Josh," Laura said, referring to their grown son, who lived nearby with his fiancée, Maureen. Laura continued to remove wads of newspaper from the box. "They want something old," she went on, "for their wedding table. We're supposed to pick out an old object that we think represents the most important thing for them as a newly married couple to remember."

Laura reached deep inside the box and pulled out another object. "This is it!" she cried, lifting out a large, pale, chipped conch shell and pressing it to her ear. "Remember when Josh found this? I never wanted to leave that beach," Laura mused. "We had absolutely everything we needed to be happy right there."

Erik smiled. "I do remember. We still have everything, though—we've got everything we need to be happy right here in this room." He patted the sofa next to him and added with a boyish grin, "Now, plant yourself down here and read me my poem."

A Holding Place

Home is where one starts from. —T. S. ELIOT

Laura and Erik Larsen had a great marriage. It was not, however, rare or unusual compared to your marriage or mine. They had significant differences of personality, temperament, and upbringing; they'd been through plenty of ups and downs. What was it, then, that showed so clearly that they'd found the secret of deep, meaningful partnership? The first clue to answering this question can be found by looking at Laura and Erik on a regular day. Whatever trials and triumphs came their way at other times, on a regular day, they were *centered*.

Any given evening of theirs might turn up evidence of this fact. Their comfortable grounding in each other was reflected in the small details of their shared life: the easy gestures of affection, the teasing, and the playful tossing of newspaper for the dog to chase, the little rituals such as eating their antacids together or reading a poem aloud each night. The soft sofa, the bookshelves, the fireplace, and the chest of treasured memories are all further signs of the special comfort Laura and Erik created in their home life.

In today's dynamic and uncertain world it is more compelling than ever that we learn how to create this sense of home in our partnership. Erik and Laura's shared peace of mind is not just something we yearn for. We actually need it if we are to get through the inevitable challenges of marriage. What's more, without the secure grounding that centering provides, we cannot safely embark on the greater adventures of changing our marriage for the better and seeking spiritual fulfillment together.

Feeling centered in our union is, of course, a state of mind. Still, we need concrete reminders of this spiritual abode: symbols, mementos, and rituals both light-hearted and solemn to call us quickly back to that center of contentment and belonging that our marriage embodies at its best. Nurturing a warm, loving home life that sustains our partnership is a pleasant process that begins by clearing a space for ourselves and then having a good, appreciative look around. Afterward, we can make adjustments to this physical environment that will reverberate in spiritually relevant ways.

Centering is about making a place for ourselves in the world where we can both feel safe and supported. More than the simple task of "homemaking," it involves seeing our environment with new eyes, letting it calm the mind and soothe the soul. In this peaceful context it is only natural to see past the surfaces—past the fatigue and trials of the day, past the pet peeves and bursts of temper to the deep and caring person we've married. It becomes easier to maintain our equilibrium and to be caring even in the middle of crisis. In the process we will also learn how best to soothe one another—in fact, to become sanctuaries for each other, no matter where we are.

As you begin the journey of each new day, your home is your point of departure as well as the place to which you return to rest. In part, centering also concerns your *regaining* that sense of comfort and belonging in times of separation or discord. If you are going through hard times, the feeling of being centered is often one of the first things to go. But centering is an important part of beginning the renewal process. It can be a small start (like a fresh vase of flowers or new hand towels in the bathroom) or something requiring greater effort (such as pausing before making a bitter comeback or being sure to spend some time together even when you're not getting along).

The daily habits in a loving home life are so simple in the end. My husband likes to leave his shoes by his chair at night. Maybe he's messy or forgetful, or maybe it's just his way of reminding the room he'll be back. Anyhow, in the morning the same space becomes my meditation room, and those shoes used to throw me off. "I can't even control things in my sanctuary!" I used to mutter, ignoring the fact that part of the purpose of meditation is to gently let go. I would pick up the shoes, march over to his closet, and plunk them down. He didn't seem to get the message. After a while picking up his shoes became part of my setup procedure. Eventually I began to experience this little ritual as a small act of centering—calming, accommodating, and making way for the spiritual life.

Because two is the minimal number in the architecture of relationships, the challenge of centering in marriage involves more than you alone. It is about maintaining balance between your twin needs—including finding support and compromise even when your hearts say different things. A flexible, dynamic process, centering also works even as your needs and circumstances change over the years. It heightens the quality of the time you spend and the space you share, whatever stage your marriage is in.

Whether you are newlyweds or empty-nesters, lovebirds or wranglers, remember the secret that Laura Larsen recalled holding that conch shell up to her ear: To begin to find contentment together, realize that you already have what you need right here, right now. Ultimately, to set out, all you need is the two of you. There is good reason for this.

Whenever I perform a wedding, just before the big kiss, I send couples forth to the "dwelling place of each other's arms." For in marriage, as in life, we come home to one another. We'll look at many ways of thinking about "home" in this chapter—as house, as refuge, as quality time, holy ground, and movable feast. Underneath it all, remember that *you* are the holding place for your partner. You are *home* in each other's arms.

As the first of the Eight Commitments covered in this book, centering is our starting point, our home base—the heart of a widening spiral. It encourages us, first, to create meaning and comfort within our home and then, in a wider sense, within each other and out in the world. We know that the work of centering is done when our partnership itself has become our deepest holding place.

Holy Ground

Put off thy shoes from off thy feet, for the place whereon thou standest is holy ground. —EXODUS 3:5, KING JAMES BIBLE

At home, at the park, at an artist's studio, in bed, in the car—no matter where we are, I believe it is possible to create a sense of home and of sacred space, simply through our intentions. The founder of Ethical Culture, Felix Adler, wrote a maxim that appears (with slight variations in wording) in many Ethical Society meeting rooms: "The place where we meet to seek the highest is holy ground." What this means is that any place can become a holy place, as long as we bring our most cherished values to bear there. Wherever we go, the sacredness of the ground we walk will be determined by our intent.

As I think back to my husband's stray shoes in my meditation room, I realize that I intuitively transformed a small daily annoyance into creative accommodation and then into a meaningful, calming ritual that I relied upon. At every step I was led by intent—to honor my time alone, to honor my husband—even though the lovely result was one I stumbled upon. Using supportive intent and positive attention, it is possible to broaden our sense of what is holy, to see everyday actions as potentially very meaningful. Why should our home not qualify as sacred space? It is, after all, where we rest, gather, and celebrate, where love and comfort are given and received every day. In fact, it is for many of us the single most important physical space in our marriage, a place where layers and layers of meaning are attached to common things. It is a natural place to seek holy ground.

Perhaps it's difficult to see our household in this way because we simply were not taught to think of cleaning up after each other (and other such everyday acts) as a part of holiness. And yet the notion that every place we inhabit is potential holy ground is fundamental to building a spiritually fulfilling marriage. By breathing new understanding into our normal activities, we open the door to enhancing our partnership and our sense of the fullness of life.

In certain early North American native traditions, with nomads moving from place to place, rituals helped to define the spiritual purpose of the spaces they inhabited. After everyone worked to clear a space in the woods, they formed a circle. A respected elder would then sing special chants while burning incense in four directions—to the east, then south, then west, then north. This signified that the space would be in harmony with the natural environment, so that a nurturing of the spirit of the people could occur within.

A former Hindu neighbor of mine used to light incense to "clean" the air in his apartment in preparation for entering the inner sanctum of family life. Often when the sweet odor drifted up through my window, I stopped and thought about the deeper meanings of his family home and mine. I remember thinking at the time how so many of us have cut ourselves off from the spiritual purpose of space.

There are numerous ways to symbolically lay claim to the sacredness of your home. Mezuzahs on doorposts are miniature encased scriptural passages that Jewish families can touch upon entering as a reminder of God's presence there. A bound stone at the entry to a Japanese tea garden announces that you are about to encounter another, gentler, and more ordered world. A crucifix on a wall tells you that no matter how deep your suffering, you are never alone. These images are especially powerful because they have all sprung from shared hopes and dreams about how to find fulfillment together.

In the days immediately following the tragedy of September eleventh, American flags were draped on, in, and just outside of homes all over the country. These flags were eloquent statements of sorrow and solidarity, of patriotism, hope, and protest. Some households, with equal fervor, displayed peace symbols on placards. We each have our own particular set of values we broadcast to the world. Most important, we remind ourselves of our highest ideals each time we see those symbols in our home.

You can also use your imagination to create reminders that your home is holy ground in ways that are unconnected to cultural or religious traditions. Allison and Shane, a couple who built their own log cabin, did this by carving twin hearts into the stair rails. Others have uttered words of hope upon leaving: "May this refuge of ours be safe from harm today." You can keep the lights off at twilight while you watch the dark come in together. You can open all the windows and let the air outside blow through, imagining all the places that the air has traveled. Or you can invite friends and family over to bless the place with their laughter.

Stress or tension can make it difficult to use intent to create holy ground. And yet the tougher things get, the more we need its support. Creating holy ground is really about making sacred time—that is, time when connectedness is possible. Such moments bring us message of profound comfort that we must hear if we are to get by: *Today is but one day in a long life. Beauty is complicated. Suffering brings wisdom. You are loved.*

So how can we get these messages if pain or timing makes it hard to pause and listen? Here is where rituals—conventional or homemade, whimsical or grand—are especially useful. A steady hand on the sternum and two deep breaths, a cup of tea on the porch every morning, washing dishes together at night in the quiet that descends after dinner, a mental list of wishes to recite when going to bed . . . If these small rituals are regularly undertaken, we'll need less energy to adopt them when the stresses of daily life are bombarding us.

Sometimes we have to clear the way literally in order to get rid of the disorienting anxieties of our "small mind." Whether it's a weekly dusting or annual spring cleaning, most of us can easily get this procedure right, using vacuums and bottled cleansers. But we may neglect the important next steps. Try sitting in your home after you have cleaned it and playing some recorded music that allows you to reflect on the fact that this space is holding *you,* the essence of you, as well as those you love. Notice where the sun shines in and trace its path in your mind across the sky. Think of how this space warms you on cold days, and brings the breezes in when it is hot. You will be surprised to see that the peace this small act of appreciation brings to you will last far longer than the few minutes spent in contemplation.

Rituals that involve clearing a space are especially powerful for uncovering the holy ground of relationships. The effectiveness is linked, I think, to those moments of genius that occur as we daydream in the shower or just before we fall asleep. The armor of the day, designed to keep us focused and responsible, is set aside, and suddenly in the newly cleared space—free of petty anxieties, preconceptions, and clutter of all kinds—we find ourselves opened up to new possibilities and a deeper consciousness of the abiding values that most strengthen our partnership. Indeed, acts of centering make our relationship at once deeply grounded *and* open-ended—forging a partnership in which growth and transformation are possible.

Sanctuary

"It has long been an axiom of mine that the little things are infinitely the most important."

—SHERLOCK HOLMES,
  IN ARTHUR CONAN DOYLE'S "A CASE OF IDENTITY"

It is no coincidence that people entering libraries, chapels, and forest groves fall silent. Each of these places provides respite from the bustle of life. They call forth hushes. There are hushes, too, hidden in our everyday living space: late in the evening when the dishwasher's running, during the silence of a lazy winter afternoon, while our partner fills the teakettle and we get out the mugs. Every event of the day offers up its own humble sanctuary. It's not the things in themselves so much as the meanings we invest in them by our shared, respectful silence. This is the secret to creating household holiness.

Sanctuary begins with the physical house—the literal holding place of your union. But on a deeper level it is your home, a place to let your spirit rest and be renewed. A sanctuary is a holding place that feels safe enough from harm that you can turn to the important work of personal renewal and strengthening your relationship.

One couple with whom I talked after a speaking engagement discovered a useful exercise to help them plan their move to Canada. The problem was, their new house was much, much smaller than the one they were leaving. They undertook an imagination exercise to help them decide what to bring. In it, they envisioned their new home totally empty and then selected three items that would create a sense of sanctuary there: one thing that would help them feel physically safe, one that would make them calm and contented, and one that would encourage them to grow. The husband picked a favorite quilt to guard against the freezing winters, a neck massager to reduce tension, and a cello to stimulate the mind and heart. His wife picked a baby gate for their toddler, a box of bath salts, and a cherished letter of encouragement from an old college professor. These categories helped the couple to think about their possessions in a new way, they told me. Afterward they both felt that the exercise had helped them to see how few things they really needed to have a full sense of home.

We can intentionally bring things into our home to increase the feeling of sanctuary in it. For example, if plants or tea candles soothe you, do you have enough of them scattered about for this purpose? During our wedding ceremony several decades ago, Hal and I had friends ring little bells at various points just for the whimsy of it. Afterward we strung the bells together with a length of wool and hung them on our front door. For many years the sound of tinkling bells was the first thing to welcome us, our friends, and our family. They reminded us in a wonderful way that we were entering a safe space. And, actually, the first year of our marriage they protected us from robbery when every other apartment in our building was ransacked! Though that last effect had not been intended, it served nonetheless as a reminder that physical safety matters greatly wherever we call home . . . and that for some strange reason good things tend to happen to those who follow their playful notions.

Sanctuary is about both safety and comfort. To be a true refuge, your home life together should be designed in such a way that you can rest assured in the knowledge that your needs (for health, for security, for consideration, for time alone, for solace or inspiration) will be met. Is the air quality controlled? Is there a security system, sturdy locks? Can you walk down the hall without worrying about being yelled at?

The place we inhabit can be arranged to bring other forms of solace, too. We can take the phone off the hook during dinner, for example, to allow for uninterrupted conversation. We can ensure that the lights are calming, not harsh, or we can play music to give calm. Above all, though, our holding place must give us "growing room." A sanctuary that smothers becomes a cage instead of a place of liberation and renewal. A home ought to be a place not only to start from and to return to for solace but also a place where we are made fresh again to face the world.

We need renewal on an everyday basis. But a good sanctuary also provides repair in extra measure when things go wrong. Put phone numbers of loved ones on the refrigerator; fill the medicine chest with Band-Aids, tonics, and hot-water bottles; see to it that your young children know how to call 911. Make sure you have, in advance, whatever curative tools you think you'll need to get through it all—journals, herbal tea, hot chocolate, a box of tissues in every room.

Most likely you have these resources already and need only to appreciate them to reap more of their healing benefits. Long hot baths, for example, do much more for us than keep us clean. After a trip to Japan one couple I know set up a cedar soaking tub on their deck. They claim that it has since saved them all kinds of doctor bills as well as serving as a place to return for calm when the ills of the world hang heavy. In another case, a widow whose oldest son was killed by a drunk driver allowed herself to cry once a day for a year—but only in the shower. That way her younger children couldn't hear her and be frightened. The warm water mingled with her tears and gave her strong relief.

While you're looking at the symbolic function of the items that fill your home, consider, too, those items that need repair in themselves. Those chipped mugs that you got for your wedding ten years ago—do they speak to you of being well loved and much used or of dilapidation and neglect? That towel rack that's been dangling for several months—does it remind you of the higher priorities you've chosen or of an unwillingness to face what's broken in your home? Sometimes fixing these physical things goes a long way toward mending the overall health of your marriage. But simply noticing the need for repair is the first step in accomplishing it.

The home is both a physical aspect of our union and a natural forum for building, clarifying, and renovating our love relationship. The need for sanctuary is perennial. But the particularities of how we create it will change over time. One decade you may love cozy clutter and the next crave utter simplicity. Your preferences might switch from red to black to blue as time goes by. How you and your partner spend time together for renewal also changes. It may refresh you at the age of twenty to go dancing several times a week, but at sixty the very idea may exhaust you. After a boring day at your first job, intellectual conversation might revive your spirits, but once the job takes on greater complexity, you might prefer relaxing quietly together instead. The general rule is this: Never assume that what gave you sanctuary in your marriage yesterday will work just the same tomorrow. Centering—creating a warm, loving home life and keeping your marriage at its center—is not a static but a dynamic, cycling process.

Give and Take

And now good morrow to our waking souls,
Which watch not one another out of fear;
For love, all love of other sights controls,
And makes one little room, an everywhere. . . .
Let us possess our world, each hath one, and is one.

—JOHN DONNE, "THE GOOD MORROW"

Perhaps the most ironic truth about lifelong partnerships is that the best-bonded couples are made up of two distinct individuals who respect and support one another's differences. Marriage is not a merger of personalities but, like the circular symbol of yin and yang, is the balanced union of two complementary forces. This "one and one" of partnership makes an extra-resilient two.

Each partner brings a somewhat different viewpoint to any given situation. Mike hears the call of duty, while Nelly sees the importance of taking a healthy break. Together they are able to eat a restoring dinner *and* get things done. In marriage we have the advantage of two pairs of eyes to survey the scene, each noticing different aspects of a problem. If we can learn to harness this strength, our decisions and the foundation of the marriage itself are sounder. A marriage is strongest when it is able to achieve a *dynamic* balance, one that involves both give and take.

This balance requires creativity. Two artists I married who lived in a studio in New York's Greenwich Village improved their relationship significantly when they adjusted their apartment to allow for what they called "nooks of solitude." They built a sleeping loft, then put his-and-hers armchairs at opposite ends of the room. Next to the armchairs each had a rolltop desk and small folding screen. Then they came up with a creative time-sharing plan. He went out with friends every second Tuesday night, and she went out every other Wednesday evening, each alternately leaving the whole space for the other to roam. It is important to set aside physical space as well as pockets of time to indicate that both individuals in this marriage are separate, sovereign entities, whole unto themselves.

"Separate sovereignty" makes life easier because of our different personalities and different preferences. These disparities will be reflected by the many details of our daily living—in the arrangement of our belongings, in our social life and our spiritual practices, in how we prefer to discipline our children, and so on. Our differences won't go away, so they must be allowed free expression, or else they can become bottled up and turn into resentments. As we affirm our partnership in the daily rhythms of give and take, we begin to discover what it truly means to love one another for who we really are.

Couples need to find a way of continuously, actively balancing the two parts of their union to prevent it from falling into discord. But this does not mean meticulously measuring our "share" on a scale, as Bruce and Delia did toward the end of their marriage.

They usually like to tell acquaintances that they split up over a set of sheets. (Actually this was just the final skirmish in a long war.) Delia loved floral patterns and remembered fondly the pink roses on her coverlet in the room she occupied during her childhood years. Bruce was into black: black sheets, black pillowcases, black comforter. Battling over this, they managed a temporary truce. First and third weeks "hers," second and fourth weeks "his." When Delia claimed the fifth week as hers, Bruce packed his bedding and left. What Delia didn't discover until sometime later, when she met Bruce's sister for lunch, was that despite his objections, his mother had made him feel like a child by putting superhero sheets on Bruce's bed right through high school.

The problem in this case was that Delia and Bruce's solution was mechanical. Even if it *had* been followed more rigorously, it never touched upon the underlying issues and values that had caused the problem in the first place. We all have something that feels so important, we don't want to compromise. And that's okay. As many couples discover on their own, irrational responses are usually linked to larger issues. These triggers, and the issues behind them, don't get resolved until we begin to discover the deeper reasons behind such behavior. If love is our goal, rote approaches to home-building conflicts will ultimately fail. Couples need to plan in time to discuss what each partner needs and *why.* For it's not about the sheets—it's about the people under them.

Homemaking, like money, is wrapped up in meaning, and so it naturally raises issues all the time. This is especially true for newly-weds, who must discover each other's strengths and weaknesses, whims and pet peeves, and put it all together for the first time. The Larsens, for example, had particular difficulty with neatness issues at first. Erik's childhood room had an embroidered wall hanging that said in both English and German, "Cleanliness is next to Godliness." Laura, on the other hand, spent the first eight years of her life in a converted bus while her freethinking parents drove from rally to rally. For years she threw her barbecued-chicken bones in the woods and believed that "We Shall Overcome" was a lullaby. It took Erik and Laura a long time to create a harmonious balance between being loose and being organized.

Issues of neatness can actually erupt into civil wars if not properly addressed. But neatness is only one issue among a great many that can make it hard for couples to keep their daily home life mutually soothing and sustaining. How much money will you spend for the maintenance of your home, for example? How will you divvy up chores? Daily conflicts of preference—over food, television watching, pet care, or sleeping patterns—can be especially difficult for couples moving in together for the first time. As you get to know one another on the level of everyday living, you find that you must adjust to another's desires on a constant basis in order to work together as a couple over the long haul.

Nelly had always heard that the first year of marriage was a great challenge. A year after her wedding to Mike, however, she was delighted to see that some initial hard work of theirs had already paid off. "Mike and I had a much tougher time moving in together than we ever had being married," she told me. "It was the learning to compromise that was the real hard work." When searching together for their first house three years later, Nelly and Mike found they still wanted different things: Nelly wanted a charming, smaller place in the city; Mike wanted a large house with clean lines and open space, and he looked forward to a calmer life in the suburbs. To succeed, they learned to openly and honestly check in with each other, even when it was difficult. "Once," Mike told me, "I had to say to Nelly, 'You don't seem happy with this house idea, but I haven't heard a complaint. How do you really feel?'" Thanks to this emotional vigilance, they were eventually able to find a home that deeply suited them both: a big old Victorian immediately outside the city, with cozy rooms and a view of the river. In the end what made this solution possible was their commitment to express their desires clearly and to check in with each other whenever one of them was feeling ambivalent.

The give-and-take quality of scrupulous care in our partnership is especially critical in times of transition or disruption—when you move, when you change jobs, when children are born or go off to college. What criteria should be used to choose a new house? How will the "rules of the house" (dinnertime, bedtime, levels of neatness, use of spare rooms) change when guests come to stay, during vacations, holidays, snow days, or times of crisis? It's impossible to set the answers to these questions in advance, for the questions themselves are always changing. But a steady habit of loving compromise will make us increasingly comfortable with working together. Thus grounded in partnership, we find ourselves better prepared for the stimulating task of balancing our marriage on the high wire of the changing world.

Ritual Time

We must get back into relation, vivid and nourishing relation to the cosmos and the universe. The way is through daily ritual, and is an affair of the individual and the household, a ritual of dawn and noon and sunset, the ritual of the kindling fire and pouring water, the ritual of the first breath, and the last. —D. H. LAWRENCE

A centering sense of home is a general attitude as well as a style of daily living. It is expressed by the physical spaces in a couple's life— the photos of loving family, the planted balcony, the candles around the bathtub—but it can also be expressed in the *time* a couple spends, both separately and together, to foster a sense of peace in their lives. Ritual time helps couples to focus on their marriage both in and of itself and as it centers them in the larger world.

You have no doubt automatically created some Centering rituals: mowing the lawn or vacuuming on Saturdays, making love on Friday afternoons, catching fireflies with your children on summer evenings. Each one of these repeated actions has the potential to bring you calmly back to your inner selves and to each other. When such events are absent, we often feel a sense of disconnection and displacement. Everyday rituals give us grounding, calling us back to the familiar, the comfortable, the ordered.

Time spent in quiet contemplation is a deeply centering activity and an important part of any spiritual life, be it a daily occurrence or one reserved for special days like the Sabbath. It may be called personal reflection, meditation, prayer, ritual, or retreat, depending on the customs of those around you and your own temperaments. Solitude, early-morning quiet, the children's nap time—these nourishing pockets of time can take many forms. But, especially if done regularly, they contribute to a sense of peace and comfort, a sense of home.

We come home for restoration. One is literally nourished by the food one eats, whether it is a bowl of rice or a five-course dinner. But spiritual nourishment also is present when we break bread with our loved ones. Whenever possible, it is good to share meals on a regular basis. This may be difficult, but it's worth the effort. Food and fellowship bond us in very deep ways. Though sadly often absent in contemporary life, mealtime is a critical part of a family's home life.

Perhaps the best meals are ones that intentionally carry a symbolic message. Every Friday evening my close friends Sharon and Dmitri take out the lace tablecloth they received as a wedding gift and spread it on their dining room table. They set out an old candelabra from Sharon's grandmother. When "Bubbie" was fleeing from oppression in Europe, she'd had to use old carved-out potatoes to hold the Sabbath candles. Now Sharon lights long, elegant white candles and says the blessing she learned as a child. Then they sit in silence for a moment before eating. Dmitri says he has come to look forward all week to this moment when the sacred space of their home is reclaimed.

Some days are deeply unsettling to our regular routine, no matter how centered we are. It is at such times that rituals give us the greatest solace. When the entire world feels upside down, that regular dinner or sunrise run can be just the thing we need to get turned back around. In fact, during tough times in a marriage, when it's hard to talk everything through, small shared rituals can be a wonderful way to feel our way back home to each other—to walk the dog together in the evening, for instance, even if in total silence.

Many couples, like Erik and Laura Larsen, find that the ritual of reading out loud to each other increases the sense of their partnership as a sacred holding place. This is one of my favorite centering rituals—taking such a small amount of time, but bringing true contentment and dignity into the home. Rituals remind me of what physicists tell us: that space and time are the same thing. The constellations of regular time spent together for the conscious purpose of recentering our union are just like the constellations of items we gather about us for security and comfort and renewal. They are the small details adding up to the warm, intentional arrangement of our home life. If we want them to, they can transform any room we inhabit into holy ground or any meal into sacred time.

Home on the Road

Those who go overseas find a change in climate, not a change in soul.
—HORACE, *EPISTLES*

Centering is an ongoing process, but one that can give us immediate results. It is first practiced in the safety of our home with loved ones. But inevitably, at least for short periods of time, we must take up our staff and turn to the open road.

The old saying goes, "You can't take it with you." But where centering on your partnership is concerned, I disagree. You can take the deep sense of "home" you have created together with you wherever you go. I have a colleague whose work requires extensive travel, and wherever she settles in for the night, she sets out a mahogany-framed photograph of her husband and children. The heavy frame itself carries a personal significance: It's a woodshop creation by her youngest son.

Pictures are so often considered important to centering that people have been known to risk their lives to save family photos from flood or flames. Refugees often cite the loss of these precious mementos as one of their greatest regrets. My niece through marriage—once a Vietnamese boat person—*still* tears up when she speaks of losing the family album in a terrible storm at sea. So, if you have old family photos, prize them. Collect new ones and bring along a few favorites wherever you go.

Carry other things, too, to bring you back to your partnership. It is not only toddlers who drag along blankets and well-worn teddy bears. I used to carry a furry monkey named Sammy with me when I went away to conferences. People thought it belonged to my son, but it was actually a gift to me from my husband. Sammy was the look-alike of my husband's first stuffed animal. He was our link to each other's need for comfort when we were unavoidably beyond the reach of each other's arms.

Once you understand that the place that physically holds you is actually a symbol of loving partnership, home can be wherever you find it. Karina and JJ, for example, never felt as much at home as when they lived one summer in Tuscany. Now they look for a cozy espresso place in every city they travel to. And two of my dearest married friends, who are chaplains, seek out chapels as homes-away-from-home when they go traveling. Donna and Ron, who met and later married in their college bookstore, told me that wherever they go, they get a deep sense of belonging by browsing around local used bookshops. This sense of "books as home" goes way back: When they were each little, their public libraries were special, safe places.

Often when we leave home, it's not for a vacation or a business trip. We may be moving to a new house entirely, to a new neighborhood, an unfamiliar city, a faraway locale. Or we may be separated from each other for a time. We might need to nurse an ailing parent. Extreme weather conditions, health emergencies, or other tragic, unforeseeable events may keep us apart. We might be stationed abroad on a long-term professional project or even separated metaphorically from each other because we have become emotionally isolated or because the stresses of daily living are just keeping us apart.

In times like these we need to find the familiar thread to take us home. We can undertake little rituals even when all else is askew—calling every night, dropping a postcard in the mail once a day. We can see the familiar curve in the mountains in the distance as a reminder that this new neighborhood is not so far off from where we began. A smooth stone we saved from our first long hike together may make us mindful of what it felt like to be truly connected. Or the wooden bench in the hospital garden may remind us of the one in the park back home, the one where we used to go to return to ourselves.

The Pilgrimage Back

Give me my scallop shell of quiet,
My staff of faith to walk upon,
My scrip of joy, immortal diet,
My bottle of salvation,
My gown of glory, hope's true gage
And thus I'll take my pilgrimage.

—SIR WALTER RALEIGH, "THE PASSIONATE MAN'S PILGRIMAGE"

Our first commitment is to establish our home base, a sacred center of nurture and tenderness to which we can often return. A strong sense of home in marriage gives us a deeply personal, calming wellspring from which we can always draw joy and understanding. The next step is to take inside of us this sense of home so that we can establish it anywhere with our partner by our being present to each other. Then we take the gifts of our partnership out with us into the world. Like the turtle, which brings its shell everywhere, we bring our spiritual values out with us as we go. But wherever we are, our thoughts drift toward return.

In the Middle Ages many Europeans sought spiritual sustenance by taking pilgrimages to the Holy Land. Travel was extremely dangerous, so it is speculated that the elaborate labyrinths from that time were designed to provide pilgrims with a less treacherous route—a symbolic journey to the center of their spiritual lives. A special kind of path, labyrinths were laid out in cut stone along the floor of the cathedrals that the pilgrims were likely to pass. Each labyrinth began and ended at the same point, allowing pilgrims to take a slow journey around and back to a safe place.

Like the medieval labyrinths, centering our lives on one another takes us on a sheltered, circular path of discovery—leaving us more grounded and calmer by far than we were before. Its goal is not just to soothe us, though, but to ready us for the greater journey of finding spiritual fulfillment in an uncertain world. In marriage we walk that winding path together, hand in hand.

At workshops I often have participants make a list of pilgrimages they'd like to take at least once in their lives. Here are a few categories that couples have come up with over the years: where each of you was born or spent your early years, where you both experienced important life changes, and where you each achieved a sense of deep happiness. These can be locations near and far, humble and grand: The river where you caught your first fish. The cathedral that was stunning in snow. The playground. The billiards hall. Granny Palmer's kitchen in the third-floor walk-up, where you could smell the spices on her stove even before she flung open the door. Only you know the names of these places of the heart. Retrieve them and savor them, separately and together, literally going there or perusing old photographs or revisiting them however it feels comfortable.

You can also make pilgrimages to the meaningful places you've created together over time: where you met, the site of your first kiss, where you got engaged, where your children were conceived or took their first steps. Go back to the place where you had your wedding, where you honeymooned, or to any place where your life together changed significantly, for better or for worse. Go back to these places especially when new memories are being forged—for family vacations, for renewing your vows. Pilgrimages remind us of where we've been and who we are. We cannot create holy ground in our present lives unless we feather them with bits and pieces of the best of our past.

As we have seen, wherever we join together with our highest values in mind is holy ground. Pilgrimages give us the chance to directly experience this fact. You've felt it in a warm bed on a cold winter morning. You've felt it in each other's arms after a long separation or a hard loss. This feeling tells you that this very moment, with all its imperfections, is joyful and right. You can't go back again, it seems to say, and yet, and yet, you always can.

For years I found the solace I desperately longed for as a child by traveling each summer to a simple converted farmhouse near the New Jersey shore. When I took the long train ride from Manhattan, it was with expectations of Mecca in mind. My Aunt Jerry would always be there at the station and her large arms, the smell of her creams and makeup, and her inviting alto words—all of which provided a kind of sanctuary I could never quite find in my family's crowded apartment.

Aunt Jerry, to whom I still speak at night when my soul is troubled, was a character who could have upstaged Auntie Mame. Raised by a Baptist minister, Aunt Jerry was a high-spirited child who defied family expectations, modeling as a teen for Saks Fifth Avenue and eventually joining the Ziegfeld Follies. To top this off she married a salesman who was Catholic, and, adding insult to injury, who smoked cigars. I can still smell that overpowering odor, which actually spoke to me of order and calm as I drifted off to sleep in my aunt and uncle's safe attic retreat.

Sometime ago I drove out to see "the old place," and it had been renovated beyond recognition. So, in my pilgrimage back, I am now confined to a journey of imagination. To get there I look at a 1941 photo of her house in the snow. I love that old picture. In my mind's eye I see Aunt Jerry standing behind the door. She is just about to open it and throw her arms wide in welcome.

Out of our repeated quests for true home we come to distinguish our love from the places where love happens. Annette and Ziya understood this difference well. After their double wedding—first in England and then a week later in Turkey—they moved far away from all family to a town along the Mississippi River. Just four months later, while crates of their wedding gifts were still unpacked, the river swelled over its banks and flooded their entire village. Annette and Ziya were first in the long line of people gathered to pass sandbags. But despite the brave efforts of many they lost their house and everything in it.

Years later, after moving many times, they celebrated their anniversary by visiting the town where they had first lived together. Toward evening, as Annette and Ziya walked along the muddy river, they were struck by its silent, mysterious message. Once upon a time the river had swept away all of their earthly possessions. But now, watching its flow, they understood that it had given them

back something, too: a precious awareness that we do not live by the grace of strongholds alone but by the flow of our love within them. As long as we have each other, we are always home.

Keys to Creating a Warm Home

- See your home as holy ground.
- Find and increase the details in your home that give you safety, contentment, and renewal.
- Be on the lookout for items in need of repair.
- Make sure both your preferences are in evidence around you.
- Take time to be alone now and then.
- Share a regular activity that you both find meaningful.
- Take a pilgrimage to a place with special memories for you, your spouse, or both of you.
- Bring one cherished item with you on the road.

Centering Questions to Ask Yourself

1. Does your home provide you with adequate sanctuary and renewal?
2. Does the arrangement of your home allow you to make choices according to your different preferences?
3. Are all those within your household encouraged to be truly themselves?
4. Are the values you hold most dear expressed in concrete ways in your home?

5. Does your home offer resources for both of you to be inspired, learn, and grow?
6. Does the atmosphere of your home support repair for both body and spirit?
7. Does everyone feel heard in your household?
8. Is this a place where deep meanings of life can be celebrated, where you are made ready to return to the world?

Your Dream House: A Centering Exercise

Has working on physical changes to your home ever knocked you or your partner off balance? In Mo and Jessie's case it did. When I met them, they were in a lethal deadlock. Mo was an interior designer, and Jessie was an architect. Both had a definite and very different picture of the kind of place they wanted to live in. When they came to me for help, they were planning their getaway home in Pennsylvania and trying not to kill each other in the process. In the course of our work together we discovered an exercise that you can adapt for your own Centering needs—whether you need to solve a similar conflict or simply want to bring more personalized comfort into your home.

I asked them each to imagine a perfect site for their getaway, putting practical matters aside. Where would it be? How big? What shape? What kind of special rooms might it have—a woodshop? a dance floor? What sort of furniture would fill it? I told them that anything was possible and that they should be as fantastical as they wished. They spent a week making separate drawings, complete with rough floor plans.

At the second meeting I asked each to give a "tour" of their

drawings, free-associating as they went about what important values were expressed in the furnishings and spaces sketched out. Mo wanted wide-open areas and lots of glass to compensate for a childhood spent in a tiny apartment. Jessie longed for rooms that exuded a warmth that was lacking in her childhood home. Talking through these details, Jessie and Mo learned which design elements were important to adopt and why. They were also able to address the few remaining conflicts with increased compassion and understanding. Above all, they were able to make their real home a better sanctuary for both of them, because they had learned more about themselves and each other. In the end Mo and Jessie's getaway wasn't a glass castle, nor was it fully furnished with pillows. But it did have the sustaining power to comfort that both Mo and Jessie had wished for, and it definitely expressed their very distinct personalities.

You may not be building a new house, but you can make tiny changes to your current home. A little more purple, perhaps? A new sewing kit? Try dreaming up your own pleasure dome and sharing your ideas with each other. If you want to, make it a hands-on project . . . or just swap ideas verbally. First, play with locations, special rooms, gadgets, or environmental settings. Then see if you can tease out *what* it is about that fully equipped gym that so strongly appeals. Consider together if there are any ways to incorporate those daydreamed fireplaces into your current home (more candles, maybe?). If you can't move to the woods, maybe you can buy a ficus tree. See if you can give something to your partner that reflects the deeper needs behind the fantasies. And remember always, your home is an expression of yourselves and of your love for each other.

Choosing

☙

I will cultivate the discipline of choosing wisely.

Josh Larsen and Maureen Maria Brady showed up at my door on a cool September day after their plans for a wild Halloween wedding bash had been vetoed. Their relatives, not surprisingly, had hoped for something a little more traditional. They had referred Josh and Maureen to a local wedding planner, who in turn had referred them to me.

I was concerned that the circumstances of the referral might have left the taste of coercion in their mouths. As we started off our first meeting in my wood-paneled Brooklyn office, I was extra careful to impress upon them that they were free to choose me—or not—as their officiant. Once they knew I was "on their side," they visibly relaxed. At that point I asked them to give me a brief rundown of their life stories. I find this to be a wonderful way to get to know a couple and also to identify any family patterns that may affect the planning or problem solving we need to address.

The only son of Laura Cohen and Erik Larsen, Josh was born in Wisconsin and raised near Jones Beach on Long Island, New York. Josh carried in him the blood of previously sworn enemies and allies alike: While his great-grandfather was piling jagged rocks along Norway's coast to ward off Nazi ships, a German second cousin was joining the führer's army, and a Jewish uncle was fleeing to America. Following in his father footsteps, Josh was a chemical engineer, but he secretly longed to become a social worker.

Maureen grew up in Queens. After her mother's divorce her two full-blood brothers went to live with their dad. She had a room next to her stepbrother, who was never in much, and she missed her real brothers badly. Maureen coped with her loneliness by writing. As an adult she wrote for a Spanish-language daily newspaper and prided herself on a reporting style that provided the facts without messy opinion. Maureen's forebears were mostly either Irish cops or Mexican field workers. Lengthy debate was not a part of the general family habit—not even when Maureen broke the family mold by being the first female on either side to go to college.

After this glimpse into Josh and Maureen's life stories, we turned back to their original desire for a raucous Halloween wedding. What was it, I asked, that had inspired this choice? As it turned out, their answer was linked to some of the very family patterns we had just discussed. Josh admitted to anxieties about all the conflicting family rituals, and he just wanted to make light of it all. Maureen had acted on impulse, simply wanting to get the plan over with and "not think so hard about the whole thing."

I explained to them that ceremonies, and wedding days in particular, are a kind of spiritual inkblot test writ large. The poem read by a friend, the candles lit by the mothers of the bride and groom, and the personal musical selections are all bits and pieces of a rich statement that is broadcasted to every guest. Weddings, done properly, are a model of good choosing and an affirming statement about who the bride and groom are as a couple.

Toward the end of the meeting I asked them if they were planning to use rings. "I wouldn't feel married without one," Maureen said without hesitation. But Josh wasn't too keen on the ornamental aspect of it.

Maureen then shared the bitter memory of her uncle's sneaking off to singles dances on weekends, leaving his wife alone. Not having a ring had made it easier for him.

Gazing into Josh's dark eyes, Maureen said, "I like to think that when we put on our wedding rings, we'll be wearing each other's commitment right there on our hands."

Hearing this, Josh looked at me with a little smile. "I see what you mean, Lois, about every little choice being important," he said. "I think I'll wear a ring after all."

The Daily Task of Choosing

Life does not give itself to one who tries to keep all its advantages at once. I have often thought morality may perhaps consist solely in the courage of making a choice. —LEON BLUM, *ON MARRIAGE*

A man I knew many years ago spent his twenties in a different woman's bed every week. One day, noticing a few gray hairs in the mirror, Liam decided to try marriage. Not long thereafter, he proposed to a feisty redhead he'd bumped into on the street. Now funny as this sounds, for some time they had a pretty good marriage. I asked Liam over coffee one afternoon why he thought it had worked for so long.

"I had to *choose* to stay with Lilly over and over again," Liam answered. "And I had to keep choosing Lilly every day of my life." He went on to tell me that this conscious decision had made him feel "like a man and not just a hormone machine."

I don't recommend Liam's approach for selecting life partners, but I do believe he stumbled across a crucial aspect of the good life—and the good married life in particular. A spiritually fulfilling marriage is a relationship that we choose and rechoose, again and again. This foundational act of courage is what signals our becoming fully human, our actively taking part in a shared life.

The First Commitment of a spiritually fulfilling marriage is to locate a center of nurture and tenderness to which we can often return. The Second Commitment sends us out into an ever-changing world. Consider that timeless centering tool, the labyrinth, which guides pilgrims meditatively around a network of paths. Such safe havens do have their place in our lives, because they allow us to find restoration and once again go forth. All the same, real life is not lived in a womb. Rather, in truth, the world we live in is less like a labyrinth than like an open-ended maze, with paths that are just as apt to dead-end or to lead us astray as they are to guide us to our goals. In a maze, as in the real world, we *choose* our way through.

Whether we realize it or not, we are always choosing. Day by day these decisions add up, coloring our whole lives. We choose a partner, and then, as Liam did, we rechoose this companion repeatedly, every day of our life. Our daily decisions range far and wide: whether to call if we're running late, how to celebrate our anniversaries, whether to stay faithful despite temptation. Every choice we make affects the direction of our life together. At the time we make them, many of these choices may seem insignificant, but they form a trail as we go along, like bread crumbs along the floor of a mythical forest, leading us back home to each other, as long as we've chosen wisely.

Lifelong Patterns of Choice

I learn by going where I have to go.

—THEODORE ROETHKE, "THE WAKING"

My mother-in-law, Betty, knitted beautiful things for the family. Watching her knit a blanket or a vest or a sweater for a new baby, I would notice how she often held the item high up in the air. "What are you looking for?" I asked one day as she lifted up a soft, many-colored creation. "I'm just making sure that what I did today fits in with what I did yesterday," she'd say, "and that it will all fit in with the sweater in my head."

No matter how large or small the issue, the artful discipline of choosing wisely begins with a look at the big picture. This look alone has helped me numerous times. Long ago I sought advice from an elder I deeply respected. I had prepared lists of pros and cons about a choice I had recently made in my marriage. I developed elaborate arguments and was busily making my way down column two when he interrupted me. "You haven't asked the right question," he declared. "What was that?" I wanted to know, turning to a new page in my notebook. Looking me straight in the eye, he said, "Is this or is this not messing up your life?"

When beginning my work with couples I often ask, "What is the story of your life?" If there was ever a question to bring out the contours of the big picture, this is it. When I'm leading groups on the subject of choosing, I always have participants break up in pairs to tell their life stories. They have only ten minutes each, and putting them on the spot brings out the twists and turns of their lives in ways that can be fascinating and surprising even to the speaker. More important, it is a splendid shortcut to perspective.

Once the tales are told, I have participants go into a little more detail by examining their *choosing patterns*. I explain that I am looking for patterns of action and reaction in their childhood homes, things they themselves caused, and things that happened beyond their control. When, if ever, did they learn to be proactive in their lives? As you think back on your own life, how did your family's choices affect you?

We first become conscious choosers when our desires conflict with family preferences. Maureen learned this early on. She missed her brothers so much after the divorce. A few times she actually got on the subway without telling her parents so she could meet her brothers for pizza in Brooklyn. She made an even bigger decision on her own when she was seventeen, when she became the first woman in her family to go to college. She knew it was a great opportunity, but many of her relatives didn't believe that college was an appropriate choice for a young woman. Since the family never discussed issues, Maureen used her confidence and enthusiasm about her choice to bring her concerned relatives around in the end.

Many of us blossomed late as independent choosers, waiting until we were on our own, off at college or a first job. With our newfound freedom we could pick hobbies we liked, make friends whether or not others approved of them, go to a school not recommended by anyone, and take risks both calculated and reckless.

What do the patterns in your life suggest about your habits of choosing? Have you often chosen the pressures of work over the pleasures of close family and friends? Have you let opportunities slip by because you were afraid? Have you chosen to stay with your partner even when you couldn't seem to stop fighting? What types of choices do you seem to make over and over again?

Repeated choices may clue us in to typical styles of reacting or to long-standing desires that we may never have known we had (aways choosing the hard road, to cite an example, may indicate a love of challenge). What's more, recurring choices point us toward what we consider most important—excitement, spontaneity, intimacy, peace. Knowing what we choose again and again tells us a lot about why we do the things we do, about what matters to us—in short, about who we are.

More than this, seeing the recurrent broad strokes of our life helps to keep the pressures of the daily grind in perspective and offers new clarity for getting by. When we're going through hard times in our marriage—when the bills pile up, the bickering doesn't stop, and there never seems to be enough time in the day to sit still—an awareness of our choosing patterns can sometimes provide a view toward a way out. Conscious choosing involves knowing our priorities, and so it enables us to select solutions that will be the most supportive for us personally. If intimacy is your priority, for instance, why not pick just a couple of those holiday parties to attend and stay home for the others?

Reviewing the story of your life, however briefly, is a handy way to tap in to a potent source of insight. Usually we need to recognize an unhealthy pattern to dismantle it and a healthy one to nurture it. You may find that some patterns spring from your family life in childhood, and some may go back even further. So, if you wish, broaden your story—go back a few generations. See where some of your current choosing styles were born: Whence comes your bent for adventure seeking or justice fostering, your call to teach or to heal? Especially when you're dealing with an unhealthy pattern such as emotional withdrawal, compulsive behavior, or bursts of temper, it helps take the edge off guilt to know that you're not alone. Sometimes just having that little insight can be enough to get you started on the path out of your troubles.

Ask yourself about all the many choices you've made. Then, like my mother-in-law, Betty, with her knitting, examine the story that unfolds for patterns that repeat themselves time and time again. The choices you've made are the basic substance out of which you've woven the story of your life. This ability is central to our sense of who we are in many ways. As one sacred mystery tale has it, once in the faraway Garden of Eden, lost in the mist of early group memory, it was an act of choosing that distinguished us as a people. This persistent story reminds us that, like the small children we once were, our ancestors had to go out into the world and learn to choose wisely.

Choosing for Two

The water is wide, I cannot get o'er,
Neither have I wings to fly.
Give me a boat that will carry two,
And both will row, my love and I.

—OLD AMERICAN FOLK SONG

We love the songs that promise us that when we step over the threshold on our wedding day we will be One: one hand, one heart, one life together. While there is poetic truth to this image, two is really the primary number in marriage. Our life together is made up of the day-to-day interactions of two distinct individuals—we each have desires, feelings, and experiences *of our own,* no matter how strong the bond of our love. In relationships we choose not just for ourselves. We choose for (at least) two.

Benny learned this the hard way when his marriage with Rosalie was in trouble. Anxious to find out what he'd done wrong, he came to my office with a friend who was a member of the Ethical Society. "I'm an ideal husband," Benny lamented. "I'm never macho. I give her whatever she wants. Do you think I should buy her a present or something?"

As it turned out, neither Benny nor Rosalie had learned to make decisions *together.* Rosalie's wit and will had made her a leader in life—competitive victory was the game, and she played it flawlessly. She knew what she wanted, but the way she got it left only room for one. Benny, the youngest son of a bedridden mother, had learned early on how to cater to the demands of a strong-minded woman. He spent much of his time covering up his own needs and desires.

When Benny finally got Rosalie to come in with him for a chat with me (he managed to convince her it was her idea), she said how frustrated she was at having to make all the family decisions. And to make things worse, she added, Benny had begun to challenge her judgment lately. "But I feel like your dishrag," Benny blurted out when I finally coaxed him from his sulking silence. Then, more softly, he added, "Rosalie, I just feel like I can't ever give you enough."

Learning how to make choices is a basic human task. But the dynamics of decision making shift significantly when we marry. The general task during our growing-up years was to achieve independence as we learned to make good choices on our own. The task of adults in life partnership is to achieve *inter*dependence, to cooperate in building a life together, and to share equally the fruits of our labors.

Complicating the task yet further, the process of choosing shifts and changes during the various phases of life partnership. When lovers first meet, they may operate for quite a while on parallel tracks. Equity can be sustained for newlyweds by taking turns on decisions—deciding which concert to attend, whose friends to spend the evening with, whose decorating preferences are followed in which room. Choosing in such a way that we please our partner (as well as ourselves) is a hallmark of early success. As the years go by and we settle down, we must make decisions concerning how to divide up the tasks of daily living—how to budget, when to take vacations, whose relatives to spend holidays with. Inevitably over the course of these deliberations, we must discover how to disagree respectfully and to make decisions jointly despite conflicting opinions.

Later yet, if and when kids arrive, we really need to pull together as a team. There simply isn't enough time to make every decision jointly, and we must count on each other to be mutually considerate in order to get on with the day. The shape of choosing expands yet again to include a teaching aspect, as we help our growing children to choose wisely. Even as couples circle toward the far side of life, after the well-oiled machine of our partnership has served us for many years, decision-making habits must shift to accommodate the changing circumstances around us. No single style of cooperation, however smoothly it has worked in the past, can sustain us unless it leaves room for flexibility.

In married life our choices (and mistakes) affect not only our partner but the future of our children and grandchildren and, through them (grand though it seems), the future of the human adventure in general. Once we have learned to choose wisely, stopping to consider the dignified autonomy of others as well as our own, we can venture safely out into the future, with deep confidence in our relationship.

Guidelines for Wise Decision Making

Let every soul look upon the morrow for the deed it has performed.
—THE KORAN, 59:18

Strategies and particulars change as you choose your way through life. But there are important keys—general constants—to keep in mind in the Commitment of choosing, no matter what stage of life you are in. We'll take a brief look at these strategies one at a time. You can use them whether you're making smaller choices, such as settling an argument, disciplining a child, or making plans for the weekend, or bigger ones, like deciding whether to take a job offer, where to move, or when to retire.

Maximize the future freedom of all involved. Choosing is always a process of opening one door and closing another. What we do has consequences, and they reverberate beyond ourselves. We're never choosing in a vacuum, but must consider the outcome of our choice as it concerns not only us but also those around us. This concept is related to the "choosing for two" that goes on in marriage, but it is always at issue, no matter the context. Keeping freedom in mind is, in fact, the foremost consideration for making a wise choice.

To begin with, a real choice is made freely—without force or undue pressure. It is important, then, to feel that we are free to make our decision. It's also important to keep an eye out for our own *future* freedom. If we are not continuously free to engage in the process of selecting our actions, then we are not choosing but merely going through the motions. It's easy at times just to give in to a forceful lover . . . a charismatic leader . . . a way of living or of seeing the universe. Hardly realizing that we chose not to choose, we bind our own hands in such pseudochoosing processes. This relinquishing is a choice, but a potentially repressing one.

The independence and well-being of others must also be considered when making a good choice. How will your partner's sleep be affected if you stay up late reading in bed? How will your daughter feel if you work late rather than attend her recital? If you have two cars and one breaks down, do you automatically take the working car, leaving your partner without transportation? The best choices maximize the freedom of those we love.

Maximizing freedom, paradoxically, does require a little structure. For some, choosing rules or standards—an orthodox perspective—allows for more freedom within the context of everyday choices. As long as the basic dignity of each person involved is respected, rules provide guidelines for our behavior so that we don't have to spend all our time figuring out what to do in every little case. We develop many of these rules without even realizing it—such as determining chores for which one spouse is generally responsible.

Wise choosing comes from that part of us that has learned how to be loving, despite fears, inconveniences, insecurities, and unhealthy old family patterns. Mike, who takes many business trips in the course of a month, often chooses to pick up the phone and call Nelly from the road even though he isn't "required" to do so. He just wants to keep in touch, to tell her the small details of his day.

When Mike forgets to call, Nelly is tempted to pick up the phone and yell at him for it. She's taught herself to pause and count to ten, twenty, thirty. After that she tracks Mike down and tells him how much she misses him. Both Mike and Nelly respect each other enough to override their unthinking instincts and to freely choose an action that will make the other feel loved and appreciated.

Freedom in loving partnership is not "freedom from" but "freedom with." By consciously choosing with freedom in mind, we come to embrace our full humanity, and we become increasingly worthy of one another.

Temper desire with respect. Once, when I was six, my father took me to a new playground in the neighborhood. It was the 1950s, and I was thrilled at the row of shiny metal seats hanging by thick chains. Just as I had plopped down on the swings, two black girls in matching red coats ran over and begged me to get off because I was on the wrong swings. The first four belonged to white children, they explained, and the last four belonged to coloreds. We would all get in trouble, they added. Well, I had just warmed up the seat and was darned if I was going to move. I stuck my tongue out and began to pump belligerently with my bare legs. It was then that one of them pulled me off by the hair. When I ran back to my father, sobbing, he wanted to chase after them, but I begged him not to. Even at such a young age I knew in my heart that my choice to disrespect the girls' urgent warnings had caused the problem.

Sometimes we want something so much that we ignore helpful warnings from others. Or, alternately, we take an "any means to an end" approach. In the heat of clashing desires, couples can often turn disrespectful or dismissive of one another, sticking out their tongues (at least figuratively) at each other. As some couples find out too late, no choice made in a contemptuous frame of mind is worth the making.

Know your priorities, and act accordingly. "You are what you eat" is an old saying. And it's not just about physiology. What you choose to eat often says a lot about your basic values, as the following story illustrates.

I met Shanti, a doctoral student, at a Wednesday-evening values-clarification course. Most of the class hung out afterward at a café. One evening, Shanti, who was a health nut, told me that she hated going home on Wednesdays. Apparently both she and her fiancé, Jim, had late classes that night and so had agreed to take turns bringing home prepared food. On her Wednesdays she brought in nutritious bits of this and that, each carefully selected. Jim, on the other hand, never varied in his contribution: He always came home carrying two stained bags full of his favorite greasy burgers and fries.

The next time we talked, Shanti reported that she had complained bitterly the previous week about the "junk" he kept bringing in. After suffering through her lecture on abused cattle and cholesterol, Jim had walked out, saying she could fend for herself on Wednesdays.

Two lonely Wednesdays later, as she was aimlessly poking at her tofu patty, Jim burst in carrying a bag full of health food items. "I want to be with you more than I want the burgers," Jim said, unceremoniously plunking down the bag.

As Shanti and Jim's experience shows, all of us can accommodate one another's differences—even big ones—as long as we can find some spiritual common ground and take the time to deliberately prioritize what matters to us most: each other.

Acknowledge regrets to prevent them in the future. There were so many people at the "Choosing Your Way Through Life" workshop I was running in a colleague's living room that people were sitting all over the floor. I began by asking if anyone had regrets they wanted to share.

Five-year-old Alexander, seated amid several squirming children, piped up. "What's a regret?" he asked.

"I'll tell you a story about that," Sadie, a feisty ninety-two-year-old widow, reponded. "I look back over my growing-up years and I don't have any big regrets. But much later I sure got one. See, all the children but Mimi left our old walk-up when they were grown. She stayed behind to take care of Mother and Father, and she did that till they died. Then she started to have trouble going up and down the stairs. Mimi loved that old house, but my husband, Shep, said it was too dangerous for an old woman to live there alone. When she broke her leg, while she was still in traction, he sold the house out from under her and put her in a nursing home. After that, things were never the same between Shep and me. I regret not standing up to him. My sister died within months. I believe it was of a broken heart."

As the saying goes, the road to hell is paved with good intentions. Shep was acting out of concern, but because he neither waited for nor conferred with those he loved, he truncated someone else's freedom and deeply hurt the woman he cherished most. But Sadie knew that through her inaction—her lack of courage to stand up to him—she, too, caused harm.

"So, young Alexander," Sadie concluded, "a regret is being so sorry for hurting someone that you don't ever want to make the same choice again." At that, Alexander got up and said he regretted not giving his sister the red pillow to sit on. Red, he explained, was her favorite color.

Seek wise counsel. It's important to stay open to wholesome new approaches to making decisions together, and that can't happen without open cooperation. Some people are in what I call "sandbox" marriages—they borrow a shovel or pour a pail of sand over the other's head occasionally, but basically their togetherness involves a lot of parallel play. They watch the kids separately, watch TV separately, eat and sleep and awaken at different times. When decisions have to be made, these couples often adopt primitive strategies—a do-it-or-else approach or narrow tit-for-tat sharing schemes. Sometimes they give up negotiating altogether.

Luckily, by the time Josh and Maureen came to me, they were far beyond parallel play. Through smarts and instinct and one summer living together, they had found their way to a great choosing habit: They tended either to consult each other directly or else to bear the other's preferences in mind whenever a decision had to be made alone. When tough decisions came their way—such as where to hold their wedding ceremony—they were able to ask each other for feedback and turn to me and others for guidance.

Emile and Anthea, whom I counseled during the same time period, were not so lucky. Both of them had acted as little adults when they were young. But all of us humans, and children especially, need help choosing. At the tender age of six, Emile had been designated by default to make most household decisions, since his parents were usually too high on crack to function. Admittedly, his judgment was probably the best available, but he lost his childhood in the process. With a lack of guidance from wise elders, Emile eventually found the act of constantly choosing to be overwhelmingly scary and ultimately paralyzing. When he grew up, the prospect of selecting one woman felt so difficult to him that he assumed he'd never marry. He was just now coming to me with his fiancée, Anthea, at age forty-two. Independence is all well and good, but it needs to be balanced with proper guidance from those who love us and can help.

Bart and Mary Jane had the opposite problem. They came to me expecting me to tell them what to do with their lives, because as kids they'd had *too much* direction. Unfortunately, much of this direction was threatening or punitive, neither wise nor supportive. Bart's family attended a strict church where the preacher regularly banged on the pulpit and jabbed his fingers at the congregation. Mary Jane was ruled by the beer bottle that her abusive father too often had in his hand.

Bart and Mary Jane's identity was strongly Christian, so I introduced them to a local church known for kind co-ministers and offbeat study groups. It was a place where they could get warm, personal guidance without being sternly told what to do. One of the healing groups they participated in was a drama workshop. The idea was to explore the hidden meanings of ancient themes by enacting scenes from sacred stories.

It was December, and the story they were dramatizing was the birth of Jesus. Mary Jane played the Virgin Mary. She sat on a folding chair in the middle of the room holding a rag doll in her arms. As she cradled it, she found herself whispering clumsily into the little cloth ear, "I will hold you, I will rock you, I will keep you safe from harm."

"Lois," she told me afterward, "I understood so many things. I saw that suffering is a part of any life—even the mother of Jesus couldn't protect her child from it. And I also learned that when we grow up, we get a second chance—to choose to start again."

Later Mary Jane and Bart took lots of baby steps, making small decisions and little by little freeing themselves of the harsh voices inside their heads. On a final check-in session with me after they had spent some time with a family therapist, Mary Jane handed me a bookmark with pressed flower petals and a quotation from Deuteronomy: "I offer you the choice of life or of death, blessing or curse. Choose life and then you and your descendants will live." She thanked me for introducing her to the church and the therapist and for showing her that real loving support can be found as long as we learn to look for it in the right places.

Whether we have been given too little or too much direction, good advice or bad, our passage to proactive and wise choosing can be a joyous and empowering journey. And a safe one. Seek the counsel of your partner and others to help light the way.

Pray with your feet. There was once a sage who lived deep in a forest preserve. He was asked one day which was more important, the inner life of prayer and contemplation or the outer life of service to others. He retired to his hut for three days. When he emerged, he declared that neither alone was right but that both together composed a full life. "If you pray with your feet," he added, "you can accomplish both at the same time."

Some of us do better separating out the thoughtful inner and dynamic outer aspects of choosing. But for many, contemplation and action are one and the same. Physical therapists working with people with special needs, Catholic Maryknoll Sisters who attend the terminally ill, Buddhist activists meditatively circling a war memorial, and women marching on behalf of their children's education all understand the meaning of "praying with your feet." They know how possible it is to nurture the inner life while working for goodness in the world.

A civil discussion of your political views, breaking bread with an elder, or supporting teachers in their work with your children—all can enhance a feeling of closeness as well as a sense of larger purpose in your lives. If our patterns of choosing are wise, they will bring partners both to increased intimacy and also to increased community participation.

When you have several choices about things to do but time for only one, ask yourself which activity will help you to "pray with your feet." Almost anything you do mindfully is actually a prayer of this sort. That includes driving, changing a diaper, putting in the extra hours of work to secure your job, and all the myriad other things that make up an ordinary day. In the larger scheme of things, partnership is not an end in itself but a means of nourishing two caring people so that they can each return to themselves, one another, and the community of flesh and spirit that sustains them.

Daring to Be Counted Upon: Commitments

Men are all alike in their promises. It is only in their deeds that they differ.
—MOLIÈRE, *THE MISER*

A fundamental premise of this book is that certain commitments—profound ethical commitments that bind us together and energize our marriage—are so important that they are at the heart of any relationship built to last. But those big commitments are only as solid as the base of the many hundreds of little choices that undergird them. The way to learn how to choose is, simply enough, to start choosing. Ideally, you begin with small decisions and then work your way up from there. Commitments flow from this concept. A late-life diabetic, for example, may first choose frozen yogurt over ice cream, then cut sugar out of her tea, then go on to consider how to balance her daily diet. That naturally will lead toward a general, firm commitment to be responsible for her health. Committing to take responsibility for a healthy marriage happens in much the same way.

It feels wonderful when a partner promises to do something, no matter how small, and then does it. Andrew tells Tess he'll be home at six, and there he is as promised in the doorway as the wall clock chimes. Tess tells Andrew she'll mop up the water on the sink counter after she washes in the morning. A few false starts later she manages to keep it up a whole week. To show his appreciation Andrew greets her with flowers Friday night. These are small acts that, accumulated over time, will lend a higher sense of faith and loving care to their married life together.

To choose something is to freely affirm it, believing that the choice will have a positive effect. By formalizing your choices into commitments, you highlight this affirmation and increase your ability as partners to make and keep regular, clear agreements with each other. Out of such "certified" choices, mutual trust evolves.

A commitment is a particular conscious action we take after reflection. It says, either literally or figuratively, "Here is what I intend to do, and on this firm promise I stand." When breakthroughs happen with the couples I serve, commitments are often the result. Imagine your partner near tears, explaining to you how hard it is to get out of bed in the morning, how exhausting everything feels these days, and how much it would mean if you could give a little more support right about now. Assuming you're not in the same exact boat, your response will most likely be "Of course."

Your commitment to each other in general is an underlying reason your partner can open up in this way, to ask for help and nurturing and to count on a positive response from you. A spiritual marriage is one in which partners commit to asking for assistance when it's needed and to giving assistance when asked for. Promising to make a loving, supportive choice on a regular basis or for a certain period of time is committing at its finest, especially where marriage is concerned. In part this is why commitments are so powerful for marriages at any stage—thriving, making transitions, stagnating, or hanging by a thread. Commitments are by definition to be kept by one partner and to be depended on by the other.

Couples can bear in mind a number guidelines for making and keeping a good promise. These tips can help partners with the process of commitment making, whether that promise is as trivial as not answering the phone during dinner or as challenging as being more appreciative overall. Of course, they will work for commitments outside the marriage as well. So, as you begin to improve your committing skills, see if you can bear the following guidelines in mind:

Choose to commit out of your own free will without feeling coerced. Though they'd felt some pressure about the ceremony from family members, Josh and Maureen were very clear about their independent choice to marry. They may have had some rough edges, but Josh and Maureen had leaped through high hoops to arrive at my door—staying together despite a jealous best friend, six months living in different cities, and the inevitable challenges of moving in together.

Choosing does not take place in a vacuum. Genes, the state of your parents' marriage, pressures of family and friends, fear of loneliness, unexpected events—such as pregnancy or the illness of a parent—all necessarily play a role in both your daily decisions and your larger ones, including the decision to get married in the first place. Nor should it be otherwise. Commitments are never devoid of context, and our consideration of others is a natural part of mature decision making.

In beginners' relationship-building workshops, I often hand out slips of paper with statements meant to stimulate conversation. One slip reads, "When people scold you about not keeping a commitment, they usually mean you didn't do what *they* wanted you to do." I find that couples who were treated this way in early life often have a more difficult time making commitments. They confuse their own assertions with memories of coercion and have to untangle that inner mess before they can step forward with confidence and say, "I choose to do this." Eventually it's possible to learn to make life choices with this confidence, responsibly acknowledging outside forces and others' opinions without being unduly constrained by them.

Don't bite off more than you can chew. Don't make a promise that you know is impossible to keep. If it's too ambitious, not only will you fail, you will discourage yourself and upset your partner. What you *can* do is promise to work toward a larger promise and look at the steps of commitment needed to get there. When Josh first moved in with Maureen, they agreed that they had to work on making little decisions together, like sharing housecleaning and setting policies about not accepting late-night phone calls. In fact, they took almost two years on that project before they thought about the larger life decision to get married.

Make a clear promise, and be sure the promise is understood by your partner. If, let's say, you promise to do the laundry but don't specify the time period ("sometime this month"), it can create unnecessary hard feelings. And, on the other hand, if your partner is still half asleep when you state your plans, you're not much better off. The devil is in the details here. I know how many times over the years I've broken a small promise, taking unfair advantage of my best friend and partner. I may have secretly, privately changed the parameters of my commitment after breaking it, just to make myself feel better. I rationalize to myself, "Oh, he'll understand." Don't get me wrong—he usually does. But *he* shouldn't be the one held responsible if he doesn't.

Keep your promise. This is, of course, the whole purpose of making a commitment. Still, it's difficult to keep that promise if the foregoing strategies—being clear and realistic—haven't been followed. If you habitually have trouble with promise keeping, try making a small promise and sticking to it. Make it silly or meaningless if it helps: Promise to make the bed, eat a salad for lunch, call your wife at 3:00 P.M. sharp. Once you've felt the satisfactions of sticking to your word, you may find it easier to build up stamina for larger and more serious commitments.

Acknowledge when you have failed, and then recommit to your promise. Anyone who has ever tried to keep a promise knows how difficult it can be to fulfill in practice. Don't be discouraged by failure—it is part of the process. On the other hand, honestly admit it so you can move on and earnestly try again. Even when you're going around in circles, those circles may be slowly winding upward, like a spiral that may just take you to success. When recommitting, don't forget to revise your promise clearly, as necessary, keeping it realistic and in line with the desires of all involved. Your failure may be due to confusion over shifting contexts—the lighter tenor of your daily interactions, the heavier stress level at work, the changing state of your health.

Ask for help in keeping your promise and for slack if you need it. It is much easier to keep a promise if your partner and others close to you are supportive. Know your weaknesses (do you lose track of time? are you a bit of a scatterbrain?), and brainstorm about how to work around your foibles (an alarm watch? a string around the finger?). Set up a system of reminders, including periodic calls from friends or check-in conversations with each other. Give yourself visual cues: Post-its on the front door or a big promissory note on the refrigerator bordered with hearts. When these little things don't work, try to figure out why. Failure often comes from weakness or fear rather than unconcern. Attentiveness to small broken promises can give you an early warning signal to a deeper problem that you could work out now, before it gets worse. If necessary, seek out professional help, such as counseling or therapy.

Affirm good intentions. Of course, we could commit to nasty things: avenging a brother whose wife is cheating on him or promising to destroy your friend's soon-to-be ex. Commitments without good intentions are just sharp tools in the wrong hands. Loving intentions, on the other hand, create commitments that build a sturdy marriage, undergirding it and strengthening it with reliability and healthy growth.

Making commitments is both exhilarating and anxiety producing. How you choose and what you promise, from the tiniest to the grandest of your decisions, indelibly weaves the spiraling story of your life. One of the primary purposes of this book is to help you start being *conscious* of the process of choosing—intentionally shaping your life for the better, making and keeping commitments (eight of them in particular) that will enhance and protect your marriage whatever the circumstances.

From Small Steps to Leaps: Covenants

The ring so worn as you behold,
So thin, so pale, is yet of gold:
The passion such it was to prove;
Worn with life's cares, love yet was love.

—GEORGE CRABBE, "A MARRIAGE RING"

Where long-term relationships are concerned, there are moments that require us to take a deep breath and then wholeheartedly leap into love. It's like standing on the high dive and mustering the confidence to jump. This declaration is a chosen act of courage—a daring to be counted on in more than just small ways.

Weddings give couples a chance to accomplish this brave deed publicly. There is a special exhilaration in seizing this ritual day and boldly claiming its promise. It is the enactment of a special blessing that comes with being human: Because we can envision a future, we can commit to it.

This kind of Commitment—"with a capital C"—I refer to as a covenant. Marriage is one such sacred promise. The word "covenant" is often used in situations involving formal legal contracts, suggesting the seriousness of the pledge. But the word's roots go back to a time when life-binding agreements were made between holy people and their conception of God. Marriage agreements, in addition to being legal contracts, are covenants binding us to what is deepest and best in our potential.

For those creating a spiritually full marriage, a covenant goes beyond written documents. It is an implicit promise to create the conditions that enliven and strengthen both people in a life partnership. This highly intentional kind of decision is made by partners who are mindful of the profound impact of their determination to wed. They have power over the shape of things to come. As Maureen expressed it in a love letter to Josh that we ended up tailoring for the wedding ceremony, "Love is not just a feeling. It is also a choice and an action. Today I choose to give my love to you for the rest of my life."

As you may recall, it was especially important for Maureen to have a double-ring ceremony. In her case it was for very personal reasons, a visible sign of what she knew in her heart: that unlike her wayward uncle, Josh would be a devoted husband. Like many wedding symbols, rings can stand for many things. Although they are not a universal or even an ancient tradition, they have taken on a special power in recent times. Not so long ago a ring in Western tradition was the ceremonial sign that the husband now "owned" the wife. These days an *exchange* of rings suggests the spiritual equality that couples plan for their partnership.

The ring has been poetically described in many ways, and sometimes officiants are asked to preface the ring exchange with a discussion of the meanings that the rings carry. I've heard many meanings described: a symbol of endless love that encircles your partner and you; a sign, as pure as the gold out of which it is cast, of your highest aspirations; evidence to others of your chosen bond and of your fidelity to your partner; or a reminder and physical "transition object" to bring you comfort when the two of you must be apart. Ultimately the ring of gold or platinum is simply a powerful symbol of our life commitment—our covenant—with each other, a sign of our binding engagement with and promise to one another.

Initially a marriage covenant is a profound life-passage choice, verbally expressed in the wedding vows. These words set the direction of a couple's path, taking them across a threshold and publicly expressing both their free choice to become life partners and their unconditional, sacred commitment to one another. Every ten years or so, many couples choose to reiterate their covenant with one another in an affirmation ceremony where they renew their vows. They may use the original words of their wedding-day covenant, or they may write new ones that reflect the changes the couple has undergone over time. This act is a formal, public version of committing to strengthen one's partnership—emotionally, spiritually, and in many other ways.

Rereading your wedding vows is one good way to easily remind yourself of your marital covenant. Your own vows no doubt reflected things that still profoundly hold you together—friendship, respect, support, fidelity. You may want to pull out your wedding video or, if you have your vows written somewhere, take another look at them. Did you choose traditional wording or write your own? Would you choose your vows any differently today or not? Are there any aspects of your covenant that you've let slip, any promises that don't seem relevant anymore, or any areas you wish you had included in your vows? What would you change, if anything, in order to make your vows a source of inspiration in the present? Some couples I've known have been inspired by this activity to put together a reaffirmation ceremony to update and strengthen their commitment to each other. Others have found that it provides perspective during hard times and reminds them what their marriage has always fundamentally been about.

I remember a moving story I once heard in which reading his wedding vows aloud helped a husband to make a courageous choice. George and Paula were referred to me by a hospital social worker. They had been married for fifteen years when Paula developed Hodgkin's disease. Her program of treatment left her exhausted, and Meg, their oldest child, often had to care for the young ones as well as continue her after-school job. George was the manager of a local supermarket and found himself depressed and overwhelmed, bringing the kids to and from school, arranging their social schedules, getting Paula to the doctor, and keeping up a stiff pace at work.

After a roller coaster ride of a year, one day George looked at himself in the men's room mirror at work and grinned. Candyce, a cashier, had pinched his bottom as he'd passed her in the back hall. Candyce wore four earrings on each ear, one on her tongue, and two on her nose. (She'd hinted about rings on other parts of her anatomy, too.) George had begun flirting with her openly. It made him feel young again—like the swinging single he once was.

"It's funny now, looking back," he told me when he and his wife came to their second session. "When everything seems upside down, you can actually tell yourself with a straight face that the best course of action is to make things more f'd up."

As weeks went by, the workers at Thriftway were beginning to notice the blatant flirting between Candyce and George. Robin in meats told Dennis in customer service, who told George's daughter Meg what was going on. One day when George picked Meg up from soccer practice, she confronted her father. George gunned the engine and denied his daughter's accusations at first. But then, as the light turned green and he propelled them homeward through the dark, he broke down. By the time they'd turned into the drive, George had soaked both his sleeves with wiped tears.

"The worst part is," Meg went on angrily, oblivious to her father's expressions of remorse, "the very worst thing is this: Mom knows."

"Paula knows?" George shouted incredulously. "Who told her?"

"No one told her, Dad." she said cynically. Putting her fist to her chest, she concluded, "She knows it in *here*."

That night George knelt on the floor in front of Paula's wheelchair and told her what had been happening. He begged Paula to help him. She stroked his thick, black hair and reached with one thin arm toward her vanity table, plucking out a rectangle of cardboard from beneath the lace doily.

"Darling," she said softly, "why don't you read these to me?" It was a copy of their wedding vows, written in George's own hand on an index card—his wedding-day "crib sheet." Haltingly, he stumbled through the poignant phrases, pausing at "in sickness and in health." When he was through, he laid his head in her lap and cried—no longer from remorse but for sorrow and fear, and for love of his incredible wife.

Taking Charge of Your Destiny

Afoot and light-hearted I take to the open road,
Healthy, free, the world before me,
The long brown path before me leading wherever I choose.

—WALT WHITMAN, "SONG OF THE OPEN ROAD"

Change without choice is called *fate*. Change with choice is called *destiny*. We share the same fate with all living beings, and much lies beyond our control. Still, what's distinctive about us humans is our ability to shape our destiny by making life-transforming choices, for better or worse. In fact, whether we know it or not, we are always choosing, and every choice we make affects the future of our marriage.

Part of the art of lasting relationships involves moving from a sense of fate—of being a passive victim in life—to a sense of destiny. We can become active partners in seeking fulfillment with one another and in the arms of life. To assert that we can make commitments is to claim we are more than pawns, that what we do counts. We can leave the job that makes us miserable; we can move to a smaller home to ease our monthly cost of living; we can carve out a bit of time to follow our creative dreams (the novel, the painting, the cooking class); or we can even choose to submit to a higher calling that guides all our actions.

I would like to end this chapter on choosing wisely with Anna and Isaac's story, in which it should become clear that I do not use the term "life-transforming" lightly. Here is one example of why two can be better than one when tough choices need to be made. In this case a woman helped her husband to make a choice that not only saved their marriage but also saved their lives:

It was the early 1940s in Germany. Anna had heard from her neighbors that the Gestapo were searching every apartment along the narrow stone streets of their village, and they were just a kilometer away. There had been tales of missing people and murders, and Anna and Isaac had promised each other an abrupt departure if it got any worse. "It's time to go," Anna yelled, running up the steep flight of stairs. Her husband leaned on the rail as she tearfully explained the situation.

Isaac was listening to one of the rare recordings of Bach that he owned. He went back inside and began to sort through a large pile of records. "What are you doing?" Anna shrieked.

"I just need a little time to pick the best to pack," he said mechanically, turning the jacketed disks over one by one.

"Are you crazy?" she screamed. Taking what she knew to be his most beloved record, she smashed it down on the oak table. With a loud crack, it split into worthless shards. "This is us if you stay," she said in a voice suddenly grave and quiet. "I am your only music now, Isaac."

Because theirs was a happy marriage, Isaac and Anna were practiced in wise choosing. Isaac had grown to trust his wife's instincts. And Anna, knowing how important music was to her husband, was able to choose a way of communicating that would shake him out of his shocked inertia. Anna was relying on the profound trust she and Isaac had for one another to break the paralysis of indecision and seize their best chance for life. Sure enough, he followed her up onto the roof, stiff as a sleepwalker. They scrambled over vents and protrusions, scaled down into an alley, and were out of the village at last. Many crossed rivers and mountains later, they arrived safely in Switzerland.

Anna and Isaac lived to tell this story to their grandchildren and to attend numerous weddings of their ever-expanding family. This was because Anna had the ability even back then to see beyond the rooms of her and Isaac's cozy life. She envisioned two futures—one with broken promises, marching feet, and a dark fate if they stood where they were and one with the kept promise of a life together, someplace, somewhere, just a brave leap or two away.

When they attended their granddaughter's recent wedding and the groom smashed the glass wrapped in linen with his foot, the sound shook their chests with the memory of that shattered record long ago. They turned to each other and smiled. Symbolic smashing can be a good thing if it clears the path of obstacles to a fuller life, a richer marriage, the human destiny that is ours.

Keys to Choosing Wisely

- Look at how your patterns of choosing support or undermine your marriage.
- Remind yourself that "not choosing" is a choice.
- Measure your individual choices against the bigger commitment to be married.
- Be sure to include your partner in decision making.
- Make promises you can keep, and make them clearly.
- Commit to improving the emotional and spiritual dimensions of your partnership.
- Track down your wedding vows to review your marital covenant.
- Take charge of your own destiny.

Choosing Questions to Ask Yourself

1. Do your choices support or distract you from peace and comfort in your marriage?
2. Do you choose with your own and others' freedom in mind?
3. In general, are you dismissive or respectful of your partner when making choices?
4. Do you act according to clear priorities?
5. Are you faithful to your commitments?
6. Do you have any regrets that might help prevent unwise choices in the future?
7. Do you usually seek the counsel of your partner and others when making choices?
8. Do your choices isolate you or connect you to those you love?

Time Lines: A Choosing Exercise

One of choosing's great gifts is perspective. This exercise is a tremendous help in making that perspective literally *visible* to you. Again and again I've seen how turning choosing into a hands-on project allows couples to take ownership of the power they have to shape their lives day by day, year by year.

Make timelines of your lives side by side. Go from birth to today and mark any major milestones along the way. You can break up your life into eras or make separate timelines for your lives before you met, if you wish. You may choose to use a roll of butcher paper or decorate poster board with pins and glitter. You can create a custom document on the computer or simply scribble on a legal pad—

it's really up to you. Make certain to include turning points: moves, changes in school, ends and beginnings, births and deaths. Include any event that feels important to you for any reason.

The first thing to do once you've drawn up your lifeline is to sit back and look at the major changes. Where did you have some choice . . . and where didn't you? How did the important events affect your subsequent choices? Now, consider where the lines of your love life converge and where they move apart. How do your patterns of choosing play off one another? (Is one of you the primary chooser in your relationship, or are you basically equal choosers?) Can you see a clear story? Finally—and to me most exciting—use the timelines to discover exactly what you have and haven't chosen for yourself in life. What has been your fate? What has been your destiny?

Remember that destiny is not one fixed destination but a generally wholesome direction. You can navigate the course of your destiny, you can turn your ship seaward and away from fateful rocks. The course of your life, and of your marriage, is yours. It's simply a matter of choice.

Honoring

🦢

I will have reverence for my partner and myself.

Tucked safely under a thick Norwegian comforter, the Larsens were as snug as Ma and Pa on a winter's night. Erik's midnight coughing disrupted the calm and got Laura to worrying a little. She put her hand on the small of Erik's back and felt the energy of his flowing blood as it moved under her palm. As she later explained it to me, every particular thing about Erik was beautiful to her. Laura's hand traced the beauty of Erik's familiar flesh: a curving back, a little ridge of raised scar tissue on his side. Laura slid her hand up to Erik's shoulder, and he sighed in his sleep. The warmth of the covers soothed her, and she slid into a memory of lovemaking.

The very first time Laura and Erik made love, their bodies didn't even touch. They had been loaned a friend's beach house in Nantucket for their honeymoon. It was dark when they arrived. While Laura tossed their bags into the back bedroom, Erik picked out a record from a tall stack. Then they settled down cross-legged at opposite ends of the living room sofa. They sat dreamily absorbing the sounds, letting the music gradually release them from the constraints of conversation. Slowly, as the melody rose to full pitch, their eyes met. Despite their physical distance, every part of Laura's and Erik's bodies felt bonded by an irresistible magnetism—from brow to stomach to trembling legs.

For a moment neither could tell where one ended and the other began. It defied their normal expectations of what lovemaking would be like. Yet they would always count this as their "first time." It was the closest either had ever come to a mystical experience.

A Mirror for Your Optimal Self

"Well, now that we have seen each other," said the Unicorn, "if you believe in me, I'll believe in you. Is that a bargain?"

—LEWIS CARROLL, *THROUGH THE LOOKING-GLASS*

I once went for dinner at the Larsen house. As Laura finished the last of the cooking, I asked Erik what he liked best about being married to her. He said, "I could never answer that in my own words. But there is a passage from *War and Peace* that comes pretty darn close."

He strode across the living room to the huge bookshelf on the far wall, pulled out a dusty, dog-eared book, and began to read: "'After seven years of married life Pierre was able to feel a comforting and assured conviction that he was not a bad fellow after all. This he could do because he saw himself mirrored in his wife. In himself he felt the good and bad inextricably mixed and overlapping. But in his wife he saw reflected only what was really good in him, since everything else she rejected. And this reflection was not the result of a logical process of thought but came from some other mysterious, direct source.'"

In letting this passage speak for him, Eric told me volumes. After many years together, Erik could still look into Laura's eyes and feel the comfort of knowing that with all his flaws he was still lovable. In fact, he told me, somehow his flaws were actually mixed up with Laura's desire for him. The miracle was, she seemed to prefer this "Erik as is" to the dreamboat he was in his youth. Reflected in Laura's eyes he could see what she saw: his essential goodness.

In the previous chapter, "Choosing," we looked at the promises and decisions, both big and small, that make up the story of our lives. But there is one choice, one intangible characteristic, that is vital to all good relationships of every kind: heartfelt, mutual respect. Couples bound by this loving attitude are able to give each other the priceless gift of unconditional love. They are resilient in the face of the squabbles and disappointments that occur in even the best of marriages. By committing to honor each other we become free to seek out, and find, the best in each other—enfolding one another, foibles and all, in our arms.

Honoring, the Third Commitment, is at the heart of ethical living, both within marriage and outside of it. Both ethics and honoring are based on human dignity. Every man and woman, every millionaire and every person in the depths of poverty is assumed to have fundamental worth. This comes independent of status or deeds and despite our differences and is the implicit promise behind the wedding vow: "I will honor you all the days of my life."

Different cultures have different ideas about why we all have this basic worth. The ancient Hebrews—and the contemporary religions that evolved out of Judaism—said that the first man and woman were made in God's image. Hindus draw the assumption of worth from the *atman* in the soul, the part that never left God at all. Scholars and students of social systems consider affirming the dignity of each person as necessary to the foundation of civilization. Even without an underlying theory, though, we know through our personal experience how important it is to be treated with dignity.

Honoring is never the same from day to day. It may begin with basic respect or with the simple act of appreciating your spouse's special place in your life. It may involve struggling to see beyond fits of temper to the magnificent person underneath. It may deepen into savoring his or her physical body, exploring his or her quirks of personality, or finding out more about his or her memories of the past. Or your mutual respect may blossom into reverence.

Reverence comes not with perfection but with profound intimacy: the true knowing of ourselves in relation to another and the acceptance of all the joys, tedium, pain, sorrows, tenderness, and vulnerability that being deeply connected brings. Priests have told me they find reverence in a different way through their love of God. Though it comes and goes in our awareness, we know it is always there, like a gem hidden in our pocket. And while it prevails, nothing can separate us from that sensed greater love that holds us all.

Paying Attention

My hands
Invent another body for your body.
—OCTAVIO PAZ, "TOUCH"

When I worked many years ago for the Industrial Home for the Blind, I was amazed how "attended to" I felt by the gentle, noticing hands of children in the play school who would surround me whenever I came in. My lips, nose, and eyebrows seemed to love being inspected by these friendly little strangers.

In the privacy and romance of adult unions, even the lightest touch can take on a special power to exchange affectionate attention. Cultivating an awareness of each other's features creates a lasting connection between us and the miracle that is our partner. Simply paying attention often leads to appreciation, and the tug of its bond pulls in both directions. It is thus one of the most basic techniques for increasing the element of honoring in marriage.

Connie and Juan found this out the hard way. They were soul mates, they told me. Still, Connie had to struggle at times to stay connected. Sometimes when Juan came home from work, she hardly noticed him—even when he came into the same room. Connie herself admitted that she might as well have been on another planet. We began to search through childhood memories for clues to patterns in her adult life. "It just reminds me of bunking in that tiny room with all my sisters," she said, adding after a pause, "I guess I just learned to zone out, to stare at the floor and pretend I was alone."

When looking to uncover times she had successfully been attentive to Juan, we came across a New Year's Eve memory that they both treasured. "It was just before midnight and the new millennium, and the disc jockey at the party started dimming the lights and music," Connie told me. "Someone must've bumped into the knob, because all of a sudden it went pitch black. Somebody screamed. Juan's arm came around me, and I moved my hand up to touch his shoulders, his neck, his cheek. It sounds stupid but I thought, 'What if this is it?' I felt like I wanted to memorize what Juan's face felt like. Then the countdown started, everyone yelled 'Happy New Year!' and the lights flashed back on. Juan caught my hand in his and told me how nice it had felt to be touched that way."

I suggested to Connie that she try the "walking fingers" technique on Juan again now and then. They turned it into a little ritual that was symbolic of her promise to be more attentive to Juan all year long. It also served as a signal. "Could you, uh, do the finger thing?" he'd ask when he was feeling shut out.

If you want to try something like this, spend a minute or two just watching your partner. See the way her chest rises and falls as she sleeps, how he stands on one leg at the stove. Memorize the curve of her hips. Know the exact color of his eyes—chocolate? heather? Tell each other what you like best: "I love the little dimples on the small of your back." "I love the length of your fingers." No one knows these features as well as you do. Not only is sharing like this an intimate and tender act, it also helps you each to respect your own body, detail by marvelous detail, enhancing the confidence within you and the affection between you.

Together and Separate: Celebrating the Music of Marriage

Sing and dance together and be joyous, but let each one of you be alone, Even as the strings of a lute are alone though they quiver with the same music. —KAHLIL GIBRAN, *THE PROPHET*

No matter how attentive we are, there is a limit to what we can know about each other deep down. At some point our ability to figure out our partner's inner workings breaks down. "How is it," we ask, "that this amazing person can cope so well in a situation where I know I would fail?" In good moments we are confounded with admiration for this "other" who is so close to us and yet so unfathomably different.

Every commitment in a spiritually fulfilling marriage requires us to acknowledge our partner's needs and interests, even if they conflict with our own. The special quality of "two" in the commitment to honor one another is the *celebration* of these differences. Honoring calls us to deeply appreciate everything that makes us as married individuals separate and unique—an attitude that helps us bring our differences into harmony in married life. The most fulfilling relationships succeed in large part because of complementary distinctions of personality that are essential to the relationship: These differences energize us, coax us out of complacency, and encourage us to grow.

Honoring requires us to maintain a certain distance between us. The profound comfort we find in the marriage embrace is related to the fact that caring partners can often know us better than we know ourselves. Paradoxically, their dissimilarity from us, their ability to step an arm's length away, lets them see us whole. They are able to catch us when we trip over things in our blind spots and to bring us swiftly back to the safety of lasting love.

Grace and Gordon, whom I met through my work with a youth group, were so similar that they had trouble maturing as a couple. At first, as long as they were together—and they were always together—they soared on the wings of love. At sixteen, Grace, who was an emancipated minor, married Gordon, who had dropped out of high school to organize a band. After they married, Grace joined the band, and both enrolled in a home-study program to earn their GEDs. They looked alike and did everything together. Grace's mother called them the Bobbsey Twins.

Then Grace got pregnant and, only seven months later, gave birth to Adam. Gordon visited Adam every day, peeking into the incubator and worrying about how thin his arms and legs were. He was overwhelmed at the prospect of being the father of a handicapped child, but Grace threw herself into the new role of mother.

When Adam was strong enough to come home, Grace organized her days around his needs, and soon dropped out of the band.

By the time Grace and Gordon came to see me, they were both worried that their marriage was about to fail. "We're just not on the same note anymore," Gordon said with a sigh.

"Thank goodness for *that*!" I replied.

A shift in roles had uncovered the fallacy of "perfect unison" in Grace and Gordon's marriage. I chose to use their shared love of music as a metaphor to help them get through this crisis. First we talked about the fact that rich music usually involves more than one note at a time. Similarly, in lasting relationships we bring two melodies into conversation with each other. Tuning in to each other does not mean forcing your partner to sing your note. It means hearing the distinction so you can harmonize together.

Don't be afraid of your differences, but instead encourage and embrace them. Although it shouldn't be difficult in practice, many people do resist this idea. They are afraid that their spouses will become unrecognizable, that they will come second to their partners' hobbies, or that their own personalities will be erased. The key here is, of course, balance. Partners are in no danger of losing themselves in the shadow of each other, as long as they *both* encourage the other to follow his or her own voice.

A woman once told me at an interfaith conference, "There's a big difference between appreciating another's religious background and wholesale adopting it. Otherwise you don't have enough room to be yourself." These wise words are true not only for faith traditions but for personal opinions, interests, and any other area where differences abide. All are worthy of respect, but to respect ourselves we must also stay true to our own inner selves. Indeed, part of the reason that obsessive, all-consuming, and isolated relationships cause problems is that they don't allow each partner to be him- or herself, either within the relationship or outside it.

This understanding is fundamental to lasting love. Your utter uniqueness in the world must be preserved in order for you to live most fully in it; the utter uniqueness of your spouse must be preserved as well. By nurturing and balancing your separate needs, you become free to grow into better people, truer to yourselves and in the end more authentically and deeply connected. Even better, you become capable of falling in love with each other for who each of you, uniquely, really is.

Disconnection

Seldom, or perhaps never, does a marriage develop into an individual relationship smoothly and without crises; there is no coming to consciousness without pain. —C.G. JUNG, CONTRIBUTIONS TO ANALYTICAL PSYCHOLOGY

Clearly, appreciating each other's differences is critical for a healthy marriage—but it can be difficult at times, and it can even be over-done. (A weekend or two per month spent fishing alone is fine, for example, but more than that can eat into your time together.) There are occasions when your moods, hobbies, and workloads create too many differences for comfort. Tougher challenges to your connection come along when conflicting priorities, imbalances of power, and unhealthy instincts get in the way.

Honoring one another involves an active, ongoing quest to stay connected. We know when we are *not* truly honoring each other, because we feel the disconnection in a painful stab of dread. Often we can't tell at these moments whether we're being paranoid or if we have a good reason to mistrust. We say to ourselves, "I don't think I really like this person" or "I have no idea who this person is." At the moment that the honoring process is interrupted, our body will tell us in a number of ways: For some, stomachs churn; for others, chests tighten or they feel suddenly drained of blood. In addition to these clear visceral signals, many people find themselves muttering the most hurtful put-downs they can muster on short notice.

These moments of disruption are usually fleeting, but they're also inevitable. In order to get past them and back to honoring, it is helpful to know what caused the disconnection in the first place. If we can determine the cause, we have a much better chance of finding our way past our troubles. Let's take a look, then, at a few of the most common reasons for discord: inequality, conflicting values, anger, and fear.

Inequality. As Confucius is known to have said, "Have no friends not equal to yourself." Just as no single background can be more important than another in a mixed marriage, so no one individual within a partnership can be more important than the other.

Unequal partnerships make true honoring particularly tough. In the heat of first passion you may have what one theologian I know called "the illusion that Eve's rib is still stuck in Adam's chest." If one or the other partner is decidedly dominant, a couple can function as a single entity for some time. But eventually both parties grow weary of such arrangements. The dominated one feels worthless, and the dominant one feels alone.

More often the balance of power shifts over time, without ever being shared. I once asked a family counselor why he thought his first marriage failed. He laughed and then summed it up succinctly: "I thought of it as a contest for who's on top. I didn't realize back then that there has to be equal room for two." This is perhaps one of the most basic reasons for any marriage to fail.

To assess the equal measure of your partnership, think back to centering and choosing, the First and Second Commitments. Does your home feature your different preferences visibly in evidence around you? Are both of you active choosers—or is one partner more the decision maker? Correcting substantial imbalances of power can usually happen only slowly over time, in increments of choice and affection. But countless minor adjustments can be made to good effect if you find that the scales lean one way or the other. For example, are only the photos of your grandparents displayed? Find out if your partner wants a family picture on display also.

Conflicting Values. When in conflict, deeply held beliefs—on the issue of pro-choice versus pro-life, say, or public versus private schooling—can make it hard to see eye to eye. What happens in arguments when only one partner is the outspoken one? (Does the other one defend his or her stance, keep quiet, or change his or her mind?) If you don't respect your partner's point of view, how do you respect your partner? Here the Commitment of honoring can really help you out. Remember, you can respect the person even if you don't respect what he or she is saying or doing at the moment. When you feel the snap of disconnection, look past your partner's angry face or aggressive posture to the vulnerable, deeply feeling person underneath. Love is always there to tap in to if we remember to look for it.

It is ironic that our most prized values can drive a wedge between us. Religion, social values, and politics are some obvious areas where this can easily become a problem if not addressed openly. Laura Larsen, for example, had a high value for social equality, while her pipe-smoking, practical husband valued family safety above all. When Laura insisted on renting their first apartment in a vital but "borderline" neighborhood, it took many long conversations to iron things out. They finally agreed that the move could be right for them both: Of great importance to both of them was fostering cooperation in a world of increasing diversity. They went into their first community, though, with eyes wide open. This included purchasing new locks and window guards, getting safety tips from the local police department, and joining an active block association. Solving their dilemma with mutual consideration, they both ended up pleased with the outcome.

Anger and Fear. We all have a need to be considered, to be paid attention to, to be loved. This need is among the instincts that no human can escape and that all of us share. There are other shared instincts, however, that can fly right in the face of our efforts to be respectful. The famous "fight or flight" instinct can cause particular problems. We may unthinkingly find ourselves lashing out at our lover or drawing away within ourselves. We may do this only emotionally, or it may find its way onto the physical plane, and even into the bedroom. The two aspects of our lower self that cut us off most from spiritual sustenance are *anger* and *fear.*

Let's consider the source of our tendency toward fight or flight. These instinctual behaviors are products of the most primitive part of our brain, the part we share with reptiles and birds and other vertebrates. This ancient organ protects us by releasing adrenaline and other chemicals when we are faced with danger. Unfortunately, our "reptilian brain" can respond this way also when we sense emotional danger. But instead of increasing our safety in close relationships, our instinct to fight or flee can actually make relationships more difficult. When challenged emotionally, coming out fighting or withdrawing inside our shells like snails makes good communication and honoring almost impossible.

In an "Honoring" workshop I once asked participants the following questions to help them internalize this concept: What is the scariest thing that's ever happened to you? A mugging? A car accident? A fire? A fistfight? Or something more catastrophic? Consider how you acted in the situation. Did you have a fight-or-flight reaction? If so, ask yourself whether these instincts "saved" you or whether in retrospect it would have been better to act rationally. Either answer was okay—the purpose of these questions wasn't to judge but rather to learn to recognize fight-or-flight impulses in our actual experience.

When I was growing up, people were encouraged to restrain their primitive parts, their animal selves. One married man I know had been taught by his mother to sit in a dark closet every time he thought of hitting the bully next door. When he came out, his father would yell at him for being a coward. He confided to me one day that he feared the "bully" was now inside of him. When I asked how he knew this, he mumbled that it came up every time he and his wife talked about sex. Needless to say, their sex life was thin.

Stuffing down our negative feelings often backfires. It tends to produce brittle, somber people who don't think very well of themselves (they can't even respect themselves!). This man, as a boy, had every right to be upset about the nasty child next door. And it was natural to *want* either to hit him back or run away. No one ever explained to this man that his fight-or-flight reaction was natural—and that the route to healthy adult relationships involves honest confrontation and compromise. In real life the well that holds our anger and fear holds our liveliness, too. Most troubling, blocking it completely may actually increase the chance of violent outbursts.

Most of us have experienced moments of stark anger or fear. When your partnership is new and you've both been on your best behavior, such base emotions may well shock you at first. And sustained, these feelings get in the way of honor and caring in your marriage. So do whatever helps you to dissipate its energy: Breathe deeply, slow down. Begin to identify what triggers your responses, so you can catch yourself. And if you can step outside yourself and find a way to laugh, especially about any excessive responses on your part, it will do wonders for dispersing the poison building up in your system. Try engaging in an activity to let out your impulses: walking briskly around the block, swimming laps, biking up a tall hill, playing the bongos as though you had to get a message to the other side of the world. If you need a sustained break, go on a work vacation or attend a political rally out of town. There are many strategies for channeling your raw energy in positive and productive ways. But most essentially, give yourself time out to recover before barreling on to fight or flee.

Although our ancient load of instincts can weigh heavily on our love life, there is a way out. It is not a quick fix (especially for those with tough childhoods), but it is straightforward: See yourself, faults and all, as a fundamentally good and worthy person. See your partner that way, too. This is such a simple idea, and yet it can be so difficult to absorb. In the next section we'll address these strategies and other alternatives to help reestablish our commitment to honor each other.

Reconnection

Once the realization is accepted that even between the closest human beings infinite distances continue to exist, a wonderful living side by side can grow up, if they succeed in loving the distance between them which makes it possible for each to see each other whole against the sky.

—RAINER MARIA RILKE

We can feel down because we've been coming down hard on each other. Or we can feel down because tough breaks are getting in the way. It is particularly devastating when our usual strategies to behave like an adult just won't work. Your spouse just landed a blow right below the belt, and the next thing you know, you're responding in kind, slamming doors, yelling, sulking.

Often we aren't sure how to get to that honoring place. Life is complex, and many of us rely on instinct to get us through, when instinct is just what we need to watch out for. But there are so many ways to get back to honoring when we feel disconnected. To begin with, make sure you have some preventive measures lined up in advance so you're prepared for the threat of future rifts. Here are several possible strategies:

- Ask your partner, at a time when you're feeling safe and comfortable together, how you can be most supportive when things heat up. Prearrange to give each other specific time-out signals in order to break the tension—secret codes or hand signals that can bring you back into cahoots or the silly, almost always effective, tongue-sputtering raspberry sound to make an angry lover laugh.

Come up with one-liners, too, such as, "It's hard for me to hear you right now."

- Make sure your partner knows how you like to be soothed when you feel shaken. It is difficult to be in an honoring mode when your body is setting off alarm bells right and left. Does a sweater over your shoulders help? An ice pack on your forehead as you rest on the sofa? Do you need a little time alone? Or a steady verbal reminder, if you tend to forget, how important you are to your partner?

- Determine *what* sets off each other's alarm bells. Nelly and Mike know that hasty accusations, weight-related comments, and unnecessary restrictions of choice make them both extra testy. Now they know much better how to prevent quarrels from turning into real fights, by avoiding those "hot buttons" whenever possible and being especially careful and supportive at other times. More important, knowing what makes each other tick has helped Nelly and Mike to remain lovingly respectful of each other, even when one or the other acts irrationally—because they know the reasons behind the behavior.

- We can learn much from our fights and disagreements, as long as the thread of honoring remains intact. In situations in which you've felt frustrated from getting what you want, how have you kept from turning on your partner in the past? Do you make him or her laugh, or do you take a deep breath or two before responding? What calls you back to the honoring place? What do you usually do in conflict, when you're not feeling heard, when you're lonely or unsure of where you stand? What do you do when you are not feeling honored? Can you identify times when you handled yourself well, so you don't feel so lost when facing such challenges in the future?

- Contempt for our differences, causing discord between us during trying circumstances, often springs from a lack of understanding. So think about an activity your partner loves but that doesn't interest you much at all. Participate with your partner one day in order to learn just enough about this activity to ask intelligent questions and be of general support. If you end up enthralled with the activity, try accompanying your partner to something else until you come across an activity that really doesn't interest you. What's important here is to find an opportunity to celebrate your *differences*. When you have finished this experiment in understanding, ask your partner to do the same for you.

In addition to these preventive tactics, there are other strategies couples can use to regain connection when they're in the eye of the storm:

- The honor you show each other is the very same honor you hope to receive in return. The next time you're tempted to act spitefully, quickly imagine a time when you did evident wrong. An outright lie told for selfish gain . . . a disparaging remark you knew was a "low blow". . . betraying a confidence when you knew it would cause pain . . . crossing the line of extramarital flirtation. Think upon that act, on any hurt it caused, on how bad you felt afterward, and on any other negative consequences. Just the thought of that incident can remind you that you're not the only one whose feelings are involved and lead you toward greater consideration of your spouse. You may, as a bonus, find your partner treating you more respectfully as a result of your care.

- Humor is a natural ally of the "holy"—the force that calls us to be whole. Laughter can literally lift us up out of our lower selves, pleasurably bringing us back to a mutually reverent frame of mind when we're under the blind, mean sway of our "animal selves" (more good news: so does lovemaking!). When things get really rough, my husband will don his black cowboy hat and come out riding an imaginary horse. You can dismantle a big bad mood with one small joke, an exaggerated pantomime, or a silly sound. Or you can go to a comedy club or rent a funny movie when the job offers won't come or when circumstances are making it hard for either of you to recall your sense of worth.

- Appreciate your spouse in spite of his opposing viewpoint. Give yourself the satisfaction of realizing that your partner enriches your worldview simply by having his own opinion. Remind yourself that you don't know it all. In fact, there is only one thing in the world that you absolutely know for sure: that your spouse is worthy of your love and respect.

- Look outside the partnership for guidance. Advice can come from your mother, your pastor, your wise older friend—but it needn't come exclusively from these predictable sources. I have my own private list of goodwill guides to call upon when things get rough. A dearly departed neighbor of mine had a funny maxim for every subject. An inner voice has always told me I'd be okay. Ethical heroes from history or literature (Mother Teresa, Alexei Karamazov) remind me to love with my whole heart. And there are many books—sacred texts, novels, poetry—that I can flip open at any time of disconnection and find ready directions to get home to that honoring place. Wherever it comes from, good advice gives us perspective when we can't see the forest for the trees.

- Rather than argue, ask for actual help from your partner or from other people. Simply engaging your partner in actively resolving a crisis can keep the two of you connected. If, for example, the kids left the kitchen a mess and your car pool for work is arriving any minute, skip the accusation ("How could you let the kids do this?") and ask for a specific favor instead ("Could you sponge off the counter?"). You can have that little "how can we do it better next time?" discussion later, when the heat of the moment has passed.

No matter how prepared we are in advance, no matter how willing we are to honor one another in the heat of the moment, there will be times when big fights require more long-lasting efforts toward reconnection. Kwan and Ginny, a couple who shared a vegetable garden with us at a cottage we rented one summer, had recently gotten back together after a separation. They undertook the task of repair by working the weed patches in the garden and found that a soothing way to ease back into togetherness.

After real trials in your partnership, sometimes doing pleasant little things like this together can actually deepen your relationship more effectively than heavy-duty conversations. While our emotional selves are still tender from recent pain, somehow it's easier to appreciate each other, cooperate with each other, and experience bonding together if we quietly share hands-on activities. In other words, it becomes easier to honor each other, both in our behavior and in our hearts. Rather than using these projects to escape, couples can use them to absorb what has happened at the unconscious level and to recharge. It is the simple, lighter things of life that give us true respite after hard struggles. Wherever we are, the bigger impact will catch up to us if we linger awhile.

Loving Through the Worst

In a dark time the eye begins to see.

—THEODORE ROETHKE,
"IN A DARK TIME," FROM *WORDS FOR THE WIND*

It is tempting to cut and run after a troublesome encounter has occurred. After a period for recovery and reflection, we must take the loving leap and hold our partner once again in our arms. "You have to take the good with the bad" is an old Kellerman family saying, and it is quite true. The "bad" side of us is often a shadow of the good—like my openness to others, for example, which can actually cause me to trespass, to get too personal, or to expose my vulnerabilities before a history of trust has been established in friendship. Dealing with our flaws does not—cannot—involve wiping them away completely. Rather, it's a balancing act. Honoring one another means nothing if it does not include the whole person, up- and downside, shadow and light.

To truly *enact* our mutual, unconditional respect, we must also help each other to change for the better, to prevail in those personal struggles we all have with ourselves. We do need to wrestle with the demons that threaten our marriage: fear, anger, unhealthy impulses, bad habits. Our grappling with these shadows will lead in time to a strength of character that will make us even worthier of each other's respect. But in order to begin to conquer these demons we need the other's respect up front—as armor for the fight, as a source of encouragement, as a backup of confidence when our own self-image falters.

Relationships become forged in steel if we can express respect when our partners are at their worst, as Annie and Yoav's story illustrates. Annie, an aspiring writer, and Yoav, a poet, had been together for several years when I met them at a workshop of mine. Annie told the group that when she was six, her best friend, Liza, got a real cloth Cabbage Patch doll. "Well, this bad, wild feeling overcame me," Annie said. "I wanted it so bad. I tried to take it and kept yanking until it split right in two."

I could see by the expression on Annie's face that she was still there, tearing the doll apart in her mind. Yoav sat quietly next to her, an arm up over the top of her folding chair.

"When I saw the stuffing oozing out," Annie continued, "I suddenly felt like it might as well have been Liza's real blood. I just stood there frozen. I couldn't believe what I had done. Liza had these big tears in her eyes." Annie's voice cracked. "When *I* started to cry, something extraordinary happened. Liza reached out and touched my arm and said we could share the doll between us and sew it up." Annie began to sob as she said this.

Annie might have gone a different route in life if Liza's mother hadn't screamed and called Annie a little monster. When her mother came to get her, Annie was dragged off by the ear and spanked soundly just outside the front door. For months and years, Annie's mother reminded her of how "undeserving" she was. No one was there to help Annie forgive herself for her natural envy and yet to acknowledge the rightness of her dread recognition. No one except Liza, that is. And Liza was no longer allowed to play with Annie.

Annie missed Liza terribly. Over time Annie began to work out revenge in her own way. First there was Frank, with whom she shared a double desk in third grade. He always had thick slices of cake in his lunch box. Anyone could see this wasn't fair. Annie evened out the odds, enjoying every stolen bite she could get. At Christmastime she wore her big sister's coat and played her secret game, "Santa in Reverse," slipping items from the toy store into her sleeves. And in seventh grade she stole Regina Winger's boyfriend from right under her nose. Over the years there were many such incidents, and Annie might have been on the road to high crimes and misdemeanors if she hadn't found Yoav—who saw through all of this. Yoav met Annie in a computer chat room where struggling poets exchanged their work. As such, he saw her inside out: soul first.

If we are fortunate enough to find this center of unconditional regard early on in our relationship, it is much more likely that we'll have a healthy marriage, in which we honor one another always. One day, shortly before Annie's birthday, Yoav spotted her at the mall during lunch hour. There she was, stuffing a cashmere sweater under the trench coat she'd borrowed from him. Yoav came up behind Annie and gently put his arm on hers. She froze. He kissed the nape of her neck and whispered, "You don't have to do that, you know. I'll buy it for you." For no particular reason, Annie saw Liza's face in her mind's eye and "felt" once again her friend's gentle pat on her arm. As the warmth of Yoav's hand penetrated the coat sleeve, Annie began to cry. This memory of Liza, released by Yoav's love and acceptance, motivated Annie to enter a formal recovery program. As she bravely explained to the group, she now understood her healing process as it pertained to the workshop's theme of "mutual reverence": Yoav had given her loving respect just when she was at her worst—which is exactly what she needed in order to begin to heal.

Helping professionals—therapists, counselors, and the like—do transforming work *because* people often come to them when they are feeling unworthy, powerless, confused, or drowning in their "sins." A child needs its mother's love much more during naughty days than "goody two-shoes" days. A person needs to be able to turn to a true friend and reveal not just successes but deep disappointments and sources of shame. And life partners must love each other through the worst if they are to be deeply connected.

Honoring is an evolving, dynamic process that ranges from basic respect to self-control, to support, to all-out reverence. Because honoring isn't static, we shouldn't confuse complacency with allowing for defects or for discrepancies between us. Total acceptance should never involve turning a blind eye to each other's weaknesses. Instead it means you withhold the voice of condemnation and that you turn up the volume on the voice of support.

Honoring provides a safety net that allows us to take the risks that positive change requires. When we both feel safe, loved, and respected, what would otherwise be a terrifying risk becomes a thrilling adventure—a looping roller coaster ride built up with the steel of unconditional love. We can quit that demoralizing job or kick that bad habit, because our partner believes we can and knows we deserve better. What's more, we can really get to the task of making meaningful improvements in our relationship. We suddenly see with a stroke of pride that we owe it to ourselves, to our partner, and to our marriage to bravely change our ways for the better.

I've always found inspiration in the cornerstone maxim of Ethical Culture's founder: "So act to elicit the best in others, and thereby oneself." This is a deepening of the famous Golden Rule, which tells us to "do unto others as you would have them do unto you." To commit truly to honoring, we need not only to treat people with respect and to believe in the best potential of others but actually *to help bring that potential to fruition.* As you deepen your commitment to honoring, remember that it includes an ongoing commitment to positive change. This means growing, healing, and becoming stronger and more deeply feeling, ever worthier of each other.

A Body of Miracles

O amazement of things—even the least particle!

—WALT WHITMAN, "SONG AT SUNSET"

Honoring is serious pleasure. It requires you to relish and even stimulate your differences. It encourages you to pay conscious attention to your partner—to his or her quirks of personality, instinctual behavior, and, of course, physical body.

As Erik and Laura learned on their Nantucket honeymoon, when a couple stumbles across the inner depths of one another, they never forget the experience. Not only is such an encounter intensely pleasurable in and of itself, but it is also a reminder to the couple that they are more than just their surface selves. This understanding is critical to the spiritual health of a marriage and can give it new life during hard times.

I know of one husband who managed to withstand the repeated come-ons of a beautiful woman while on an assignment away from home. He used a two-part strategy. First, he told the woman he was happily married. Then he called his wife and said he was so needy that even doughnuts were beginning to look attractive. Taking her husband playfully up on this image, she suggested they buy strawberries and whipped cream and eat them while they were on the phone the next evening. Each night they picked something to eat and touch. They also recalled their favorite love trysts. These tactics worked like a charm, and the would-be seductress vanished from the husband's mind. When he got home, the couple discovered an added benefit: Their lovemaking was more rewarding than ever.

Sensuality helps to keep us out of situations dangerous to our marriage, such as infidelity. It can be healing medicine, transmuting the potentially destructive power of lust into permeating, wholesome desire. And it keeps a nice, warm glow on the home-fire coals. So learn the little techniques that keep pleasure alive, and find ways to express them often. You can enjoy, for example, the tiny goose bumps that rise along your lover's arm when you run your fingers down its length. Or you might take a moment to savor the smile that appears on your partner's face when you tenderly kiss each knuckle. Ask your partner often, "What do you want?" Say what it is that fires you the most—real and imagined. Explore sensual activities to find what works best: Read love poetry to each other, get up early and take a long hot shower together, give each other massages using special oils, go away to a holiday spa and, after a long soak in the hot tub, fall asleep in each other's arms. Savor the fact that you will always be, on some level, mysteries to one another. And reflect on this: Each small portion of pleasure given and gained can be magnified a thousandfold by the fact that you are experiencing it with the person with whom you will spend the rest of your life.

It is hard to connect sensually like this when the relationship overall doesn't feel right. Women, who are more likely to prefer meaningful connection as a *prelude* to physical intimacy, may want to talk things out before they'll kiss and make up. Men, on the other hand, often want to use the sex itself to reconnect emotionally. Husbands and wives can find themselves in a catch-22, each stubbornly waiting it out. Remember at such times what honoring tells you: You are more than your surface selves. Honoring *is* a connector between you—before, during, or after sex. No single sequence of events is better than any other, but all sequences can work as long as you can call upon the deep appreciation of honoring to help you.

It may seem paradoxical to link lofty reverence with physicality—but honoring is actually a critical part of a healthy marriage's sensual side. To put it bluntly, sex without honoring is rape, even in the marriage bed. And honoring without sex deprives couples of a richly pleasurable aspect of married life.

Sexual attraction, embedded in the brain, begins as a physical thing. Many of us had it good in the first flush of love, a time when we were probably more amazed by our partner than we are today. Do you ever stop to consider this connection? At its best, making love means abandoning oneself body *and* heart to someone who is fascinatingly different from us. Sex isn't just about our bodies rubbing thoughtlessly against one another. When honoring is at play, it becomes something much more. In the spirit of the master violinist who knows just how to play his instrument, we too can touch each other with deep attention—so that it's not just our bodies that hum and swell; our mind and spirit do, too.

If you've had experiences that felt like this, cherish them and build upon them. If sensual connection is *not* your strong point, know that committing to honoring will help you share such powerful experiences in the future. Whenever partners cultivate an attitude of deep reverence for each other, the high pleasure of sensuality has a greater potential to flow. When you can rest in the unconditional acceptance of the other, you are freer to abandon yourself in new ways.

Making love exerts on us a tidal pull into the *now*. As we ride its waves, the mystery of life opens before us, as naked as our lover, complex, radiant.

Wonder and Silence

Wonder is the basis of worship. —THOMAS CARLYLE, *SARTOR RESARTUS*

Once, when I was ten, I tried to rescue a small brown rabbit that my cat had hunted down. I cradled it in a cotton-ball-filled shoe box crib. As midnight turned to morning, it could no longer suck the milk I was feeding it with an eyedropper. I pressed my praying finger to its tiny chest. My own heart beat faster, as though it could somehow pump for two. In that moment the little creature's spirit entered my life forever. It was my first communion.

Wonder is the sublimation of our egos to what lies, alluringly, beyond our grasp. It is thus at the root of both healthy worship and healthy love. Most broadly viewed, honoring is a feeling of reverence for something bigger than you are—nature, music, God, anything you consider deeply significant. When shared, wonder-inspiring experiences bind us together on a spiritual level, strengthening our connection soul to soul. Whether we find this high on a mountain-top or deep in the work of everyday life, such profound experiences can renew and sustain us both over the long haul.

There is a kind of silence that draws us out of our small, separate selves into a quiet and generous realm where mutual tenderness can flourish. Like the hushed expectation I felt kneeling over my trembling rabbit or the wordless sensual experience that Laura and Erik Larsen shared on their honeymoon, this golden silence is an ally in the endeavor of honoring one another. (Not all silences, of course, are golden. The "silent treatment," for instance, is often used as a weapon in marriage.) Soaring music, an exquisitely prepared meal, or conscious, loving focus on a lover's face and body can bring us into a reverential state of mind without our ever having to say a thing.

Mother Nature is an even more powerful ally in this private realm beyond words. One couple who lives near Half Moon Bay, California, recently shared with me an experience that exemplifies nature's power to elevate our frame of mind without words:

It had been a tough year. Lydia had lost a child in the fifth month of pregnancy—no one was sure why. Then Tomás was laid off, and their old car broke down for good. Their spirits were so low that they bickered constantly. Then, on Independence Day, Lydia and Tomás took an excursion to a grassy hill above the fishing docks in town. Half Moon Bay is famous for its cold summer evenings, Tomás told me, so they pushed their chairs up close and cuddled under a heavy wool blanket. Soon they were watching the grand spectacle of exploding pinwheels and flashing bursts of color in the sky.

After the final eruption of lights, in the still darkness, Tomás and Lydia gazed upon the more lasting spectacle of a sky strewn with stars. Tomás recalled legends about the summer constellations that he'd learned from his grandfather. Pointing to the moon, Lydia said that she had read that the strings of DNA inside one human body, if stretched out in a straight line, would reach to the moon and back. They sat quietly, taking it all in. Then Tomás turned to Lydia. Without a word, they got out of their chairs and knelt down on the wet grass, facing each other, pressing the tops of their thighs, their tummies and foreheads together, and feeling, beneath their bulky sweaters, the steam of their flesh. For a long moment they remained, sensing their own responsiveness to one another, to the canopy of tiny lights above . . . and something beyond, in the primal dark.

"Somehow it reminded me of the time I went to mass with Aunt Esperanza," Lydia said quietly, as she sat holding Tomás's hand on my office sofa. "I remember her explaining about the communion wine and the host and thinking how incredible it was to taste God."

After that night, Tomás told me, they had a better time keeping their troubles in perspective. "Sharing that night brought us much closer together," he said. "I wanted to honor the experience by being more patient and trusting in life, and with Lydia."

The unspeakable beauty of nature is perhaps our greatest resource when it comes to cultivating a reverential frame of mind. At every moment it offers up strong nourishment for our souls. Even when it disrupts our lives, as with a fearsome storm, the natural world calls us to an awareness of a larger reality beyond ourselves— an awareness that helps us to be better to each other.

We can derive wonder from anything that is meaningful to us— from nature, from religious practices, from art, from each other. It is a deep, positive response that brings forth a natural generosity. Thus drawn out, we are able to breathe and take in the extraordinary person who is our partner for life. Suddenly we see beyond the surface: Before us stands this incredible, distinct universe of a human being, packaged neatly in flesh and bones much like our own, yet somehow miraculous.

The Binding Power of Memory

Memory is the mother of all wisdom. —AESCHYLUS, *PROMETHEUS BOUND*

Honoring makes use of our innate ability to experience one another as unique and precious. It starts early in life. Both Tomás and Lydia, for example, were able to draw on memories from childhood in order to find inspiration during a difficult year.

If a couple has had encounters (either together or separately) that evoked amazement, they'll be able to translate these experiences into their love relationship, increasing in it the presence of reverence. On a regular night you may say to your spouse, "Remember the view from the lodge in Colorado?" Yes, your partner will nod: We shared that. In the tension during a family crisis you can also call to mind a time your partner deeply impressed you or stood by you steadfastly, as a way to regain the honoring mind-set.

We are bundled in sustaining memories from infancy through advanced age. One such recollection still strongly cradles me—the recollection of my father's singing me to sleep. Even now I can close my eyes and hear the croaky rasp in his throat as he sang his lullabies to me in a voice that was sweetly off-tune but filled with love. What are your sustaining memories? Do you remember the first time you looked up and really noticed the stars? Or perhaps it was something else that shocked you into a reverent state of mind: the moon in August, the city lights from an airplane, sheep blocking a roadway, a day heavy with rain?

Sharing memories such as these is a potent way to see past our irritations with each other, to regain our awareness of the deeply feeling person inside. I regularly suggest to couples that they share their memories of feeling connected to the universe. One fiancé told me about watching fishing boats sail out to sea at dawn; his partner remembered waking to the smells of a cake baking the morning of her eighth birthday—and having the distinct feeling that she was at the very center of the cosmos. Did you ever marvel at the insides of some object you had taken apart? Or perhaps you sat in a meadow at night and turned your flashlight up to the stars? To really hammer in the effect of this activity, some couples have found a way to relive or reenact these wondrous experiences, together.

I used to collect pebbles. When I would show my collection to friends, I would tell the history of each pebble: where it had been found, whom I was with at the time, what had made me first notice it. This drive to gather not just precious objects but memories is great in all of us. And it serves us well in sorting out the helpful patterns in our lives that allow us to honor one another. Laura Larsen's Iranian foot chest, which held so many meaningful objects, served as a storehouse not only for the past but for the future as well. The conch shell that she kept inside of it, for example, served as a reminder of a night when all felt right in the world. When she placed it in the chest for safekeeping, it also became a message of hope for the future.

We Were Not Meant to Be Alone

Every married pair undertakes to fulfill on its part the task of humanity. This is the obligation which all who enter into the marriage relation should have before their minds. But the task is not only to perpetuate the spiritual life, but to enhance it.

—FELIX ADLER, FOUNDER OF ETHICAL CULTURE,
  RECONSTRUCTION OF THE SPIRITUAL IDEAL

Love, the fruit of honoring, is reached through the continuing courage to leap into one another's arms. It feels risky to do this at times—in new relationships, for example, or when we feel ourselves changing. Committing to honoring takes stamina and vision. But without the love that honoring creates, the world itself cannot hang together. Anytime you think your marriage is insignificant in the greater scheme of things, think again. We are indelibly linked to our fellow beings through common heritage, shared concerns, and the earth upon which we stand. Where honoring is not practiced, violence and hatred happen, and all our lives change for the worse. No couple, no community in the world can ever be a "nation apart." The need to honor one another has become, I believe, the most critical issue for humanity as a whole. Keep this implicit mission in mind as you learn how to better honor one another at home.

Underlying your vow to honor each other, there is also a tacit vow to honor the world in which you reside. But how are you supposed to honor the world? You don't, you can't, except through interactions with others. You start small, practicing the art of honoring in the safety of your primary love relationship. In time the benefits naturally spill out to touch the lives of many. In fact, in a spiritually strong partnership we regularly share the gifts of mutual honoring with others.

It is not enough to share your reverence and wonder only with each other. Life calls to other life, deep calls to deep. This may take the simple form of telling a close friend all the things you adore about your spouse. It may be that you participate in a neighborhood festival or invite friends over to share dinner on the Sabbath. Have a girls' night out or a guys' night in. Create opportunities for honoring however you can to share with others.

The adventure of creating a spiritually fulfilling marriage begins by putting aside the idea of a solitary journey. Together we stand, called into life in twos and threes and more: a couple dancing, a father tenderly holding his wife and infant child, four girls playing double Dutch, five buddies around a campfire—the circle ever widening. Whether single or paired up, introverted or extroverted, we belong in the company of others. This is because, from the beginning of our time on earth, we humans have been "wired" for community. We need each other to survive and to thrive. When a couple chooses to marry, they are publicly making manifest what is invisibly true for every one of us: We were not meant to be alone.

The greatest thing about honoring is that it's contagious. Whenever you act in an honoring way toward someone, you are most likely to be treated in kind. So smile at your postal worker. Honestly thank your bus driver. Help someone who needs it across the street. Bring bottles of water to people on work crews. And tell your friends why you like having them around. Do it all jointly, together. This is your ongoing meditation. This is your prayer to life.

Keys to Strengthening Mutual Reverence

- Prize every feature of your partner's that you find endearing.
- Make "harmony" out of the many differences between you.
- Don't let your marriage be all-consuming; allow yourselves to be yourselves beyond it, too.
- Arrange for time-out signals in times of conflict.
- Help each other to heal and grow.
- Enfold your whole partner, foibles and all, in your arms.
- Pleasure one another.
- Treat golden silence as an ally.
- Revisit memories of amazement and wonder.
- Turn to nature to raise your spirits.
- Spread the seeds of reverence far and wide.

Honoring Questions to Ask Yourself

1. Can you find comfort in the assurance that you encourage each other to be your true selves?
2. Have you stood by your covenant to honor your beloved for better or worse?
3. Do you imagine both your partner and yourself as fundamentally worthy human beings?
4. When you don't agree on priorities, can you respect your partner's different opinion?
5. Do you have ways of getting back to respect when you feel unsupported or alone?

6. Do you help each other heal those old wounds that keep you from being your best self?
7. Can you see beneath the surface of your partner's words and behavior—to the fascinating person underneath?
8. Is your partnership all-consuming, or does it free you to be yourselves both within and outside it?

The Lover's List: An Honoring Exercise

As we've seen, honoring is an essential element of a spiritual marriage. And though it can be serious, the tricks in this exercise—which can help you get into the habit of consciously honoring your spouse—are anything but.

The gist of "The Lover's List" is as follows: There are countless methods for reminding yourself why you chose this one person above all others. It may be her bright blush, his cowlick, or that cute vein in his forehead—the one that pops up when he's laughing hard. It may be the way he mumbles when doing math or the way her hips sway as she walks down the hall. Perhaps you've always admired his dancing skills—or maybe you love him for *enjoying* dancing despite his two huge left feet. There may be a small number of highly specific things you adore, each of which captures the essence of what you love about your partner . . . or, on the other hand, it may be difficult for you to stop thinking of new "favorite things" once you've started, and your list may never end.

Allow your own style to determine how you do this exercise. There are about as many permutations of it as there are quirks in your partner to love. The basic format is to write out ten traits or habits and use them either as a springboard to expressing your affection to your spouse or as a private reminder to treat him or her with respect (or both!).

One of the versions that I like best is as follows: Take out two legal pads, and each of you write down ten funny little features. Carry the list around with you for a week, and try to look it over every day. Then set aside time on the weekend to sit together over cups of hot chocolate and read each other's lists out loud. Alternatively, see how long you can come up with a new favorite quirk each day. Leave it in a note under your partner's pillow. Or make up a new list each week and keep it in a private closet or your underwear drawer.

Yet another version is to laminate your list and carry it with you wherever you go. When your partner has done something to disappoint or frustrate you, sit in a quiet place, perhaps closing your eyes. Notice any negative feelings you are having, and one by one let them go. Enjoy the empty space this leaves. Now take out the list and visualize each entry one by one. End by letting the positive, more honoring feelings you've just elicited fill that empty space.

Caring

I will be a source of loving care for my partner,
setting my heart upon what matters most.

"The trouble with secrets is, you can't tell anyone. If you do tell, it gets you into trouble. But you're in trouble if you don't tell, too."

Josh was keeping a secret from Maureen. As he sat with me in my office, he told me that it felt like a pit in his stomach. The truth can hurt. What good would it do to hurt someone you love, Josh wondered—especially when that truth wouldn't really change anything? Yet deep down he knew that it would be wrong to keep quiet.

Finally one night the dam broke. Josh and Maureen had rented a movie, a hilarious but tragic tale about a blizzard of lies really messing people up. Afterward Josh pointed out that if the heroine had just told the hero the truth, they might still be together. But the hero had needlessly suffered by keeping his own secret, Maureen replied.

Josh realized it was now or never. "You know," he said, searching Maureen's eyes for some clue as to how she might react, "I'm a lot like that guy. I'm holding something back, too."

Before he knew it, Josh was rapidly recounting his story. During the intermission at a jazz festival he had attended with his father, Josh had hinted that he thought Maureen was "the one." He was expecting his father to be elated, maybe even a little bit proud of him. Instead Erik *bristled and, maybe thanks to his second cup of red wine, actually went into a tirade.*

Was his son going to betray his own heritage? Erik wanted to know. Didn't Josh realize that a thousand years ago his ancestors in Norway had been forced to convert to Catholicism or have their heads roll? What about the pope's strange silence during the Holocaust? Was it back to prayer beads and magic, then, instead of science and reason? Would rigid old men in robes be telling his future grandchildren what to do?

Josh was shocked by his quiet father's sudden vehemence. "And don't go running to your girlfriend and telling her I said all this," his father added.

On the ride back they had a brief discussion about the jazz scene but soon settled into silence. Josh recognized that his father was turning his temper inward. The night Josh and Maureen came over to show off the engagement ring, Erik stiffly shook Maureen's hand and then retired as soon as dinner was over.

"I should have defended you, but I guess I was too stunned," Josh concluded. "I'm really sorry."

When he looked up, he noticed the tears in Maureen's eyes. She reached over and put her hands on his. She was glad Josh had told her about this, she said. After all, Josh's father's feelings were not Josh's fault.

"And don't feel bad about not telling me sooner," Maureen added. "What matters to me is that you cared enough about me to find a kind way to tell me the truth."

Loving Care

The whole idea of compassion is based on a keen awareness of the inter-dependence of all these living beings, which are all part of one another, and all involved in one another.

—THOMAS MERTON, SPEECH GIVEN IN BANGKOK, 1968

What happens when you love two people and one of them rejects the other? Hearing the hard truth from his father really hurt Josh. He had always read his father's silences as admirably contemplative, even as a kind of tacit affirmation. Now he knew otherwise.

Stepping back to identify the underlying values of our conflicts helps us to disarm anger and fear and get to the heart of the matter. Josh knew that underneath it all, his father was worried that he had failed as a parent—that Josh, by his choice of life partner, was rejecting hard-won family values. But when Josh began to think seriously about all this, he realized it was actually his father's value for objectivity and his openness to new ideas that had allowed Josh to build such a strong relationship with a woman from a very different background. Also, though Josh's father had blurted things out in a hurtful way, his words pointed to issues that Josh and Maureen would eventually have to address. How *were* they going to raise their children? (Church one week, jazz festivals the next?) What *was* most important to each of them? (Pleasing their elders? Choosing a religious identity?)

Differences of vision and value between us and our loved ones are as inevitable as rain, and just as beneficial in the long run. When we're soaked and shivering from a sudden downpour, it doesn't necessarily seem so. But even though it can be tough to deal with our differences, whenever we boldly face and resolve them, we strengthen our partnership and our other important relationships. And we learn to care for each other in ever deeper and more lasting ways.

To begin to disentangle ourselves from our conflicts, it is helpful to take a step back from the net of hurt feelings and to retire to a place where we can think things through. What is most important to us, not just when dealing with conflict but all the time? Figuring this out will help us on regular days to do right by each other, to face transitions, and to weave up our values—both shared and divergent—into one integrated way of living together. In a sense, by looking at our values, we are intentionally undertaking an act of loving support for each other, our marriage, and all those we love.

Committing to care has two parts. The first is identifying what matters to you—what you care about, what you value. The second is acting according to these values—which inevitably takes the form of treating your loved ones well. Caring in a spiritual marriage is not only *feeling* love for your partner but *giving* love as well through your daily acts of consideration as well as your larger acts of support.

A motivational counselor I know likes to say, "You can't get what you want till you know what you want." He feels (and I agree) that if you identify what matters to you, you'll find yourself acting for its fruition. Think about the fact that "to care" means both "to be concerned" and "to nurture." Once you consciously realize that, for example, you are greatly concerned about the welfare of children, you may find it a matter of course to study to become a teacher or to spend extra time with your orphaned niece. Indeed, giving of ourselves—whether through vocational training, activism, or simply everyday kindness—is a natural result of pinpointing our values.

In a good marriage we count each other among the most precious gifts we have. Because we cherish each other, we are loving to one another both emotionally and actively, both concerned in our hearts and nurturing with our arms and hands.

"The Art of Ought"

We must use time wisely and forever realize that the time is always ripe to do right. —NELSON MANDELA

After the incident with his father, Josh felt torn between his desire to protect Maureen and his feeling of being cut off from her by the secret he held. Was it possible to be both kind and honest at the same time, or did he have to make an impossible choice? Were there any guiding principles that could tell him what he ought to do?

Nowadays when it comes to figuring out how to do the right thing, we can no longer get away with unquestioningly submitting to a narrow, prepackaged base of authority. Having grown up in today's diverse and dynamic world, we've learned to think more and more "outside the box" and to adapt quickly to changing circumstances. This resiliency is good in both the workplace and our marriage. But as a result of all this freedom we have in a sense been left to raise ourselves. We've got a lot to figure out on our own—especially if we wish to create spiritually fulfilling relationships.

The bottom line to loving care is the guiding force of ethics, the guiding force of doing what's right for one another and being as *decent* to each other as we possibly can. Ethics is what one of my professors called "The Art of Ought." What ought I, as a caring person, do? How should we humans live our lives? How *can* we treat each other well?

In addition to these broad questions, other sources of guidance are always available to us. Whether we're conscious of it or not, we've been exposed all our lives to guiding principles and sets of cherished values: those of our community, our social class, our religion, our country; those of our school, our industry, the organizations we join; those of our friends and mentors and, of course, our family. We will have adopted many of these principles (but not all) as our own. Since the principles come attached to cultural trappings, we often need to examine and reshape them as deeper new questions surface. The better we get at refining our personal values, the more surely they will guide us toward a confidence about what's right.

To help sort out all these things, it is useful to talk with our partner about how we were raised and what we were taught to believe. Each of us has brought into our adult life helpful and unhelpful models of how to be a caring person. By looking at the models a bit more closely, we can find guidelines for both navigating conflicts and acting with care.

My great-grandparents immigrated from Alsace-Lorraine to New York City the year President Grover Cleveland died. My grandmother's father, a top-notch engineer, had to work in an unregulated, soot-filled factory because he spoke no English. It didn't take long after settling down in Hell's Kitchen for them to appreciate the meaning of that neighborhood's name. My great-grandfather quickly eased himself into the oblivion of alcohol, and he died of tuberculosis not long thereafter. My great-grandmother then formed a tight-knit circle with her five growing daughters. They scrubbed the stone steps outside their tenement; they sewed hundreds of hats for rich ladies; they cried in each other's arms. Three generations later I've received the value-laden message of their earnest lives: Keep clean in a dirty world, do whatever honest work is offered, and stick together no matter what. These lessons formed a part of my family's rich, informal moral tradition.

The *formal* traditions in which we were raised can also help us to figure out what is right and to be better sources of loving care to each other. For example, if you and your partner were brought up to believe, as many Christians do, that loving your God and loving one another are almost the same, you may be more inclined not to yell put-downs over the phone when a telemarketer interrupts your dinner or you may stop yourself from shouting at your partner for getting up to answer the phone. Alternatively, if the Buddhist Eightfold Path (including Right Speech and Right Understanding) more closely reflects your spiritual heritage, the next time the telephone rings at dinner, you will breathe in, breathe out, and resist the urge to fight about whether to answer the phone. The resultant "right" behavior will be similarly mindful and kind.

We can look back as well to history, to literature, or to traditions other than our own. Humble and great people alike have wrestled with questions of ethical living throughout the ages, trying to sort it all out into something one can actually practice in our daily lives. The greatest rabbi of his age, Hillel, summarized Judaism as follows: "What is hateful unto you, don't do unto your neighbor. The rest is commentary—now go and study." St. Augustine declared that the whole of Christianity could be summed up in this directive: "Love and do as you will." And the Dalai Lama declared at a gathering of faith communities, "I practice the religion of kindness."

Despite the common thread of caring in these epigrams, there have always been questions, confusions, and hard choices to make when it comes to trying to live them out. Here is where ethics steps in again, as a way to make sense of these quandaries in a relevant and responsible way. Ethical inquiry tells us, for example, not *which* choice to make but *how* to choose (with good intentions) and *why* (so as to bring out the best in ourselves and others).

People often use the word "ethics" when they really are talking about "morality." In practice, these approaches provide meaningfully different answers to questions of "ought." Philosophically speaking, morality connotes a set of relatively hard-and-fast rules to live by, as promoted by a particular group. Every community has rules of this sort, and often they have been thought through for generations. Some rules regarding right and wrong, such as Muslim and Jewish acts of submission to a greater good by refraining from eating pork, are not practiced everywhere. Other moral rules, such as that against bearing false witness, are more broadly embraced.

Ethics, meanwhile, fosters a certain skepticism toward rote conventions and prefers general, evolving guidelines to rules. It asks, When am I justified in confronting my partner? What are the right means for us to use in achieving our goals as a couple? In situations when hand-me-down rules of conduct no longer work, couples may find richer, more adequate resources for developing meaning in their marriage by getting comfortable with such open-ended questions.

When things get really bogged down, such penetrating inquiry can help us to see our problems in a more balanced light. For example, a man from a fundamentalist background may be considering marrying an urbanite but not be able to get past differing family ideas about premarital relations. Ethics can help break the impasse, by posing questions that get to the heart of the matter. What would he think of a woman he marries who breaks his community's rules? What would she think of a man who forced her to conform to a system of belief that wasn't hers? What common standards of behavior can they follow to give them the best chance at a lasting marriage? In practice, ethics becomes a process of reflection and subsequent action that helps people to nurture their relationships in the layered, dynamic context of a complicated world.

Of course, we need both morality and ethics. Seasoned moral rules—the time-tested conventions of decency in our community—are stepping-stones that get us started. But when they clash with rules of other groups, or with our own hard-won experience, then the broader vision and versatility of ethical inquiry is needed.

We live in a world peopled with those who disagree with us. No matter how absolutely certain our beliefs, we still have to share the world with people who march to different drums. Often enough our own spouse may be one of these dissenters. This idea is critical to remember as we sort out our understandings of what is right. For practical purposes it's usually good to take a stance of openness and to refrain from blanket judgments against certain behaviors, at least until we have a fuller understanding of the context.

Sometimes we must do not what we want to do or feel like doing but what we believe is right—for us, for the group, for future generations. When I became a parent, this truth really hit home for me. It was as though a door had opened, and in my son's first cries I could hear a call to make the world a better place, for his sake. That type of call leads us all down the ethical path to the question of how to live.

Acting on Principle

Our deeds determine us, as much as we determine our deeds.
—GEORGE ELIOT, *ADAM BEDE*

Asking ourselves the big questions leads us toward general guidelines. But being caring partners and parents also requires us to deal with the specifics. It helps in several ways to get crystal clear about what really matters to us—and to our loved ones. We can use that inquiry as an aid in self-help and self-knowledge. We can explain why it is that our partner behaves a certain way—irrationally, angrily, or resignedly, say, when an in-law finds fault in a decision. We can be more understanding when our partner succeeds in some endeavors and fails in others. And we can find firm common ground on which to shore up our partnership.

It is easy to slip into squabbles, half-truths, and standoffs when we're not paying attention to our behavior and to the reasons behind our behavior. Petty habits, such as putting off chores because we want our partner to do them, can and do add up without our really noticing. Suddenly we find ourselves disconnected or even silently warring over the most inconsequential things.

Your actions are the true measure of your values. If you value cooperation, you must demonstrate it. Is doing the dishes with equal frequency really that important to you? Perhaps it symbolizes something precious (gender equality or teamwork) and therefore *is* that important. Then again, maybe your bitterness on the subject is just a bad habit worth trying to let go, now that you've noticed it. And the fastest way out of that habit is to put your head down and do those dishes.

Identifying what matters is useful for disentangling petty knots. It's even better for helping the two of you in making decisions together, be they daily choices or life-transforming ones. Whenever you ask yourselves practical questions, your values are underneath them: How much time should our child spend on homework and how much in the playground? (Where do we each draw the line between play and diligence?) Should we send our child to public school (for diversity and thrift) or to private school (for more guidance or a specific curriculum), or do we do home schooling instead (to ensure safety, control, and the most personal touch)? Clearly, these questions are not about values per se—and yet they are fundamentally driven by values and answered because of them in the end.

A shortcut to uncovering our core values is to think about what we have chosen again and again. This gives us a starting place. When Hal and I were first married, we rented a small apartment in Rockville Center, Long Island. Everyone (except us) agreed it was perfect. It did have practical virtues. It was on the second floor—easy to mount the stairs, but too high for robbers to climb in the window (as my mother-in-law pointed out)—and it was exactly halfway between our jobs (we had actually measured the distance on a map). Six months later we broke the lease and moved to a smaller apartment with higher rent, right behind the Museum of Natural History in Manhattan. Opera within walking distance, Central Park, cafés galore—who cared if our living quarters were cramped and we had to step over garbage to get in the door? We realized then, and not for the last time, that we were hopeless romantics who valued rich experience over practicality. This became a living values-clarification exercise for us.

To begin to find out what our values are, we must ask ourselves, What have we chosen time and again? *What really matters to us?* There are multitudes of enjoyable ways to answer these questions. Here are just a few brief alternatives:

- Pick an object from your home that you absolutely love, and see what it says about your values. For example, I love old things—washboards, hay hooks, whatever links me to the past. They speak to me simultaneously of continuity and change over time. In other words, they remind me that I value both tradition and new growth.

- Start with a list of what you don't like, and then infer from this the opposite. Flakiness, emotional distance, and superficiality are some of Nelly and Mike's worst peeves, for example. From this it is easy to infer that they prize dependability, warmth, and sincerity.

- Make a list of a dozen or so virtues, such as courage, loyalty, or diligence. Then number them in order of priority. Afterward compare your lists with one another, discussing differences and similarities. You and your spouse can come from the same town, ethnic background, social class, and religious denomination and still have vast differences in the way you see the world. Find out what those differences are.

- Look at the honoring exercise, "The Lover's List." What do your favorite things about your partner say about what matters to you? If his constant jokes tickle your fancy, then humor is important to you. If his determination to exercise every day impresses you, then perhaps it's discipline that matters, or physical health.

- For a virtual crash course in relationship building, each of you can ask the other: 1. What do you cherish most about me? 2.

What drives you nuts? 3. How are these two responses linked in terms of your moral code?

Deeds speak louder than words when investigating your values. You may say and even think, for example, that you treasure patience, and yet you find yourself leaving job after job in short order. Perhaps you actually value creativity more than patience. Or perhaps you do value patience but don't know how to make it real in your life. So be honest with yourself. Make sure when determining what matters to you that you are being realistic about your behavior's adherence to those values. When there is a discrepancy between what you say or think and what you do, it's not necessarily hypocrisy at work. It could be fear that is slowing you down. For instance, it takes staunch courage to be honest at all times. Or it may be a conflict between opposing values—such as free-spiritedness and dependability.

I've never met two couples in my years of work that listed the same exact set of top priorities. If I had, wisdom would counsel me that their situation was likely to change some over time. Even if your preferences match perfectly at the moment, there's no guarantee it will always be that way. Besides, this changeable quality is often a result of maturity and a perfectly good thing. Lives and values don't pop up ready-made. They grow and stretch and twist with the bends in life's road.

However useful it may be to identify our most grounding values, it's never worthwhile to be stiffly definitive about them. Ultimately, like Josh Larsen with his secret, you'll know it in the gut if you are breaking one of your highest principles. The real answers to the question "What are my values?" are to be found in your track record and in your heart.

Whatever your core values, in a spiritually fulfilling marriage two of your highest priorities will be your spouse and your partnership. But cherishing each other is not just a state of mind. It is also a tacit commitment to do right by each other, literally taking care of each other and acting so as to support each other's desires.

In your daily encounters, acting on principle is a humble endeavor. Here it's the little things that count: a box of favorite crackers for your partner even though it wasn't on the shopping list, a heartfelt apology offered ten minutes after you've exploded at him or her, remembering to drop the toilet seat down or throw away those wadded-up tissues on your bed stand. . . . There is no end to the tiny acts of consideration you can perform to express how much your companion matters to you.

When misfortune comes along, there are other gestures you can make: Offering to cover for a couple of extra chores, bringing flowers on the anniversary of an old trauma, e-mailing a little love note during stressful times at work, or just giving an old-fashioned back rub will bring a little extra TLC to this person whom you've chosen above all others.

When we know what our loved ones care about, we automatically know better how to care for them. When we know where we *agree,* we have the delightful ability to move confidently toward our jointly cherished goals. When we know where we *disagree,* we can be prepared to treat choices related to these issues with extra care.

Navigating Values in Conflict

There is no road or ready way to virtue.

—THOMAS BROWNE, *RELIGIO MEDICI*

When we are little, we are taught the ABCs of virtue: "Be kind, be brave, be honest," and so forth. But as we mature, we discover the complexities in carrying out these directives. Is it brave or foolhardy to run onto the highway to rescue your neighbor's cat? While it is kind not to make a fuss about your friend's dandruff, might it not be more caring to warn her as she goes out for a job interview? A girl runs past you and hides; a scruffy, concerned-looking man follows and asks if you've seen her. What do you say?

There are countless difficulties in putting our principles into action in our daily living. There may simply be confusion: Which value should I choose? There may be fear: What will happen if I risk telling my best friend (a police officer) about my wife's drug problem? Expediency, insecurity, and flat-out powerlessness all can hamper efforts to make ethical choices. What guidelines are there for doing the right thing when the complexity of life gets in the way?

Some of the most rewarding challenges in marriage come from navigating those conflicts between us that can't easily be resolved. I once knew a man who was pretty bad about giving presents on birthdays or Christmas. Sincerity and spontaneity carried much more importance for him than did conformity to social tradition. For him, the joy of giving required spontaneity. (Once he bought his wife an exquisite—and expensive—music box, just because. These were the kinds of gifts he'd enjoyed receiving as a child.) Meanwhile, for his wife, traditions served not only as a genial reminder to give but also as a chance to heighten the pleasure by anticipation. She found it impossible not to feel hurt and angry when her husband came home empty-handed yet again on their fourth anniversary.

When they first met with me shortly thereafter, he was feeling manipulated and she was feeling uncared for. After a few sessions she was able to "hear" that he was only acting on his own principles, and he was able to "hear" that preplanned gift exchanges can give joy and needn't be meaningless ordeals. This kind of below-the-surface understanding of what is fueling our partner's perspective helps prevent hard feelings. It is a necessary aspect of our ongoing marital conversation about what's most important.

In time this couple came to a compromise: On nonholidays he would continue to get gifts as often as the fancy struck him. She in turn would plan the events on official occasions, and he could get her just a card. Now and then on these holidays he actually surprised her with a present—such minimal expectations freed him to be more spontaneous! Of course, when children came into their lives, the gift-giving scenario had to be examined once again. But this awareness of how their values differed allowed them to prevent pain, to care more for each other, and to reshape compromises together over time, all the while preserving their individual preferences.

Differences of this sort may be the result of cultural upbringing, of family history, or of personal inclination—but both of your interpretations have validity and deserve respect. You and your partner may basically agree that thrift and generosity (for example) are virtues you should have, but you may not prioritize the same one over the other if they were to conflict. Nathaniel, for example, liked fancy dinners while his wife, Breen, who worked at a nice restaurant, liked something more fun and casual. He loved to bring her flowers or a negligee as a special treat, even though, as she finally told him, she would have much preferred an extra day off from watching the kids. Their discussions about these conflicts were successful because they involved compassion, honesty, respect, and open minds.

Already you are well armed to defuse situations charged with conflict: Simple mindfulness of your highest goals helps to solve many a problem—especially if you two share those goals. If you both feel that financial security is a must, for example, then despite the lure of that weeklong Hawaiian getaway, a weekend road trip will easily suffice as soon as you stop to think about it. (Money, by the way, is a symbol in some of the biggest values conflicts couples face, so conversations between us on this topic should be undertaken early, often, and carefully.)

Most of the time our own priorities and those of our spouse are in accord. They may not be identical, but they can harmoniously coexist. If your spouse is a vegetarian on principle and you're not, you may still eat meat—but you know better than to fill the refrigerator with bloody steaks. Chances are you'll simply eat most of your meaty meals at lunchtime and at restaurants. In this way you show respect for your spouse and her choices while still living according to your own. This is caring in action.

Caring is taking the garbage out late at night because your partner values a clean kitchen or leaving ten dollars on the counter "just in case" because your partner values preparedness. Caring is not, however, being demanding or using guilt to get your partner to do such things for you. The key here is that these acts of love are voluntary. It's natural to want caring from your spouse, and it's appropriate to ask for it respectfully if you feel unsupported. But controlling or otherwise manipulative tactics are incompatible with caring (and with a spiritual marriage), because the intrinsic worth and autonomy of both partners needs always to be in place. To receive the kind of caring that really gives you comfort, your partner must give it to you on his or her own, from the heart . . . because your well-being *matters.*

When navigating conflicting values—whether it's disagreement in your relationship or whether the conflict springs from an outside problem—there are several activities I've seen work well with couples I've known. One is to imagine what your favorite ethical hero or heroine would do. Another is to try to imagine yourself as an objective third party, whose job it is to come up with a solution that's fair to all. But perhaps the most powerful shortcut-in-a-nutshell is to *pick people over things.* To cite one clear-cut example, if your car loses its brakes and you won't be able to avoid crashing, you will do it in such a way to minimize injury to the passengers rather than damage to the car, no matter if it's your brand-new car that cost you half a year's salary.

Henri and Kris's story shows what can happen if we forget to put our value for each other up front. Henri and Kris were both very politically active. But when Kris switched party allegiance in order to support a third-party candidate, Henri had a fit. When he failed to convince Kris through an assault of reason, Henri fell into a long sulk. His candidate lost by a narrow margin, and that signaled the beginning of an all-out war. Henri couldn't heap blame on obscure millions, so Kris got the blame instead. It got so that any sentence between them was sure to have a curse word in it. In their passion to change a harsh world, they themselves had become hardened. Both of them cried profusely the first time we met. They had forgotten to value *each other,* and being devalued hurt.

If we get distracted from caring *about* our partner, it makes it much more difficult to care *for* our partner, especially during conflicts. A good marriage is one in which we both keep an eye on what matters, for the sake of the other's well-being as well as our own.

The key to navigating conflicts is to consider first our intent and then the likely consequences of our actions. When in doubt, we can return to what preserves our human dignity and the intrinsic worth of our counterpart. In marriage this translates to an impregnable respect for our partner. Our spouse wants to be treated well and deserves the truth. What should we do? In such moments I often fall back on a variation of a prime maxim of Ethical Society, which urges people to make all their decisions in the context of caring relationships: "Act so as to bring out the best in your partner, and thereby yourself."

Compassionate Truthfulness: The Tabernacle of Virtues

A "no" uttered from deepest conviction is better and greater than a "yes" merely uttered to please, or what is worse, to avoid trouble.

—MAHATMA GANDHI

In a letter from 1703 the philosopher John Locke wrote, "To love truth is the principal part of human perfection in this world, and the seed-plot of all other virtues." But if truth is the flower bed, compassion is the sun.

If we think back to Josh's dilemma about whether or not to tell Maureen about his secret, his struggle was not so much about whether to take care of her, but how to take care of her *best*. Kindness and honesty seemed at opposite ends of his list of options. This is a common issue for couples. After many years of struggling over such problems in my own life and in the lives of others, I realized that honesty without kindness is too often cruel and that kindness without honesty can be blind. From this insight a potent guiding principle emerged for me that I call "compassionate truthfulness."

This multifaceted ethical standard has been helpful and even transforming for many of the couples with whom I've worked. It gives teeth to the principles of kindness and respect for others and also helps resolve many conflicts. Compassionate truthfulness is especially powerful because it mirrors partnership, forcing equal values into constant "dialogue." It serves as an overarching concept for organizing dozens of virtues, from thoughtfulness to courage, openness to reliability. Consider: A habit of dishonesty, even to oneself, can lead to a breakdown in the very spirit of the partnership. Conversely, a habit of compassionate truth telling creates a trusting sense of safety and a feeling that we generously care for one another as if by instinct.

Compassion encompasses many of our most loving values: It is always an act of *generosity*, and through it we also exhibit *responsiveness, empathy, sympathy,* and *kindness.* By concerning ourselves with the welfare of others, we prove our openness to *cooperation, thoughtfulness,* and our *willingness to share.* By thinking of others instead of ourselves, we reveal a certain *modesty.* And, when broadly understood, compassion includes an intrinsic sense of *fairness* in one's dealings. Out of compassion, the social principles of both *mercy* and *justice* are born.

When it comes to *truthfulness,* there's an equally long line of connected virtues. *Honesty, openness,* and *forthrightness* immediately spring to mind. As Josh proved to us earlier in the chapter, *courage* also comes into play, especially when the truth is hard to tell. *Reli-*

ability, trustworthiness, and *loyalty* follow naturally in the footsteps of truthfulness. *Individualism* or *distinctiveness* is the result of being truthful to and about oneself. And finally, both knowing and telling the truth indicate *awareness, attentiveness,* and the *capacity to be observant.* From this humble beginning such great principles as the search for universal truths—in both religion and science—were born.

The practice of compassionate truthfulness provides a foundation for building unshakable trust. When Josh came clean to Maureen about his father's harsh judgment of her, he was intuitively practicing compassionate truthfulness. Though Josh was tempted to protect her from an unpleasant fact, he knew deep down that, kept secret, it served as an impediment to their intimacy. His being compassionately truthful with Maureen actually provided greater protection for them both in the long run.

Lying, even "white" lying, throws a roadblock upon the path to caring. Have you ever told a little lie that spiraled out of control? As a preteen my young friend Timothy used to exaggerate every possible detail of his school day: Lobster was served for lunch on the field trip; he got A-pluses on all his tests; ten girls asked him to his first sock hop. Habitual liars like Timothy have an inner defense that says, What does it matter? I'm not hurting anyone. This, too, was a lie, for Timothy was hurting himself. In his case, as in so many others, he didn't trust his own sense of worth to show his true self to others. Perhaps he didn't think others would respect him enough if they knew he'd had a Quarter Pounder for lunch, a 3.4 grade-point average, and no date to the dance. But when we see the details, the truth is sadly clear: Those facts are perfectly respectable—it's only his fibs that lessen him in our eyes.

Or consider Paulo and Tina, whom I met at a fall couples' retreat. There had been an unusually strong sense of camaraderie, so they didn't hesitate to volunteer to reenact a scene from their life. The skit was called *The Last Straw.* "Actually," Paulo said, laughing while vigorously mixing an invisible salad, "this should probably be called *The Last Mushroom.*" As the drama unfolded, the group came to understand how even a small fib can undermine a relationship. Six years earlier Tina had told Paulo she loved the raw mushrooms in his salads, and she'd never had the heart to tell him the truth. But that didn't emerge until the day of the big fight. As it turned out, Tina had chosen to be kind rather than honest; but in the end Paulo couldn't help mistrusting everything she told him. At the time of the workshop they were on the verge of a separation.

After months of squabbling, another couple rather prematurely hit upon the powerful notion of scrupulous honesty in marriage. Marnie had read that husbands and wives should tell each other the "microscopic truth" and pressed Chuck for a tell-all sit-down. I happen to agree that we should be totally honest with one another—but *always with compassion.* Unfortunately for Marnie, Chuck was still burning from the pain of a decade-old fling of Marnie's. He lit into her, substituting contempt for compassion, in a bitter truth-telling bout covering everything from Marnie's artistic integrity to her incompetence in bed. Thanks to cruel honesty, Marnie suffered numerous invisible wounds that night, wounds that were deep and slow to heal.

Clearly, compassion is just not enough without truth, and truthfulness alone can sting. Compassionate truthfulness is a twofold concept that should seldom, if ever, be split apart—though it may be tempting to do so. In other words, if you feel the urge to choose one over the other, you are probably in for more than you bargained for. There's something about seemingly trivial fibs that can get the best of you. As the philosopher William Paley once said, "White lies always introduce others of a darker complexion."

There's another advantage to scrupulously kind truth telling: It's a shortcut. By incorporating values into this overarching system, it becomes easier to organize complex thinking in accessible ways, such as that which arrives when needs and values conflict with one another. When you're faced with tough decision making, try to see how you can combine compassion and truthfulness, and you may find that a number of other concerns are resolved as well. In Josh's case he refrained from demonizing his father for his harsh opinion and concentrated instead on his own real confusion and pain. Maureen in turn responded with sympathy for Josh, acknowledging what she knew was true: that his father's opinion was not Josh's fault.

Ultimately, what we do when values come into conflict can actually open us up to new ways of living healthily together. With a sigh of relief Josh realized that he and Maureen could present a united front against his father's disapproval. Perhaps together they could bring him around. It requires agility to solve conflicts like Josh's, and inventiveness, too. But compassionate truthfulness gives us an edge.

Finally—and to me the most delightful by-product of compassionate truthfulness—there's the reality check. When we find ourselves telling a hard truth with relative ease, we know beyond a doubt that the fiber of our partnership is solid and strong. When we care for each other as if by instinct, exposing our fears, supporting each other in conflict, admitting faults and accepting them in each other with loving hearts . . . then we know that our marriage has truly become spiritually strong.

By committing to the values we hold dearest and by facing the tough stuff instead of hiding it, we find at last how to move beyond a rule-based approach to relationships. No skeletons, no lies, no prescriptions or strictures like "Always be polite" or "Never complain." Just a steady inner voice guiding us home, to each other. The unlikely duo of the Gospel preacher St. John and the social critic Karl Marx had it right when they declared, a millennium apart, the power of truth to set people free.

The Hard Truth

I was angry with my friend:
I told my wrath, my wrath did end.
I was angry with my foe:
I told it not, my wrath did grow.

—WILLIAM BLAKE, "A POISON TREE"

It is clear, then, that telling the truth—even a hard one—is crucial. It is also crucial that the truth be told with kindness and respect. This isn't always easy but is always worth it. One woman I know got herself to the tough task of confessing a mistake to her partner by promising herself a reward: an entire Toblerone bar with a big mug of full-fat milk. This technique worked well (at least until she stepped on the scale). In another situation a man who had been asked to critique his girlfriend's poems began his truthful reply by leveling the playing field and admitting to some unflattering facts about his own writing.

As an approach to living, being truthful in a caring way is often a great challenge. It's a fine art, fraught with complexity. As I've found in countless workshops, talking the talk and walking the walk of compassionate truthfulness are very different things. When it comes down to it, many couples need a little extra help getting started telling a hard truth. When something's not being said, even if one of you is unaware of the "elephant under the rug," there is still that ineffable strain to your conversation, a stiltedness and insecurity that makes it even harder to speak your mind and clear the air. Singles cope with this every time they go out on a date. Ironically, if they don't risk being candid, they can cut off the possibility for an open and honest relationship to develop.

Fatima, who met her future husband while resting by the ninth hole of a golf course, was tempted to lie when he put down his clubs and sat next to her. After they had chatted about the beautiful view and the weather, Richard asked, "Out for a day of golfing?" She hesitated a moment, then replied, "No. I work here." She was sure this information would end the conversation. But actually Richard appreciated her straightforwardness. Soon he was telling her how he had just been laid off. "One last game," he said with a sigh. They ended up going out for pizza that evening, and, as Fatima would later say, "The rest is history."

Brand-new relationships require courageous honesty, because you run the risk of losing a potential friend. In marriage the stakes feel even higher when you need to tell your partner something tough. The following guidelines may help you move past the discomfort you naturally feel when bringing up such topics. They're based on the premise that telling a hard truth is the surest way to *maintain* our connection, not to break it.

- Begin with small talk. You'll have an easier time if you keep from hitting your partner over the head. Don't ever broach hard truths before you have made a positive connection.

- Make absolutely sure you can establish a state of mind in which you can respect the person to whom you're speaking, while you're speaking. This may be a challenge, especially if the hard truth involves your own anger or pain at your partner's hands.

- Begin your critique with honestly positive statements about your partner. Phrase the rest in self-responsible ways, acknowledging any part you may have played in creating the current situation.

- Give a brief history of encounters that led to your concern. Describe any sensations and feelings this evoked in you.

- Brainstorm and be tentative in your analysis; acknowledge that it may be off base. But when presenting your main point, be direct and firm. Express what it is you want and what you will do to help make it happen. For example, you might say, "I'm not sure if I'm right in thinking you don't care. But what I do know is that I feel deeply hurt by your actions, and I need things to change. I'll let you know next time I feel this way, and I promise to listen to how you're experiencing things then."

- Ask for feedback. Use questions such as, How does this feel to you? Does it ring a bell? Do you need time to take it in, to mull it over for a while?

- Always end by reaffirming your care for your partner, repeating this thought several times in different ways.

It's up to our closest friends and loved ones to tell us what they believe we need to hear. Only these companions know us well enough to honor us fully even in the face of the most difficult truths. "Since we're being frank with each other . . ." my dear friend began as we drove toward a restaurant. I interrupted her. "You mean we usually lie?" I asked. We both laughed. What she was trying to say was that she hated being harsh with me, but in this case she thought I needed to hear it anyhow. The truth is, even before she told me her concerns, I was already grateful for her help. Those that love us best know us best and bear the responsibility of telling us what we need to hear—*for our own good.* I knew that my friend would speak out of concern for me and a desire for me to be as healthy and happy as possible. If, like her, you're afraid of speaking up, focus on the eventual benefits your loved one will gain, even if the initial response is angry or ambivalent.

Robbie also had a hard truth to tell. He had noticed the extra wrappers and boxes in the trash, and he knew that Rebekah had started her overeating cycle again. He considered pretending not to notice but chose instead to broach the subject lovingly. "My darling, beautiful wife," he murmured in her ear as he hugged her, "I want you to know that I know you're going through a hard time again. I'm here for you, and I want you to be able to talk to me about it whenever you feel like it, but only if you feel like it. Okay?"

Perhaps the hardest truths of all to tell have to do with sex. Dissatisfaction and dysfunction in the bedroom are tough but important to discuss, and infidelity even more so. But not admitting to it can in fact ruin a relationship. The basic guidelines offered above may at such times be inadequate. We might want to seek the support of a professional counselor, especially if we aren't sure of our motivations for bringing up this painful subject. Perhaps we want to spill out our feelings just to get rid of them or in some way to get even. Deep down, do we want to end things or save them?

Some couples try to go it on their own, with widely varying results depending on the circumstances and the overall health of the relationship. Daring to face each other lovingly is an important part of the process. Letters left on bureaus usually backfire—though sometimes it helps to sort out one's feelings on paper first.

I know a woman who spent a whole week composing a letter to her husband, rewriting it many times. Finally she arranged a meeting with him. After first explaining that what she wanted to say was too important to leave to a nervous tongue, she requested that he consider replying in kind. Then she read the letter out loud. It began by asking her husband to hold their love in his heart while he listened. In their case this approach worked. A week later the husband gave his reply to her, and this opened them up to an extended exchange. What helped here, I think, was the deliberate care with which each partner communicated to the other, including the intentional slowing down of the interchanges. The manner in which they approached each other helped create a healing buffer zone that is required for both telling *and* hearing really hard truths.

The Pattern of Protection

When I was small, curled up in my father's lap, I loved to listen to his deep baritone narration of "The Three Little Pigs." At the end, after the Big Bad Wolf had blown all but the brick house down, I would complain that bricks were boring (we lived in a fourth-floor walk-up apartment built of brick upon brick upon brick). Surely, I asserted, those clever little pigs could have figured out a way to reinforce straw—by wrapping it in wire, say. Or what about a mixture of wood and cement? Closing my eyes, I would think up sturdy huts of gold and giant marble towers that no wolf could ever blow down.

"You're missing the point," my father would say, spelling out the moral for his wayward child. "This isn't about real houses. It's about building your life in a way so that you can grow old and still laugh." This didn't make the slightest sense to me at the time.

But it does now. The lesson latent in the mean old wolf and scared piggies has gotten much clearer in my mind. For you, the Big Bad Wolf may be the slow process of aging (as it was for my father), or financial hardship, or addiction. And the building blocks of your partnership, that home in which you're safe from the wolf, are your ethical values. However you stack them up, your value system is there to protect you. But if you do a sloppy job of it, the protection may not last long. As with the three pigs, you may have a terrible threat huffing and puffing outside. Take a little time to carefully address the values at the core of your marriage: Be conscious of what you care about—your priorities, your partnership, each other—and build it all up with nurturing attention. Now look that wolf in the eye and let him know he can puff till the end of time. Nothing can blow your house down.

Keys to Being Compassionate and Truthful

- Count your partner among your very highest priorities in life.
- Make your behavior an embodiment of integrity, as you envision it.
- Find out what your partner desires most.
- Put people ahead of things when resolving conflicts.
- Practice honesty as an act of love.
- Consciously cherish what matters to you—including your spouse, family, and friends.

Caring Questions to Ask Yourself

1. Does your home life generally reflect an atmosphere of tenderness and care, feeling safe enough that hard truths can be told lovingly?
2. What do your actual life choices say about your values? What wise choices have you made to further your most cherished dreams?
3. In what ways does your behavior indicate your respect for one another?
4. Do you show your partner how much you care?
5. Can you rely on each other to be truthful and kind, no matter how hard the circumstances?
6. What attempts have you made toward reconciling conflicting values?
7. What unlikely figures from history, literature, or the real world serve as role models to you and why?
8. How do you attempt to cultivate your shared values in the larger world?

"Thanks": A Caring Exercise

Here's a method for investigating what you care about. It also doubles as a true gesture of caring (with a little bit of healing sprinkled in, too). You can modify it however you like.

Each of you take some time to write up a list of "thanks." I often have couples do this in preparing for their wedding day. My conviction is that you can't become a full-fledged adult until you can appropriately separate from your parents (or parental figures). This individuation can occur only once you have found something your parents gave you for which you are genuinely grateful. Focusing in this very specific way will clarify and highlight your most cherished values as individuals and as a couple.

Once you've determined the "gifts" you most prize, take another look: They will reflect your highest values. Gratitude for the gift of, say, your family's many wonderful trips may reflect your value of family togetherness, or learning, or perhaps adventure.

If you have had a rough childhood, this can be a difficult exercise, but all the more important since such a childhood makes it much more difficult to lovingly move off into a new life of your own. Sometimes all a person can say is "I'm glad they gave me the genes that helped me to survive my childhood" or "I'm glad they made me get good grades so I could have the job I have, even though they did it in an abusive way" or simply "I'm glad they brought me into this world." Even these limited thanks belie the valuing of (respectively) perseverance, diligence and worldly success, and life itself.

One bride I know said that the only thing she could say to her mother, a person with a major emotional illness who had been institutionalized many times, was how glad she was that her mother could be there in person on this special day. The remarks inspired me to speak to the mother directly during the ceremony about the long voyage she had made—in fact, it had spanned her entire life—in order to be present at her daughter's wedding. She wept, and for the first time in years they embraced.

In repairing, the Sixth Commitment, I'll talk about moving beyond thankfulness to take on forgiveness. Here, simply consider that gratitude is an attitude that helps reveal us to ourselves. Whatever it is that we are truly grateful for, we should consciously appreciate and strive to nurture it. When I read the list of thanks at a ceremony, I can usually tell by the tearful smiles it evokes that an important release has occurred on all sides.

To enact this exercise within the private sphere of your love relationship, you can also give thanks to each other. This rendition of the exercise is just as informative for identifying your values. Consider this activity for birthdays, anniversaries, or other special occasions you plan to celebrate privately.

Fifth Commitment

Abiding

❦

I will have faith, patiently persisting
through life's many changes.

The jangling telephone next to my bed jarred me out of deep sleep. I blinked my eyes in the still-darkened room.

"I'm sorry to call you so early in the morning, Lois—"

Though the words came out huskily, I half-heard Maureen's lyrical voice. It was the week before her wedding day, a time when off-hour panic calls are not uncommon.

I rolled over to switch on the light, and as the fog receded from my head, I made out a much deeper voice on the phone. It was cracked and breathy—not at all the light young voice I was anticipating. "Lois," the woman let out in a low moan, "oh, Lois, he's gone. Erik is gone. He died last night."

As the words settled into my sleepy brain, I belatedly responded. "Is that you, Laura?"

But how could it be Laura—Laura Larsen, Erik's beloved wife, Josh's caring mother? Isn't there a rule, I desperately thought, about tragedy not being allowed to happen the week of your son's wedding?

But it was Laura. Laura Larsen, who just weeks ago had been gathering mementos for Josh of her own wedding day: a photo of Erik in a tuxedo, looking as though he couldn't wait to get it off . . . the bride-and-groom figurine from atop their wedding cake . . . the program and their written vows, all bundled up together in a stretch of Laura's veil. There I was with the phone against my ear, plunging into the shadows of a woman's grief.

Laura told me the details of the evening's ordeal. They had just begun their Sunday-night chess match when Erik suddenly felt severe indigestion, cutting short the game. His sleep was interrupted in the wee hours of the morning by sharp, sudden pains in his arm and chest. He attempted to stave off what was then clearly recognized as a heart attack by holding a pillow to his torso and coughing rapidly. Finally there was the ambulance ride. Laura's voice grew calmer as she recounted how, after the paramedics had stopped trying to revive him, she had taken Erik's cool hand in hers. Her ring had lightly clinked against his.

"Lois," she murmured in a voice sounding at once faraway and near, "I knew in that moment such a deep truth."

"Yes?" I said, encouragingly. But Laura's voice was momentarily clogged with pain.

"What is that deep truth, Laura?" I gently probed again.

Laura cleared her throat and said in a whisper, "I will never be alone."

This Spinning Earth

Nothing is permanent but change.

—HERACLITUS, QUOTED IN DIOGENES,
  LIVES OF EMINENT PHILOSOPHERS

If you have a terrible day, you can console yourself with the knowledge that while you sleep, the earth will turn and the day will eventually end. But this is true, too, of wonderful days and, in time, even of the most enduring relationships. This was the stark reality that Laura Larsen absorbed as she sat in silence in the ambulance with the wail of the siren obliquely penetrating her thoughts.

Change is the way of all things. From the air in a room and the blood in our veins to emotions we can't keep bottled up, *circulation* is both natural and necessary for a healthy state of being. Our whole self—body and soul, flesh and spirit—needs to be set in motion and exercised regularly. In relationships we experience a continuous flow of interchanges, give-and-take—receiving and, yes, letting go.

For many people the ongoing flow of life constitutes God itself—Christians call this life force the Holy Spirit, or love; Hebrews refer to it as *nashoma,* or soul. For others this moving force is more an essence of being: Yogis use the word *prana;* the Chinese say *chi.* Some humanists use terms like "spiritedness" to convey a sense of energetic transience. As R. Buckminster Fuller once said, "God, it seems to me, is a verb." This life and goodness in motion flows in and around us, infusing everything.

Change makes way for new knowledge and experience: We deepen our relationship by getting married; we deepen it further by buying a house, or having children, or facing unforeseen challenges together. Every day along the way offers opportunities to learn and grow—but we also struggle together and against each other as these changes shake up the status quo. We are compelled to readjust our relationship and the comfortable patterns of our married life to accommodate "new additions" to the scene. So it is perfectly understandable that we can experience change as threatening.

This chapter is about growth—a constant in our lives—and how to make the best of it. How do we ride the waves of motion without feeling powerless or out of control? And how do we retain a sense of safe constancy without shutting ourselves off from life's dynamic pulse?

There *is* a way to nurture the resilient frame of mind one needs to achieve this task, an art to living that eases our burdens and helps us cope with uncomfortable change. I call this artistry "abiding," and there are two parts to it: having faith and being flexible.

First, there is *having faith*—a confidence of the heart—that whatever challenges come, they can be handled. Faith in your child's talents and intentions, for example, might make you more supportive when her report card is less than perfect. Faith in the teaching power of adversity might help you to console your best friend during his or her marital struggles. And faith in the lasting power of your *own* marriage can help you hang on, whatever difficulties may come.

The second aspect of abiding is *being flexible* through life's tough circumstances. When conditions take a turn for the worse, we need to find new and appropriate ways to hang in there—to be present to our partner and ourselves. In order to have lasting resiliency, we need the flexibility to learn new things, to know when to let go, to be childlike and open, and to turn to others for help when we need it.

Having Faith

We don't see things as they are. We see things as we are. —ANAÏS NIN

I fondly remember the day Desmond and Marie, friends of the Ethical Society, stopped by the Brooklyn building to announce that they had both been laid off from their jobs and had decided to go out dancing. When I expressed surprise, Desmond laughed with a deep roll. "Lois, back in Jamaica we learned that when we're most afraid and uncertain of the future, we can dance our fears away." Marie chimed in, "Life should always have joy in it. It's enough that we have had our livelihood taken away. We can't give up the joy, too. Tomorrow we'll look for work." To this day I take comfort in the image of them walking down the block, arm in arm, Marie's bright red dress swirling about her knees.

To get through the many decades of a lasting marriage, we will have to seek out continuity through the disruptions life brings— the overbearing in-laws, the career change, the troubled child. On good days we simply trust that we will get through it all, even though we don't know what lies ahead. In this sense the expedition of marriage is really a faith journey in which we find our way in the dark.

What does it mean to have faith? For many, an interior sense of faith is experienced not so much as an unshakable truth but as a hunch—a hunch that there is something bigger than us, something to which we are curiously drawn—a feeling as much as a thought, a longing to be connected to what we sense cannot be bad. At its root, faith, or deep hope, is about goodness and our attempts to be in touch with it. Faith in marital situations is also a yearning for the

partnership to be more than it currently is and a confidence that it can be. Finally, faith is the heartfelt perception that (all appearances to the contrary) our resources of knowledge and love will be adequate to meet our evolving needs.

To me, whatever we personally hold true in our heart and mind and live out in our life—especially as it pertains to our conception of goodness—is faith. I am not using the word "faith" here to mean "creed" or the specific beliefs of a particular religion or religious denomination. The beliefs we hold in our heart may be closely aligned with the religion we practice, but they needn't be. Ultimately, faith is not just a set of beliefs; it is a permeating awareness of where we personally find profound purpose and meaning.

When I was twelve, I told my mother I needed a therapist. She told me to pray to Jesus. And I did. But, later, I reached out for a therapist's help as well. I was the youngest in a family in which there was much screaming and yelling. Our mother seemed to slip in and out of a private universe and couldn't always be counted on as a caretaker. I knew early on that I needed more than a child's pleading prayers.

At the end of my first therapy session I was afraid to leave and feel alone again. My therapist, sensing this, slowly and firmly reached out across the coffee table and grabbed my hand. "I'm here," he said. For months afterward I would stop and touch my hand—at a bus stop, during a lunch break—clasping it in a repetition of that act of first touch, letting myself feel connected to his healing presence. To this day I occasionally do that ritual of reconnection. To be touched and to touch; this is the heart of life.

Do you have memories like this—of being kindly touched—to draw upon? Saul of Tarsus once said that faith is "the substance of things unseen." *Substance?* Yes. Because faith has a curious solidity to it as it is experienced moment by moment by individuals: Laura's wedding ring clinking as it touched the ring of her dead husband, the heat of holiday candles calling us to continue another year.

Like the canopy that the nomadic sabras carry on four poles under a desert sky in order to protect a wedding couple from both the heat of the sun and the chaos outside their community, faith is that which shelters us as we go. It is at once intuitive and primal, individual and communal—the sense that whatever the appearance, help is near. You are not alone.

Enact Hope in the Present

Be bold and mighty forces will come to your aid. —BASIL KING

The Dutch painter Vincent van Gogh, whose life vacillated between hope and despair, once said, "Hope for better times is not a feeling, it is an action in the present." And so it is. You can bravely *enact* hope. Discover what inspires hope in you, and find a way to actualize it. Hang a photo of a favorite ethical heroine on the wall. Plant a lily in a pot in the midst of winter, and make watering it a holy act. Give a friend in pain a soothing CD, wrapped up in linen and tied with purple twine.

Hope is experienced specifically: a phone call, a long hot bath, a prayer handwritten in calligraphy. Both Nelly and Mike's work lives were in turmoil when their tiny apartment, which hadn't been renovated in thirty years, began to fall apart. Almost daily, it seemed, a closet door would come loose, a towel rack would fall, the sink would stop up. There was little that either of them could do to rush, or change, the outcomes of their outside dilemmas, but it was definitely not the time to move. Nevertheless, Nelly came up with a way to sustain hope: Every few days she found a new inspirational quote to stick to her computer screen. She wrote in her journal religiously and bought candles, art supplies, and flowers . . . and a few do-it-yourself tools for repairs. She had a set of songs to listen to that could serve for solace or celebration—whichever way the wind blew. It's not enough to make wishes vaguely, but when hope is enacted like this, it can offer real, usable support.

Often we discover our true locus of faith in crisis. Where do we really turn when the chips are down? A married man I know (a doctor with several other doctors in his family) successfully battled colon cancer in classic abiding fashion. Early on he found his family's "stiff upper lip" attitude and medical jargon inadequate for his battle. So he joined an innovative program that treated the whole person, offering many alternative therapies from music to pets to tai chi. His neighbor, who had conquered cancer some years earlier, turned out to be of more help than all his professional relations, talking him through his fears, offering mental strategies, and simply being around for support. In the end the many techniques he used gave him hope that he could see, hear, and touch, and the flexibility to address new challenges (including a brief relapse) in new ways.

What such living faith, such high hopefulness, "feels like" may be different for you and for your partner, as it was for Sherry and Manuel. Driving home late one night, they got involved in a pileup crash between an oil truck and a bus. Amazingly, their car wasn't crushed. During the incident Sherry, a churchgoer, called out to God and felt held by an incredible warm presence. Meanwhile

Manuel, a skeptic, was moved beyond words by a sudden overpowering love for his wife and children. Both told me they felt at that moment, no matter what the outcome, that everything was all right. The crucible of the accident had revealed to them separate sources of well-being, distinct but equally valid and equally powerful.

Once I was staying overnight with a friend who was suffering great distress in her life. I thrashed around on the guest cot, finding it impossible to sleep. How could you do this? I addressed the universe. Where are you when I need you most? I railed, dredging up images from an early picture book showing a king in a ruby robe looking down from a cloud. In time I fell into a troubled sleep.

Awakening toward dawn, I felt strangely held. Lying still, I suddenly realized that I was humming a tune—a wonderful oboe piece by Ennio Morricone proclaiming the utter simplicity and sacredness of love. The tune stayed with me two days and nights, soothing me all the way, and freeing me to give my friend the full support she needed so badly.

William and Sami, agnostics who were struggling to raise a couple of unruly teenagers, once asked me to write a prayer for the family to say before dinner. Here are the words I wrote then:

> *You, closer than our own breath*
> *And deeper than our dreams,*
> *Abide with us*
> *As we abide with you*
> *In freedom and understanding,*
> *In truth and in commitment,*
> *In acts of fairness and loving care*
> *That flow from these, our listening hearts.*

William and Sami used this prayer for grace. You could use it, too, as you awake on a gray morning, before a stressful event, after a fight, as a wish for a troubled friend, or on retiring after a hard day. Better yet, you can compose your own prayer or select a passage from any source you choose, sacred or secular. Any formal call for spiritual sustenance has the capacity to help us to build up hope in times of ease and to restore it during life's heavy transitions.

Be Faithful

To keep our faces towards change and behave like free spirits in the presence of fate is strength undefeatable.

—HELEN KELLER, "LET US HAVE FAITH"

No matter how tough it gets, you *can* get through. My Great-aunt Mabel used to say, "Change is actually one part agony and nine parts opportunity." But when you're on the steep side of the hill, it may not seem so. Keep in mind the fact that uphill doesn't last forever. There is always energy in reserve when you've been faithful to the climb.

If the first step of abiding is to cultivate deep hope, the second is to be faithful. Faith in a marital environment quite literally is confidence in the loving culture we have developed in our home life. This culture includes spiritual practices, shared memories, and promises kept. In time this special holding place becomes a third party to our covenant. We have a commitment to ourselves, to our partner, and to the marriage we have created together. Being loyal to our marriage, which is utterly unique in its flavor and loveliness, leads to a feeling of integrity, strength, and being true to ourselves. This is unconditional love—committed connection, come what may.

If you've been bickering a lot with your partner, it may be difficult to stop midfight and ask, Am I being faithful to this marriage? Instead think of some of the commitments you've made—to try to see the best in your partner (that is, to be honoring) or to maintain a loving environment for your children's sake. When your bond is strong and outside forces challenge you, the reinforcing power of dependability can be deeply sustaining. Whether it's homemade hot meals for her the month after the miscarriage or driving him to and from work every day while his broken ankle heals, being faithful takes many forms—but it is always supportive.

Fidelity has lost its larger meaning in recent times, being equated solely with sexual abstinence outside of marriage. Whatever your convictions here, I believe that most of us are just too insecure to handle extramarital affairs, and there are health issues, too. Sexual urges (women's as much as men's) are perfectly natural—but we don't need to act on them. Most times extramarital attraction is at the surface, fleeting. After noting and enjoying this sign that we're still alive and kicking, it's best to tuck such feelings away and remind ourselves how fortunate we are to have a real person in our life. One who is counting on us.

If the attraction does not go away, it is speaking to us of something profound that we have not yet tended to—an old resentment, a need for more adventure, or a hidden part of us that needs letting out. We need to ask ourselves, What am I missing? Then we must dare go to our partner and ask for it. It is imperative to have the courage to talk about what we are missing and try our best to work it out. This is not an easy problem to solve—it has to be handled sensitively, and again we may need outside support. But left unattended to, such problems can destroy a marriage.

What if it is not you but your partner who is inappropriately engaged outside the marriage? Let's say you notice a flurry of e-mails to your spouse from the same person. Perhaps it's a mild flirtation (although this in itself is a slippery slope), or perhaps it's a real temptation. A situation like this is both a crisis and an opportunity: If together you can abide through it with understanding, you have a chance to bring your marriage to new depth and fulfillment. In the end, our most painful struggles will greatly strengthen our marriage, as long as we continually stay present to each other.

Madey and Les understood this intuitively and went against the advice of all their friends in retrieving their relationship. Madey's scriptwriter associates told her to cool it and look the other way. Les's buddies at the art studio told him he just needed to be more discreet. He couldn't, though, because part of him *wanted* to be caught. The day Les came home for the third time with long black hairs on his sweater, Madey knelt on the floor in front of him and cried profusely. They embraced and promised to work it through. They were asked some years later, at the end of a long, bumpy road, what they'd had to do in order to save their marriage. Les responded succinctly, "We had to look at each other, to really look, and keep at it until we could finally *see* each other again."

Not everyone has the experience Madey and Les had. A partner may continue to be unfaithful or be unwilling to work at repair. Still, this is not automatic license for you to react in kind. The power to make the choice of how to respond to infidelity—or to any painful situation in which you're seemingly powerless—is always yours. In the time of crisis it may be hard to remember that.

But if you can access the basic sense of autonomy that is there, underneath, it can help you to feel much better.

What is the right thing to do when something this jarring happens? In part the answer will depend on your values and circumstances, but in general it will involve *sticking by your chosen commitments.* Whatever your priorities, remember that the by-product of freely choosing your commitments is a responsibility to uphold them. This may include, for example, extending an olive branch to your partner or comforting your children.

Doing routine things can also keep hope alive. When my husband was between jobs, we found repetition to be a blessing: sending out résumés and checking for e-mails every day, the back and forth of shopping, the going on toward a brighter tomorrow even when we hardly had the money to pay the rent. It's little habits like these that get us through each trying passage. When you're having problems you must try, try, and try again to solve them as best you can. Then, when you're really tired, try once more. Repeat to yourselves encouraging words: "I choose this, I choose this". . ."Lord, Lord, give me strength". . ."This, too, shall pass."

Do your best, then, to be reliable for all those who rely on you. During hard times we need the comfort of intimate companionship more than ever. It is then that the foundation of our relationship is tested, as we grab each other's hands and leap into the unknown. The dependable return of the wave to the shore or the day to the nighted earth: These age-old images of fidelity have been available to humankind for a long time. Emulate them as much as you can.

Use Reverence to Keep You Connected

Hold on to what is good, even if it is a handful of earth. And hold on to what you believe, even if it is a tree which stands by itself. Hold on to what you must do, even if it is a long way from here. . . . Hold on to my hand, even when I have gone away from you. —PUEBLO VERSE

Most of us have experienced moments of fright and disassociation. In the swirls and eddies of stormy circumstance, many of the tools we learned in honoring can be used to keep us connected as we abide. Often, in harrowing cases such as Laura Larsen's ambulance ride or Sherry and Manuel's near-fatal car crash, qualities of reverence—peaceful clarity, keen appreciation of detail—spontaneously occur. In these moments awe and wonder conjoin so dramatically that we may see our faith with new eyes. Our understanding of the universe is forged in these moments. Our lives change.

In a major crisis awe, wonder, reverence, or faith may arise spontaneously. However, life-defining moments can also be recalled intentionally for strength in the daily grind. What were those major experiences for you—the fall off the horse, the wild turbulence over the Pacific, the bomb scare? How did you cope then? Did any insights strike you—"I have a purpose in life" or "I will be all right no matter what" or "Nothing is more important than my children"? See these memories as life preservers that can keep your spirits up when you're struggling in the choppy waters of challenge.

Sometimes we suffer together. Sometimes one of us is under attack while the other one offers care. And then there are the times we suffer alone. It is devastating, in the midst of crisis, when our partner is not in there abiding with us. What can be done in these cases?

You and other loved ones can try calling him or her back to your original covenant, to that sacred honoring place, by engaging in compassionate truth telling—and by inviting such kind honesty in return. If such loving, respectful attempts to connect fail at first, remember that it often takes time. It may require repeated efforts, and the strictest maintenance of respect in the face of pain. Accept the process as necessary. Tears and loving struggle are as sacred as smiles.

The assistance of reverence is critical for abiding in a spiritually fulfilling marriage. Recall the honoring exercise "The Lover's List"— that enumeration of the quirks you love in your partner. When times are tough, this list becomes so much more than a sweet exercise in appreciation. Whoever may be to blame for, say, the break-in of your home, the botched dinner party, or the broken relations with your in-laws, the temptation inevitably rises to pull away, to find fault, to block your companion out, to shut down. Needless to say, in hard times this is exactly what you *mustn't* do. Calling up your helpmate's wonderful qualities and putting that list in a retrievable place for yourself (physically or metaphorically) are other forms of life preservers. So are memories of when your wife or husband *did* stand by you when you needed it. Remembering reverence during tough times helps to keep you from turning on each other when you need each other most.

Trust Each Other

"You are not tired, are you, Little Bear? Little Bear," said Grandfather, "—are you tired?" Little Bear was not tired! No! Little Bear was fast asleep.
—ELSE HOLMELUND MINARIK, *LITTLE BEAR'S VISIT*

I used to fall asleep reading copies of my son's *Little Bear* series whenever I felt the need to reparent myself. These stories present the ideal loving family everyone longs for but no one has to perfection. Falling asleep in someone's arms is a basic act of faith, requiring that we believe wholeheartedly in the good intentions of the person holding us. Thus, finally and fundamentally, having faith also involves *belief in each other*.

In an atmosphere of hope, fidelity, and reverence, trust can truly flourish. It is the natural outgrowth of caring for and honoring one another. But it can be hard to access when life is a struggle. There is a joke that reminds me how to break through the paralysis of mistrust that crisis can bring: A preacher, a mechanic, and a housewife found themselves in a lifeboat in the middle of the sea. "Let us pray," the preacher bellowed. "Only God can save us."

"I don't believe in your God," the mechanic shot back. "What we need to do is row."

A fight broke out. Fortunately, the housewife was a seasoned expert in diplomacy. "Dear sirs," she said, placing one hand on each man's shoulder, "let us pray with our oars."

This joke reminds me that we tend to trust only the people who acknowledge our worth and agree with our thinking. We often withdraw our trust when someone disagrees with us, confusing another's objection with being attacked. True trust means you will give your partner the benefit of the doubt, knowing that once in a while he or she may not, in fact, deserve it. If you find that you cannot believe the words coming out of your partner's mouth, trust that there are good intentions. If you are unable to believe in your partner's good intentions, then trust your partner's heart. There is a good but hurting person in each of us, a need for compassion when we're at our worst. An old bad habit may rear its head, for example, bringing with it shame and lies. Remember to believe in the basic worth of your chosen mate. Trust in *that,* and it will help him or her—and you two as a couple—in weathering that particular passing storm.

And if with all this, something hard still happens—outside the two of you or in between—trust in the universe itself. There is always some spare room to recoup from the unfair hurts as well as from the mistakes we have made. With trust you may find a hidden purpose, a deeper growing wisdom, in the trials of the day.

Remember that the narrative line of your life is long and winding and that this is but one phase of it. With distance and perspective old wounds can be seen as precursors to important lessons, hard but worthwhile. It is more difficult in the midst of challenge to maintain that perspective, yet still you *can* remind yourself that this is a small portion of a long experience. Tomorrow, or someday soon, you may receive the surprise of newfound promise. Trust that the bigger picture always has more in store for you than you can possibly foresee.

Being Flexible

To hold on too long may only be obstinacy; letting go too soon may only be inconsistency. —ARTHUR DOBRIN, *SPELLING GOD WITH TWO O'S*

Flexibility is about yielding. It is the elbow bending, the knee raised high, as we push each other up the hill. There is a false security in rigidity, though, for something that is brittle takes much less pressure to break. Ask any tree. A marriage that lasts is one that learns to bend with the wind.

I have seen marriages at many different phases of development. Most couples go through six in particular that require certain types of "bending" to meet new challenges. As you read through these typical phases, think about how closely your actual experience reflects them. In the discrepancies you notice, you may find clues to improving your relationship.

Honeymoon. The challenge of this phase is to learn to please each other. How can I make both of us happy? What do we both enjoy? How do we encourage each other to become all we can? At this stage it is a thrill to help out our best friend, as it was for me when I helped my husband set up a darkroom in the bathroom of our tiny apartment. Later he bought me a huge easel, and I can still recall the giant smile on his face when he brought it home. Some couples are shortchanged on this phase, being prematurely faced with major responsibilities—home buying, conceiving a child right away. Others may need to learn how to allow each other in, letting go of the control of a "me only" mind-set, and finding out how to think of another person first.

Responsible Living. Now you begin to make important decisions together. Not every moment is pure happiness. Do we go to a movie or pay the rent early? What? You had an accident in *my* car? Here you are learning to work together, to solve problems in mutually considerate ways, and to gain the deep satisfaction that effective teamwork brings. Suddenly there are two of you to get one chore done. Depending on age, values, chance, and other factors, married couples may find themselves at this stage very soon after the wedding or several years into it. Couples who resist this level by spending *too* much time playing can find themselves unprepared for the challenging tasks to come.

Creating a Family. Suddenly everything is upside down. Carrying three beers and a bowl of pretzels to the television at once no longer qualifies as multitasking. This phase includes dressing with bleary eyes, a general loss of privacy, and forced separations (due to the new "divide and conquer" policy). Of course, there's an absolutely adorable little being that has conned you into being a willing diaper slave. But the neat divisions of labor that marked the success of the "Responsible Living" phase are in shambles—and sometimes you feel you are, too. The task here is to maintain balance in your partnership with your attention so deeply diverted. Many a marriage stumbles at this point if it lacks a good support system.

Teen Duty. When the kids were young, you each could do your thing. They'd be just as thrilled to go to the game with Dad as to attend a mom-and-child yoga class. They didn't mind accommodating to your routine—such as it was. Now you and your partner must present a united front. The challenge here is to support each other when you are being significantly challenged: Your values, your rules, and your past history of wrongdoing (remembered in ruthless detail) are all grist for the mill. The first job of teens is to distinguish themselves from their parents—and a parent's first job is to make sure they don't maim themselves in the process. Even if you went through the first three stages effortlessly, this drawing-the-line thing can get you down. Are you being too soft? Too tough? You don't always agree. Hey, part of you wants to join in the rebellion.

Full Calendars and Empty Nests. Well, you've done your job, and they've left you. You're glad they need to borrow money, because you suspect you otherwise might not get a call. Or they're calling you all the time, and you're not there to protect them from the world. Decades have passed, and the person you married, now that you have a chance to take a good look, is a bit more frayed around the edges than you'd previously noticed. (So are you.) You won't go back to being the way you were when you were twenty or thirty, so you have to make space to get to know each other again. One or both of you may be at the peak of your careers. One or both of you may be entering the job market again. You'd like to have each other all to yourselves, but public voices call. The challenge of this phase is to redesign your life for an equilibrium between marital togetherness and engagement in the world.

Silver Linings. These are the harvest years, the time to savor what you've achieved together. But they are also a time to adjust to inevitable restrictions in your life: a prostate problem, creaky bones, and more serious ailments that you pray surgery or meds can fix. How come there are so many candles on your birthday cake? You always had a bad memory, but now it shows. If it doesn't on you, it does on your partner. Fortunately, you can finish each other's sentences, because you remember the important things, matters of the heart. And little faces are beginning to appear at your door. They all have the very same smile as your firstborn. Suddenly your grown children are seeing you as wise (well, sometimes). The scent of the grandchild lying next to you under the sheets is warm and sweet as summer. For this alone was the world made.

Each of these six phases of marriage offers you an opportunity to deepen your connection to life and to one another. If circumstances and choices have caused you to cut short or skip a stage, you might want to experiment creatively with the lesson tasks of that missing phase. A couple who married due to an unplanned pregnancy, for example, might try the enjoyable task of pleasing each other more (the Honeymoon stage), which might have gotten short shrift. Make sure to go to the park, blow bubbles, or tickle each other silly. If you can find equivalent experiences, the later phases may be experienced less like rude awakenings and more like ripening into marital maturity.

Every phase of partnership requires adaptations in behavior, shifts in agenda. It is as though your marriage covenant covers a series of separate contracts. If you're in a second marriage or have stepchildren, you've got even more agreements to manage.

And don't think you're off the hook if you've chosen a companionate marriage (one without children). "Creating a Family" is done in spirit as well as fact—building a community, mentoring, fighting for a cause, creating art—and "Empty Nests" can happen any time a long-term goal is reached. Marriage is always about growing and learning and bringing out the best in each other through all the variety of experiences that life offers. To abide, you must be flexible and have faith in your ability to live things through together, knowing that the benefits of all your perseverance will exceed any wish you ever made upon a star.

Learn and Grow

You're never too old to unlearn. —A WISE DOG

Maintaining the liveliness of your marriage means teaching yourselves new tricks at each bend in the road. Sometimes this means
unlearning things in order to clear the way for new habits and attitudes. A weekly hike to the top of your hilly street may help you to
see the bigger picture for years but lose its effectiveness over time.
Attending religious services may help you to get in touch with
forces unseen, but events, personality clashes, and shifting beliefs
may require you to find new sanctuaries or rituals. A spiritually fulfilling marriage evolves, like a sacred scroll unrolling. It's a joyful
undertaking, but it takes a little planning and preparation.

The word "education" comes from the Latin *educere,* "to lead
forth." We need to be led forth by one another. We need to learn new
things in order to respond constructively to changes in our marriage
and our life. We also need to be led forth out of our narrow nagging
minds into a broader-minded sense of faith and connection.

It's best to love the work of learning. Part of that involves figuring out *how* you learn best. My husband is a voracious reader, an
almost-instant expert on any subject he picks up. But for me the
apprentice style works best. That's how I learned to drive—sitting
in the passenger seat and consciously watching my husband's ma-
neuvers month after month.

Some gardeners learn by reading about gardens first, others by
making a mess of their little patch of backyard earth. Try to discover
the kinds of learning environments that are most comfortable for
you. Maybe a wine-tasting course would make your nights out

more satisfying. An ethics lecture could get you into a spirited debate about your beliefs, or, then again, maybe a single class in ballroom dancing would do more for the two of you than five lectures on communication skills.

The great teacher and thinker Albert Einstein once said, "Imagination is more important than knowledge." That is because imagination leads us out into new terrain and encourages us to build upon our own philosophy of life. Erik and Laura Larsen treasured poetry as a means of learning and of gleaning responses from one another. You will have your own preferred modes of learning—surfing the Internet, experimenting with arts and crafts, watching documentaries, exploring your families' genealogies. The message at the heart of many of these activities is that often the most important thing to do in response to change is to change yourself. *To grow.*

Over the years I've discovered that the kind of learning that helps me to make the most of my marriage is learning that fosters an attitude of reverence and responsibility toward life. A passage from T. H. White's *The Once and Future King* talks about the sustaining power of learning to pull us through even the toughest of times:

"The best thing for being sad," replied Merlin, beginning to puff and blow, "is to learn something. That's the only thing that never fails. You may grow old and trembling in your anatomies, you may lie awake at night listening to the disorder of your veins, you may miss your only love, you may see the world about you devastated by evil lunatics, or know your honour trampled in the sewers of baser minds. There is only one thing for it then—to learn. Learn why the world wags and what wags it. That is the only thing which the mind can never exhaust, never alienate, never be tortured by, never fear or distrust, and never dream of regretting. Learning is the only thing for you. Look what a lot of things there are to learn."

In my family I was often expected to know how to do things without any instruction or practice. While this high expectation stretched me significantly, and for a long time my natural talent kicked in, it also often filled me with dread. You should not assume that you have to know everything up front—about yourself, about marriage, or about any other profound topic. Give yourself a break.

Remember, the odds are stacked in your favor. Your brain is designed for learning, and your natural human spunk can make it fun. Take advantage of that. You two were meant to know more today than you did at birth. And to *be* more as well.

Decide When to Let Go

Patience is bitter, but its fruit is sweet. —FRENCH PROVERB

What makes abiding necessary in the first place is inevitable and constant change—which means that tomorrow's atmosphere will be different from today's. For this reason any effective process for perseverance must allow for the flexibility to change your mind. Healthy doubt can tell you when to hold fast and when to let go. You might think of this special kind of sorting as doubt in action.

Healthy doubt does not sabotage relationships but rather fosters their deeper potential. It asks, Does this (habit or belief) really work for us? Has this style of coping outworn its usefulness?

In dark times I have often been led by doubt. Doubt whispers in a quiet voice that something is wrong. It is a "soul sense," a "not-rightness" that leads you to leave the small constricted rooms of your present habitat. Because the culture in which I grew up taught me that doubt was bad, I used to feel guilty whenever I doubted something. My elders portrayed doubt as an obsessive need for literalism—and I agree that overclinging to material proof can certainly be a problem. But mature doubt, born of the longing to escape stultifying beliefs and situations, can actually be a vehicle to deeper faith.

Susan and Jocelyn, a lesbian couple for whom I wrote a letter of recommendation when they were adopting a child, despaired at first of being able to bring their son up in their faith. After several rebuffs by local fundamentalist ministers, they finally came upon a Unitarian Universalist church with a large sign out front saying WELCOMING CONGREGATION. They were thrilled to find that same-sex unions were honored there. When they each had discovered they were "different," as Susan's mother referred to it, they'd had to look again at their childhood beliefs. Jocelyn told me that she had gone back to reread the Bible through adult eyes. She was surprised to note that the sin of Sodom and Gomorrah was never specified. A long talk with the new minister affirmed her new take on this story and confirmed what had not changed—her belief in the transforming power of love.

When couples have tried to live the Commitments and find they can't, it may be time to step back, review, and drop self-defeating patterns. Letting go of a long-standing bad habit can dramatically refresh their reserve of hope. "I'm alive!" one husband sang out over the phone to me. He told me how good it felt to part ways with a manipulative friend who had been getting in the way of his marriage for years. Addictions and codependent behavior, secrecy, going through the motions, and using guilt trips to get what you want—all these are further examples of patterns that put strains on a marriage. By releasing them we free our relationship to grow.

In struggling relationships sometimes one person abandons work on the partnership while the other one clings. It's a natural instinct to hold tighter to ambivalent nurturers, especially when we think we're too weak to go out on our own. It is oddly easier to let go of those with whom you have had satisfying relationships than those who have frustrated you. If you've been abused or neglected, you may feel so insecure that you will tend to cling to the shirtsleeves of an inappropriate partner until you're helped to disengage. And, yes, there are some unions that are "fatally" flawed. There are some abusive relationships, devoid of adequate respect or caring, that may not be fixable. If sticking with it means dishonoring yourself, there is a larger fidelity to which you owe allegiance: faithfulness to the potential of an extraordinary human being—you. Whether the trouble springs from inside or outside a marriage, you can use doubt to make sure you stay loyal to your own worth as a person.

Often at times of sudden or painful change we begin to doubt everything. Despair is likely to creep in. As the Catholics have it, despair is the only unforgivable sin. Doubt that leads us to despair is not healthy. But doubt that leads us to a larger sense of life is. Beth had once made her husband, Marty, the sun to her Venus. She all but worshipped him. After Marty died, Beth had trouble pulling herself out of despair. She succeeded eventually by questioning the model her mother had passed down to her of living for your man. While it didn't destroy the joy of her long, happy union, this new doubt of hers did help her to see that old customs such as throwing wives alive into the husband's funeral pyre were a custom itself best laid to rest.

Physicists such as Max Planck tell us that if physical laws exist, there is no reason to assume they will always be the same. Theological scholars have challenged every line of sacred text. These days we needn't take anything for granted, but we must pose the questions ourselves in order to be truly satisfied with the answers. The continuing challenge is to find our way not to absolute certainty but to a confidence that will keep us grounded without rigidity. Doubt is a necessary part of this resilient faith.

Change, as we have already seen, is life's only constant—but accepting that fact does not mean naively or indiscriminately welcoming everything that befalls us. In order for our growth to be positive, selectivity and healthy doubt are necessary. As Finley Peter Dunne put it so succinctly in *Mr. Dooley's Philosophy,* "Trust everybody, but cut the cards."

Be Childlike and Open

Whilst we converse with what is above us, we do not grow old, but grow young. Infancy, youth, receptive, aspiring, with religious eye looking upward, counts itself nothing and abandons itself to the instruction flowing from all sides. —RALPH WALDO EMERSON, "CIRCLES"

Ironically, both skepticism and childlike idealism can give us relief and loving energy in the face of tough times. Don't wait for a disaster to hit, though, to bring the critical element of playfulness into your marriage. Ask for the crayons when you go to a restaurant, and draw pictures on the place mats together. Get a set of water guns, and chase each other around the lawn. Make sand castles when you're at the beach—elaborate ones. Play hopscotch in an empty playground. Play doctor and nurse—you know how—reversing roles now and then.

Children have the ability to remind us to see the world as always new. An old friend of mine once was strolling down the block with his four-year-old on the way to the doctor's. His son looked up at the sky, pointed, and shouted out, "Purple!" My friend, always ready to instruct his boy, was about to explain that the sky is actually blue. Then he looked up and to his amazement saw the purplest darkening sky he'd ever seen.

Being grown-up isn't any fun if you leave behind the child you once were. I remember a couple who put off getting married for years because they thought that once you signed the wedding contract you transformed into the farmer with the pitchfork and his stern and sober wife. In fact, a good marriage features joy and laughter, not only on regular days but also as a way to cope with bleaker times.

Julie and Brice had the toughest year of their shared life nine years into their marriage. It started when Brice, a second-grade public-school teacher, was diagnosed with cancer. They opted for aggressive chemotherapy, which left Brice exhausted and hairless. One day their daughter Courtney matter-of-factly observed that she couldn't remember the last time she'd seen her parents smiling. Julie realized then that she had to do something more than settle for survival. She read a book that recommended watching lots of comedies and found that helpful. Courtney especially enjoyed watching the Marx Brothers. Julie then bought a juicer and made a game of it with Courtney, seeing who could grind the most carrots quickest. When little Courtney came into the bedroom with carrots sticking out of her ears, she elicited her father's first full-bodied laugh in months.

Ella and Kareem, a childless couple who came to me to help them revitalize their relationship, stumbled across the idea of reading children's books. They took turns reading aloud in my office Watty Piper's classic, *The Little Engine That Could.* This simple yet profound story of faith speaks to all generations. Ella and Kareem found that selecting their favorite childhood books and reading them to each other to get in touch with the playful, hopeful parts of themselves was a wonderfully direct way to restore their tired relationship. Sometimes they would discuss what simple truths were embedded in the storyline or whom it was they identified with most. Ella and Kareem made a list for me of their favorite books from childhood, which included the *Frog and Toad* series, *Goodnight Moon, The Secret Garden, The Sword in the Stone,* and all of *The Chronicles of Narnia.* What childhood books inspired you? Go back and read the one that sounds like the most fun to you.

Reading children's literature helps us connect to our spouse and to our child selves. Evan, who worked as a CPA, recalled while reading *The Hobbit* to his young son his own sense of mystery and adventure when his father had read it to him. At some point, Evan realized, he'd lost this fascination with adventure. How had that happened, and why? Pondering this question led to a meaningful discussion with his wife about how to find that youthful energy again. That one discussion went a long way toward reviving the romantic spark in his married life that had dwindled a bit, too.

Turn to Others and Your Community

Ideologies separate us. Dreams and anguish bring us together.
—EUGENE IONESCO

The final step in abiding is straightforward and simple: Don't try to do it alone. You don't need to be totally self-sufficient as a couple, and you'll waste your hearts by trying. There are groups to help you figure out what you believe and groups to celebrate your beliefs together. There are support groups of every stripe and flavor. There are neighbors, friends, and extended family all waiting to help you, if only you'd ask.

Unfortunately, there are some who feel extremely uncomfortable asking for help or even letting on to others that anything's wrong. More unfortunately still, these are often the very people who need help the most. If you are one of these people, I cannot force you to accept the gifts that others would likely be grateful to give. All I can say is, you're not alone. You are loved without asking for it. And maybe, over time, with a growing faith in yourself and in those around you, maybe one day you'll find that the loving support of your community has grown around you almost without your noticing it and that help is not quite so terrible a prospect. After all, things do change. . . .

How many times have you waited until a bad situation got miserable before asking advice from Mom or Dad or whomever you prefer to protect or impress? Why is it so hard to admit that we need help? The truth is that honest self-disclosure both opens your heart and gives you the strength to carry on in difficult times. As one dear friend told me recently, anticipating my hesitancy in asking for help, "Saying what you need is the mature thing to do."

Abiding requires letting your needs be known to all who might be able to help. "How many people did you *tell*?" Hal lamented after he came home from knee surgery. "As many as I could think of," I demurely replied. While our partner's privacy must be respected, I firmly believe that in order to abide in the real world, we need real help—real arms to hug us and real friends to remind us that we are part of something larger than our pain. Many comfort stories from religion have this lesson at heart. Without community, these stories tell us, a problem can be an unthinkable burden; within it, however, we can get by—and maybe even grow wiser. Every group has its weak points (its politics, its restrictions of belief), and these have distressed many reflective people enough to make them withdraw from group gatherings and live in relative solitude. But we need one another, deeply, desperately at times, and continually.

Clark knew he wasn't going to keep partial custody of his little girl, Melissa. Jobs in the tech sector were just too hard to come by. His new wife's book wouldn't sell, and his ex-wife was still so bitter that she saw Clark's troubles only as her chance for total victory. One day he wandered into a small chapel in his neighborhood, even though he had not been brought up religiously. He touched his head with the holy water the way the two old men in front of him had done. Then, after sitting in a back pew for some time observing the ebb and flow of bent bodies, he walked forward and lit an electric candle. Clark wasn't sure just what he was lighting the candle for, but he saw that it was not the only one flickering in its red cup. Each one of the lit candles had a sad story, Clark realized. As he walked back down the stone steps, he felt as though he were in the company of thousands. The echoes of their imagined footsteps filled his mind and soothed his heart. In the midst of others' sorrows he found solidarity and suddenly knew he could go on.

You Shall Overcome

Think of all the beauty still left around you and be happy.
—ANNE FRANK, *DIARY OF A YOUNG GIRL*

There are many strengths to help us stay the course through the ups and downs of marriage. A marriage based on convenience falls apart under stress: If partners have been betraying or ignoring their marital covenant, fostering despair or false hope, or insisting on the status quo, they won't have the resilience to deal with significant changes, especially those that have a tragic aspect to them. Conversely, couples who've kept faithful to the spirit of their marriage covenant, flexibly opening themselves up to continuing transformation, are ready to weather the heavy storms. If partners have been persistently supportive of one another, bearing hard times together, and being patient, they are in a position to take what comes, good or bad, and harvest it all toward fulfillment.

Abiding is about knowing that whatever comes, it will be okay. You will be okay. And the journey will be incredible.

Keys to a Faithful Union

- Change your attitudes for the better.
- Enact hope in concrete ways, such as handwriting prayers.
- Be faithful to each other in every way.

- Lift up your spirit by recalling times when you deeply admired your spouse.
- Believe in each other.
- Never stop learning.
- Sort out what's worth keeping in your partnership, and let go of what's not.
- Let the child in you out to play.
- Let helping hands hold you up.
- Hang on through all the ups and downs.

Abiding Questions to Ask Yourself

1. Is there a basic sense of comfort and security in your marriage—in order for faith in *it* to be possible?
2. Are you generally faithful to commitments you make to each other, so that you can rely on each other when all else fails?
3. Do you honor the life force of your *marriage* in the same way that you honor your partner and yourself?
4. Can your partner trust you always to stick to your principles? To tell the truth? To take good care of him or her?
5. Do you know that, no matter what, you will be okay?
6. Do you have any hurtful or unhealthy beliefs that you could stand to let go of?
7. Are you open to new resources to help you to get through life's ups and downs?
8. Do you have a regular way of sharing joy and hope with others, through the downs as well as the ups in life?

Hope Chest Journal: An Abiding Exercise

This exercise asks you to create a "trust fund" that you can count on during hard times. Using a journal or notebook, begin by thinking of times you felt hopeful and times you did not. Take a few minutes to jot down relevant experiences shortly after they've occurred. Make lists of activities that bring you back into a resilient mind-set. Search your past for memories of joy (the water park excursion, twilight on the dunes, the first time you held your child). Search your imagination, too, for things you've always longed to try (skydiving, improv class, checking out the inside of that Quaker meetinghouse or church that you pass every day). Be sure to include times when your partner stood by you or treated you especially well. These entries will be your Hope Chest journal—to help remind you when times are tough that you can count on this person who loves you.

Another effective, if common, technique is just to rent movies with an eye toward deliberately bringing up your spirits. Here are a few movies couples I've worked with have included in their Hope Chest journals: *Much Ado About Nothing, It's a Wonderful Life, What Dreams May Come, Harold and Maude, Groundhog Day, Say Anything, Forrest Gump.* Make a list of movies in your journal to choose from on hard days.

There are also many, many books you can choose from. A close friend of mine returns to *Walden, Zen Mind Beginner's Mind,* and Herman Hesse's *Siddhartha* to help her reconnect to her faith in the goodness and interconnectedness of the universe. What are your favorites? List them in your Hope Chest journal.

Keep your Hope Chest journal faithfully. In times to come you can use it to remind yourself of how you hung in there through it all.

Sixth Commitment

Repairing

🦢

I will work to mend what is broken
in my partner and myself.

How could you be mad at someone who was dead? This was the question Maureen asked herself as she sat in the chapel of the funeral parlor. Barely able to listen to the eulogy, Maureen felt a hot, bitter sting rising up in her chest and buried her face in her hands. She could only hope that people would assume she was struck with sorrow. Where were these other feelings coming from, so fierce, so unbidden?

I'd expected to be performing a wedding, and instead I was presiding at the funeral of the groom's father. Everyone had agreed that the wedding should be delayed. As I gazed out over the crowd of mourners, I noticed that Maureen was visibly shaken. Later she told me in detail what she'd been experiencing.

Maureen had admired Josh's father, had, in fact, coveted his approval. She felt robbed now of a chance to remedy his summary dismissal of her. As far as tolerance was concerned, her family members were no saints, either. Her mother was going to be miffed when she came in and had no open casket to kneel in front of. The thought of her mother's lack of compassion brought more sobs. And ("How selfish," she chided herself) his death had ruined her wedding. There was something about having her special day taken from her. . . .

Josh kept his arm around Maureen throughout the service. Afterward the three of us took some time in the empty office of the funeral director. "I guess you're crying for both of us," Josh said to her, smiling wanly. He hadn't been able to shed one tear. Maureen buried her head in his chest and cried like a lost child.

"Want to talk about it?" Josh finally asked. At first Maureen didn't answer, afraid of hurting Josh's feelings. But finally exhaustion took the edge off etiquette, and she let out her mixed emotions. To her surprise, Josh seemed to understand.

"Maybe I shouldn't have told you my secret," Josh said sympathetically.

"No," Maureen replied. "That would have been worse. If I'd found out some other way that your father disapproved of me, I would've had to wonder what else you were hiding." Suddenly she was overwhelmed by the truth of her words. Turning to Josh, she said, "I've got a secret, too."

It had to do with why she didn't want her stepbrother to stand up with them during the wedding. Josh knew that Jerry had been hurtful somehow to Maureen years ago, but Maureen always dissolved in tears when the matter came up, and Josh was hesitant to trespass.

As a teen, Maureen had found it difficult enough to adjust to a new father figure in the house. But Jerry was another matter. Built like a football player, her stepbrother was too undisciplined to make the high school team. And he had a mouth like a sewer. Jerry would disappear for hours and occasionally days at a time, although no one but Maureen seemed to notice or care.

On her fifteenth birthday, shortly before midnight, the door to Maureen's tiny bedroom opened, revealing a hulking male shadow in the shaft of hall light. Like a cornered mouse, Maureen froze, closing her eyes and desperately hoping he would go away. Instead she heard his stumbling footsteps, smelled his alcohol breath, and felt his heavy body splay out on top of her quilt. She screamed inside, but nothing could slip past her soldered lips as she watched the scene unfold with utter detachment.

"*Hope you liked your birthday present,*" *Jerry whispered in a heavy slur when it was over. He stumbled out and closed the door, leaving Maureen lying there and wondering how long she would have to hold her breath to die.*

Attending to Breaks and Bruises

One word frees us of all the weight and pain of life: That word is love.

—SOPHOCLES, *OEDIPUS AT COLONUS*

Mourning doesn't start at funerals. It begins with first loss. The night you call out to your mother and, unlike every other night, she doesn't come; the runaway cat; the rained-out birthday trip to the amusement park. Beyond these hurts there is also a deeper order of loss, as Maureen experienced it the night her stepbrother came, drunk, into her room. When your innocence is broken, if it happens violently, early, or often, you may have to seek repair in stages over months and years.

Whether the wounds of loss have been minimal or deep, one thing is for certain: We must attend regularly to repair. From start to finish, life bruises us all.

In the previous chapter we took a look at how abiding can make you more resilient in the face of challenge and change. But "resilient" does not mean "immune." However much faith you have, healing always needs to be done. Faith gives you the means to hold on until help arrives. It does not promise the absence of pain, only the ability to bear it.

I used to think there was a quota system in the universe. If I'd had three hard things happen in one day, I thought I could avoid a fourth, or I'd tell myself I'd had a lot of early grief so I'd be saved from later harm. Unfortunately, it doesn't work that way. In fact, I've given up looking for explanations of why bad things happen to good people, other than the obvious fact that to care is to be vulnerable. It's a trade-off: Vulnerability makes us capable of having love, intimacy, a full life. But the price we pay is to open ourselves up to pain.

If we are to find spiritual fulfillment in marriage, we will need to get down to the task of repair. Unattended emotional wounds breed resentment, disconnection, and, too often, further injury. The more regular mending work we do, the easier it will be to fix. But there is even more incentive to be found in that deep mending feeds the soul. When it is undertaken together, repairing not only makes our daily lives smoother but binds us closer, deeply.

Bringing Pain to Light

What in me is dark
Illumine, what is low raise and support;
That to the height of this great argument
I may assert eternal Providence
And justify the ways of God to men.

—JOHN MILTON, *PARADISE LOST*

Once a dog came up to me on the street and began licking my leg. When I looked down, I realized I was cut. I hadn't even noticed. But he had, dear fellow. Before beginning to nurse your wounds, you must of course acknowledge them. This may sound simpler than it actually is. To be open to our pain is often a fear-laden process, and our well-honed defenses run deep. People who have had experiences like Maureen's, for example, often hide the pain of such encounters even from themselves for years.

To complicate matters further, it is impossible (or at least unwise) to rush the overcoming of denial. Its purpose in the first place was to protect you, so it takes a little care to remove it without causing panic. Over time a scrupulous habit of being honest with yourself helps you to acknowledge defensiveness that leads to denial. Why be honest when it hurts so much—at least at first? Because in a funny way it feels good, like when you wiggled that loose tooth you had at age seven. Somehow your fingers were called into action, to make way for the empty space that was the precursor to something sturdier, more lasting. Candid self-examination, though occasionally fearsome, leads in the direction of health, insight, and fulfillment.

In order to do hard or scary work, we need sanctuary in extra measure. A spiritually strong marriage creates that environment of trust—the kind of safe haven in which true healing can happen. Is your partner someone with whom you feel safe enough to share your failures, insecurities, and pain? That question posed itself to Maureen before she even shaped it into words, before she allowed herself to remember what had happened when she was fifteen. As a teenager, Maureen couldn't turn to her mother. Whenever she complained about her stepfather, Tony, who was slow, stodgy, no dance left in him—nothing like her "real dad"—her mother would brush off her complaints. "He puts food on the table!" she'd snap. (And that was true. End of discussion.) It was only in the utter safety of Josh's embrace that Maureen began to bring the incident with her stepbrother out of the shadows of her memory.

To find someone we can trust is crucial. Once, when I was on a date with my future husband, I was so tired as we drove toward a distant restaurant that I nodded off briefly in the front seat. Pulling over, Hal suggested that I lie down in the back, where I'd be more comfortable. He gave me his good jacket to use as a pillow. That evening, snugly curled up, I drifted off to sleep in the sure knowledge that even before reaching the restaurant I was with a man I could trust. This fact was confirmed many times over the coming years. In time it allowed me to begin looking at my own challenging childhood and for the long healing work to begin.

Knowing we have a place—or a person—to soften our falls provides us with the extra confidence we need to make the inward journey of lasting repair. Compare a good cry in the warm arms of a trusted loved one with the stifled hiccups of a cry in the stall of a restaurant bathroom. Healing goes deeper and lasts longer if you have the chance to seek it in a place of safety, a place where you can really let go of anguish.

Sometimes, we're having such a hard time that we hesitate to spill our raw feelings in front of our partner. When that happens, we need to seek out safe places to sort things through first. After months of being turned away, Colin was so furious with Pia over her refusal to make love that he thought he well might spontaneously combust. One day he cooled off by walking down the street to the sunny wood-paneled reading room of the neighborhood library. Colin could hear a librarian softly reading to a group of children in the next room. He remembered how his grandfather had done that when tucking him in at night. As Colin closed his eyes, he felt great sadness under his anger. Suddenly he realized how cut off he had become from Pia and how hungry he was for her love. He resolved to go to Pia that afternoon and seek to repair the rift between them.

Once we're ready to admit to pain and sorrow, which can often be masked by anger, we're in a position to be more open with our partner about it. He or she is a primary source of solace and support, serving as a bridge between us and the greater love that surrounds us. When that support is removed because our partner caused harm, it is twice as urgent to accept and address the situation. Our partner deserves to know what we're feeling so that it can be quickly addressed. But remember, there's a difference between sincere expression of feelings and verbal assault. Be kind and honest. Be safe havens for each other.

With Respect to Forgiveness

It is by forgiving that one is forgiven.
—"THE PRAYER OF ST. FRANCIS OF ASSISI"

There is a special type of repair called forgiveness. Forgiveness in marriage is, of course, a necessary element. Small things can build up—our spouse snaps at us, borrows our car the day we needed it, forgets to call while away on business, or accidentally breaks a porcelain doll we've had since we were five. Angry feelings expressed in the heat of an argument, too, sting and can't be taken back no matter how sorry your partner may be later. And there are major ruptures caused by infidelity, violent outbursts, and screaming fights. At such times we may wonder who this person we married really is. We're not sure how to repair things, not sure if we even want to. How do we get to the other side of all these different kinds of disruptive situations?

Sometimes, with a small infringement, a heartfelt apology goes a long way. But while apologies can do wonders to elicit forgiveness, they certainly don't guarantee it. Heartfelt forgiveness, like falling in love, is something you feel your way toward. It often feels as if it happens *to* you instead of your consciously making it happen. But when you fall in love, you do intentionally open up, you do choose to spend time exploring each other, and you do allow your mind to linger on the mysteries of this fascinating person. Similarly, there are intentional techniques for forgiveness in marriage. The most important one—mutual respect—is a shortcut for repairing of every kind.

Recalling your commitment to honor each other helps to get beyond suffering. This is true regardless of the extremity of your dilemma; regardless of whether pain is inflicted on one of you, on both of you, or between you; and regardless of what other techniques you use to heal. "You should learn to forgive!" a well-meaning friend may have said to you in the past. But how do we do this? Keeping quiet and not bothering anybody? Repeating a string of magical words? Taking all the blame on ourselves, or accepting empty apologies followed by more and more as the hurts pile up? Of course not. Forgiveness is accepting the pain that we've suffered and/or the person who has caused the pain. It is a process by which any self-respect we may have lost is restored, and it is a return to a place of mutual honoring.

In the midst of disconnection it may be a struggle to honor our partner. In a big fight we often say things purposefully to hurt each other—and it's hard to respect that. But if a denigrating situation continues, true repair is impossible. In order to communicate compassionately in a state of interpersonal disrepair, equality and mutual respect are crucial.

You can begin to increase the atmosphere of respectfulness simply by cutting back on the put-downs. Martha, for example, taught herself to stop using put-down language when talking about Phil during their six-month separation. "Deadbeat dad," her mother's term for Martha's husband, was the first phrase to go.

If the put-downs are coming *at* you, fight the temptation to go tit for tat. Instead of responding to the "low blow" your partner just landed, respond, as Callie did, to the fact that your partner felt the need to fight dirty in the first place. Warren and Callie were arguing over the baby-sitter when he suddenly brought up their strained relationship with her parents—something about which he knew Callie felt deeply guilty. "If you weren't such an ungrateful daughter, we could count on them to watch the kids," he shouted.

Paling, Callie waited a moment and then responded, "This problem really hits a chord with you if you feel the need to cut me down like that." Warren had expected her to say, "How dare you!" Instead, she cut his attack off at the pass. When he didn't respond right away, she asked, "What have I done to make you want to hurt me like that?" When he told her he thought she was accusing him of stinginess, they could finally proceed toward resolution. Thinking past the hurtful *words* of Warren's attack to the *fact* of them, Callie concentrated not on her pain but on why her normally kind husband had been so mean. In so doing, she intuitively honored the person behind the behavior. This is a potent form of self-protection, which doubles to keep fights from becoming hurting contests.

If it's possible to hear each other out, either in private or with a counselor present, adopting a respectful attitude can have an immediate impact on a couple's daily interactions. This approach to repair works best if engaged early on. In one instance Wendy, who worked as a Legal Aid lawyer in downtown Manhattan, missed three appointments with me because of last-minute schedule changes at work. Twice she didn't even call to cancel. I asked Wendy if she treated Adina, her domestic partner, this way. "Adina needs to get used to it," she snapped. Yes, I acknowledged, Adina probably *would* have to get used to it. But that didn't mean Wendy could get off the hook so easily. *She* would have to see that acknowledging broken engagements was an important part of maintenance work in a loving relationship. As it turned out, Wendy was able to change her habit fairly rapidly, carrying her cell phone and taking time for a two-minute call whenever she was delayed. It became much easier for Adina to forgive each new broken appointment when she knew that Wendy was making a respectful effort to consider her feelings. Honoring can be as simple as a phone call.

Myra's case was more complex, involving deeper wounds, but it was still amenable to a respectful repair approach. When we first met to talk about her dilemma, we sat at the same table in Pasta Heaven where she had first happened to see Peter and that big redhead together. Myra swirled the straw in her club soda and asked me if she should tell him she'd caught him or just throw his clothes out on the sidewalk? Or was there some other way? Hurt and confused, she unburdened her pain to me, buried her head in her arms, and cried.

The outcome of this situation was not something Myra could completely control. But she *could* create the conditions in which the reconciliation she hoped for would be more likely to happen. First, she had to find a way to put herself proactively into the forgiving process: She turned her attention away from her indignation and toward the hope that Peter would want to save their marriage and that he could talk about his dissatisfaction without hurting her too much more.

Finding this place of forgiveness was not at all easy. Humiliation leaked out like steam from under a pot lid. Eventually, though, Myra mustered the courage for a conversation. This involved privately engaging in some centering activities, including deep breathing and listening to Mozart as she lit a fire and cleared a space in the living room for them to talk. When they finally sat down, Myra told Peter how sad she was that they had drifted apart and how much she longed to work with him to make things better. She couldn't hide her heartache, but she could try to solve their problem cooperatively using compassionate truthfulness to open the door. She asked him if there was anything she needed to acknowledge about her own behavior. This approach set the tone for a real conversation rather than a fight. With help, time, and a conscious effort to be respectful, Myra and Peter were able to talk about the problem in a caring way, tell each other what they wanted, and, eventually, recommit to their marriage.

It might have gone another way. Peter might have attacked her verbally or taken the chance he was looking for to walk out the door. She might have kicked him out herself, and he might have begged to come back after a hard separation. The point is, their best chance for togetherness and mutual care—and for fully healing their marriage—came from striving to respect each other even in the midst of their crisis.

Steps for Day-to-Day Repair

Marriage is one long conversation, chequered by disputes. The disputes are valueless; they but ingrain the difference; the heroic heart of woman prompting her at once to nail her colors to the mast. But in the intervals, almost unconsciously, and with no desire to shine, the whole material of life is turned over and over, . . . and in process of time, without sound of trumpet, they conduct each other into new worlds of thought.

—ROBERT LOUIS STEVENSON, *MEMORIES AND PORTRAITS*

With a centered, safe environment and an attitude of respect, we can begin to do good mending on a regular basis. Small-scale hurts are generally easier and faster to fix than large-scale ones. But small-scale injuries can and do feed on each other to create deeper wounds. So it's important to be vigilant, to move quickly, and to nip minor problems in the bud. The overall improvements you see may very well be dramatic.

If you find yourself stung by a forgotten promise or inconsiderate act, speak up. (Just be sure to maintain respect; nagging and nitpicking come from speaking up without it!) One couple I know had a small problem that could have grown much worse. After his promotion Elliott had so much work to do that he began "double-tasking" his phone calls to his wife, Lori—deleting old e-mails or filing while she talked to him over the speakerphone. She felt increasingly shut out by the clicking keyboard and his distracted tone of voice, and after a week or two she told him so. She told him how much it meant to emotionally connect with him during the day, especially if he was working late. She asked him if he could schedule a ten-minute "love break" once a day, when she could have his undivided attention. In return she promised not to call at other times unless it was crucial. In this way she was able to express her hurt feelings without being overly accusatory—and to suggest a solution that wouldn't increase his stress.

Inevitably from time to time we ourselves will cause our spouse pain. It takes a bit of humility to handle day-to-day problems when we are at fault. Still, the aftereffects of the repair will be lasting if we can accomplish three things in particular:

First, acknowledge you have done something wrong. Often your partner will tell you of a trespass. Try not to be defensive, but instead recognize that you're not perfect and may have caused some harm. You can also review your day on your own, asking yourself, Did I compromise my partner's freedom of choice or act without regard to his or her feelings? Acknowledge it to yourself, and then (this is very important), to your spouse: "I'm sorry I didn't stop to ask if you were through before throwing out the paper" or "I committed to plans without checking with you first." Show courage by facing up to any trouble you might have caused. Saying this out loud is important. And be sure the expression is heartfelt.

Second, reach out to make amends. Small-scale mending begins with acknowledgment and apology, but to last, it needs to be reinforced with further action. Ask your partner what symbolic gesture you can make to balance the negative. You can never literally undo the past harm you have done, but you can offer a gesture of goodwill and remorse. A handful of wildflowers for being late, new earrings to replace the ones you stepped on, an IOU slip promising recompense for a broken commitment, or immunity from a lecture the next time your spouse messes up the way you just did.

Third, make a commitment to change. This is very important, otherwise your words and gestures of reconciliation are ultimately hollow. You may first have to explore with your partner what kinds of interactions trigger hurtful responses—testiness in the morning, obsession with one's hobbies, bursts of temper when under stress. Find ways to avoid those situations, or else teach yourself to respond in a different manner. Do things that show that you're really trying, including taking courses, publicly asking friends for support in changing, and seeking counseling if your troubles are persistent.

Changing the way you interact—even little daily habits—can be hard work, so be kind to yourself and ask your partner for patience and understanding. Don't condemn yourself for setbacks, and don't condone your old ways or make light of their harmfulness. Accept where you are, but don't lose sight of where you want to go.

Looking at the Patterns of Your Pain

For in grief nothing "stays put." One keeps on emerging from a phase, but it always recurs. Round and round. Everything repeats. Am I going in circles, or dare I hope I am on a spiral? —C. S. LEWIS, *A GRIEF OBSERVED*

Forgiveness is an enterprise that spans generations. The little things that your ancestors left undone between them—a nod of approval not given, a lost chance to reconcile—cast shadows that extend long past their days and nights on earth. So it is with us. A hundred years from now a child may wake up crying because of a seemingly insignificant mistake we made—or wake up smiling because we had the courage to make amends.

Some emotional pains are deep down inside of us, harking back to our childhood or our family dynamics, and the usual bandages and easy-road remedies just don't work. Little hurts are happening right now, every day, every month, year after year. The same old habits and patterns drive a wedge between partners that gets wider the further in it goes. Deep wounds also come from traumatic fights and festering resentments. Grief, compulsions, habitual withdrawal, and self-blaming all need to be dissolved in order for our marriage—and us in it—to proceed with vitality.

Over the years I've learned that lasting, profound repair can be realized only over time. This sort of long-range healing begins with simply looking at the larger picture—at the repetitive injuries we've inflicted upon one another and at the "inheritance" of behavioral patterns and assumptions that have been handed down to us.

Some interpersonal hurts are fixable, situational problems, while others are not: They've taken on symbolic meaning and may carry the heavy weight of our past. As an example, not calling home when you're working late can be either a small issue or a large one. For some couples it may simply make dinner planning harder. For others it may signify "yet another" inconsiderate act—the straw on a camel's back already overloaded with disrespect. Familiarizing ourselves with the patterns of our pain enables us to tell the difference between an irritating bad habit and a major source of pain.

Inherited patterns often are not immediately obvious to those repeating them—even in the most blatant of situations. Martha, who had had to teach herself not to call her husband, Phil, a "deadbeat dad," found a remarkably obvious pattern within her pain, but only after considerable searching. "I don't know what happened," she told me the first day we set up a telephone interview. "I mean, he just walked out in the middle of dinner and didn't come back."

"Has he ever done this before?" I asked.

"Well, yes, when I was in the hospital giving birth to Brad. And then it happened again when Emily came along."

"Well, what did you tell him over dinner?" I asked.

"That I was pregnant."

As it turned out, Martha's "foot had slipped" each time she'd become pregnant. She just kept forgetting to take those birth control pills, so tiny, tucked away in a bottom drawer. Was there a pattern here, I asked? Well, yes, Phil obviously had an aversion to responsible fatherhood. I encouraged her to see if there was another pattern, perhaps one in *herself*? It took awhile to identify behaviors in Martha stemming all the way back to her tenth birthday, when her father had gotten up and walked out on the family forever. Seven months later her brother, Parker, was born. In time Martha came to see that she had been goading Phil toward that door, plainly *and yet unconsciously* creating the old familiar pattern.

"I guess I was setting Phil up for a fall," she lamented, her voice breaking over the phone. This new awareness was the first step in Martha and Phil's reconciliation.

Because patterns of behavior like Martha's often originate in one's childhood home, repairing may require a broader look at the patterns of our life before we can disentangle ourselves from present distress. Several of the other Commitments (such as choosing) involve looking at the emerging patterns in your life. With regard to the Commitment to repair, we need to ask ourselves, Do any of these patterns hurt others? Or do I find myself being hurt in similar ways again and again?

Alfie woke up one morning calling out harshly for Daisey, his first wife. "Set the coffeemaker!" he ordered.

"You've got the name wrong, but the demand right," Sue snapped back. Suddenly Alfie realized he was in a time warp. His whole life was a time warp, come to think of it. Who was he really calling out for? Who was he really angry at? His foster mother, of course! Lilah usually slept through breakfast, leaving young Alfie to climb up on a chair in order to get a cereal bowl down for himself.

Simply *recognizing* these patterns can be quite liberating and initiate the journey toward wholeness. For one thing, as we've seen, glimpsing root motivators such as underlying values or parental habits can make it easier not to blame yourself. For another thing, it can help us to change behavior that's based on ideas—separating out blind assumptions from true beliefs. Let's say, for example, that your mother raised you alone and felt that all men were untrustworthy: Acknowledging *her* opinions as the source of your own disparaging attitude toward your husband may help you to be kinder to him.

"Rome wasn't built in a day," my father said to me when I insisted that a dollhouse he was assembling for me be instantly available. I think it is actually harder to unbuild things (a city, a pattern, a relationship) than to build them up from scratch. So remind yourself of this where deep patterns of hurt are concerned: The Roman Empire—glorious, vast, and imperfect—is inside you. You'll need steady dedication, solid plans, plenty of resolve, and bold implementation to change long-standing patterns for the better.

Accept the Limits of Repair

God, give us grace to accept with serenity the things that cannot be changed, courage to change the things which should be changed, and the wisdom to distinguish the one from the other.

—REINHOLD NIEBUHR, "SERENITY PRAYER"

The "Serenity Prayer" is well known, especially because of its association with programs like Alcoholics Anonymous. To twelve-steppers one can stop drinking forever but will still always be an alcoholic. This notion relates to the next strategy for repairing.

Not every injury heals completely. In fact, most wounds leave at least a faint scar. This is natural and can even be protective as you move on in life. There's no denying that loss and failure are sad. Think upon your losses and pains. Allow yourself to *feel* the sadness so you can move on and it's not trapped inside or redirected unfairly toward your spouse.

There are limits to what we can accomplish in repairing. A deceased loved one, for example, won't be back again to confront or to hug. Edward, a man on his third marriage, sought my help in confronting the image of his dead mother, who was somehow creating more havoc as a "ghost" than she had during her actual lifetime. Edward finally came to grips with the fact that the direct reconciliation he longed for with his mother would never happen. In acknowledging this, more realistic reconciliation with the flesh-and-blood flawed women in his actual life became possible.

A hurried approach can leave us empty and increasingly frustrated. Lasting repair involves both acceptance and letting go. We can't change it if our spouse was unfaithful in the past, for example, but we can try to be loving to him or her in spite of that and to improve conditions to help prevent the infidelity from happening again.

Some of the deepest repair work we participate in during our lifetime may not reap benefits for generations perhaps. As we rear our children and support our grandchildren more attentively, or address the social conditions that contributed to our hardship, we *can* get the satisfaction of amends being made and of discernible progress. But we may have to adjust our conception of what progress is—accepting improvement, not perfection, as the outcome.

Enlist Your Imagination

Natural forces within us are the true healers of disease.

—HIPPOCRATES, *APHORISMS*

Repairing can be a long process, but it's not always hard work, because the spiritual forces within us are powerful healers. All we have to do is creatively make way for them to do their work. Here are just a few ways we can harness the imagination for repair:

Imagine your goal. Images of the end goal can excite and inspire us, giving us a snapshot of how it will be when we "arrive." When I'm conducting exercises with workshop groups, I use various images to lead participants from a confined space to an open one—walking a narrow, winding passageway through high grass, coming out to a beautiful clearing, or climbing a rocky pathway through woods and arriving at a stunning view. Sounds and smells can be incorporated, too. Then put a symbol of your goal in that airy end place: the smiling face of a person with whom you're trying to reconcile, a symbol of the new self-confidence you hope to achieve. One couple I know found the image of encouragement to be the faces of their smiling children three years hence around the Thanksgiving dinner table. Another couple imagined themselves in rockers on a porch at the Victorian hotel where they honeymooned. Others have imagined themselves dancing together at their siblings' or children's weddings.

Privately designate tokens of healing. Tokens can take any meaningful form we care to imagine—a photo, a pressed flower, a string of beads. One of my favorite imaginative healing symbols was created by the son of a Haitian baker whose father had been shot by government thugs in the doorway of his bake shop. Some years later the son returned with his new wife to that boarded-up store and reopened the bakery. He could not forgive the son of one of the men who had killed his father and refused to sell his baked goods to him. At night the baker would look up at the moon and say, "You must forgive what I cannot." He made moon cookies to privately express this. Many years after that, following numerous failed attempts at reconciliation on the part of the murderer's son, Jacques was able to let go. When he went to make the reconnection, he brought along a plate heaped up high with moon cookies, still warm from the oven.

Use repetition creatively. Repetition is a natural healing tool that can dull our pain by giving us some detachment from our anxiety. We can put this basic behavior to creative use, extending it to the realm of symbolic reality—telling the story over many times, for example. Prayer beads, rosaries, Chinese weighted balls, and mantras repeated over and over are some traditional aids used not only for reduction of basic tension but for connection to something beyond the flesh. We may improvise our own techniques, such as going the same route on a daily walk or run, or we may walk a labyrinth for a more formal walking meditation. Repetition can not only discharge built-up feelings but also help us to gain a momentum that may eventually propel us out of our cycle of pain.

Review the story through other people's eyes. As we retell our experiences, we may want to do so with attention toward the perspective of our "antagonist." This reminds us that we don't have the whole picture. Understanding the motivations of the one causing harm can be an additional aid in not blaming ourselves so much, in seeing how a hurtful situation developed, and in moving toward forgiveness.

Imagine hurtful people before they became abusive. This step takes us farther in the direction of forgiveness. When we're able to see the perpetrator of our pain in a sympathetic and respectful way—rather than with fear, dread, or anger—we're on the threshold of release. Resentment melts quickly in the fires of compassion. Rhonda, a participant in a workshop I was conducting on forgiveness (the most attended workshop every year), had brought a picture of her older sister as an eight-year-old riding a carousel. The sister was proudly displaying the brass ring she'd caught, and there was a big grin on her face. It had been a very long time since Rhonda had heard a kind word come out of her sister's mouth, Rhonda told me, gazing at the photo in a kind of visual reverie. But it had been even longer since she'd seen her sister smiling.

At the workshop Rhonda was struggling with how to forgive her big sister for her near-constant bitter remarks and her seeming resentment for Rhonda's very existence. I asked when she thought her sister had stopped smiling.

"Around the time our mother died," Rhonda responded. Her sister had essentially become Rhonda's mother at the age of eleven, losing out on much of her youth from that day forward. All at once Rhonda realized that this unfair shift in roles had no doubt caused the permanent frown on her sister's face. At the end of the workshop Rhonda said she still wasn't sure if she would ever have a warm relationship with her sister. But connecting the dots between the events and the change in her sister helped Rhonda to put things in perspective and tempered her hurt and anger with fuller understanding.

Engage in Rituals to Let Go

Woe to him who is alone when he falls and has not another to lift him up.
—ECCLESIASTES 4:10, REVISED STANDARD BIBLE

We can all creatively share our efforts to heal. A woman I counseled who goes with her partner every fall to a cabin in Maine developed an imaginative ritual for dealing with old hurts. It was inspired by a Jewish mourning practice. Walking through the woods, she collected stones, as her father had, to place on the grave of loved ones. Over time she created her own use for the stones, searching for two types in particular: small, smooth stones and larger rough ones. The smooth stones were to remind her of daily hurts. She kept these stones in her pocket for a while, touching them from time to time as a concrete reminder not to put off making amends. The rough stones represented the harsher wounds of life. A few of these stones had names and faces. Weeks or months later, when she was ready, she carried her rough stones together to a remote place. There she threw one stone at a time high up in the air, then watched it fall in a wide arc toward the earth. A couple of the words and faces on those stones reappeared on other stones and needed to be flung away another day. But others never did come back.

One man I know, tormented by the memory of his sister's suffering when their father made her sleep in pajamas she had wet, always put an extra pair of PJs by his daughter's bed. She let him continue to do so long after she was able to stay dry through the night. Though she was still very young, she sensed that somehow this ritual gave him comfort.

No doubt you already have repairing rituals that you've enacted without forethought to help you heal. Perhaps you go to the farmers' market for fresh produce on Saturdays after stressful weeks at work. Or you turn to your knitting, or your poems, or your woodshop when pain exceeds your ability to process it consciously. Think to those existing rituals; share them with your partner if you think it may help him or her. And keep your mind open for new rituals to soothe and empower you when new hurts come.

Find a Circle of Support

When you hammer a nail into a board and accidentally strike your finger, you take care of the injury immediately. The right hand never says to the left hand, "I am doing charitable work for you." It just does whatever it can to help—giving first aid, compassion, and concern.

—THICH NHAT HANH, *LIVING BUDDHA, LIVING CHRIST*

In the presence of others we can sanctify one another's suffering and at the same time share our own efforts to heal. Sometimes a circle of support is right there for you, as it was for the man with his perceptive daughter. Other times you must consciously set up a support network. One of the best resources for recovery is a trusted friend, a person to whom you can turn for support no matter what. In a good marriage your partner can almost always serve this purpose. But he or she need not (in fact should not) be the only person you can turn to. Allow yourself to get help from others as well.

Have you reached out appropriately to others for support in repairing? I know someone who used to tell anyone—stranger or acquaintance—her most intimate problems. When she came to me, she was genuinely perplexed about why she hadn't found help. One key to successful repair, as she had yet to learn, is knowing where to get the right help. Sometimes it takes us a while to find a person who is ready, willing, and emotionally capable of assisting us. We must allow ourselves to be choosy and wait until we're comfortable. But remember, no one is perfect. So we shouldn't wait to find a flawless person. There's always some risk in reaching out.

There is perhaps nothing so powerful as sharing the company of caring others. Whether it be a prayer circle, a small loving group of friends, or the many arms of generous strangers, there is an appropriate circle out there for you, offering you a safe place to cry, to breathe, to rest and recover. Be sure to be open to receiving help from those who can offer it to you *in their own ways*. Let a parishioner bring you a couple of meals a week or a close friend watch the kids while you have a good cry. Let those around you know that you're in a tough spot, and accept their creative gestures of support—a care package, a couple of errands, a card. Take down the phone numbers of others who've been through similar ordeals or of professionals who can help, be they financial advisers, lawyers, therapists, pastoral counselors, or support-group leaders. Think in advance about what you might need from each.

Finally, while you're sharing the pain and the gift of repair with others, don't forget that you can *celebrate* your successes with them, too. Do you positively mark the end of a struggle and acknowledge small triumphs? It can be so easy just to forget about a problem once it's gone. "Glad that's over!" we say, brushing off our hands and immediately concentrating on our next most bothersome problem. But we may inspire someone else by not only taking a moment to appreciate our hard work but also inviting our fellow strugglers and loved ones to witness our accomplishment. Successful substance-abuse rehabilitation programs use this technique with resounding success, celebrating anniversaries of, say, sobriety on a monthly basis, complete with such things as medals and ice cream cakes.

Maureen was wise enough to realize she needed help herself. She approached me for a special session to help ease things before the rescheduled wedding day. After a brief meeting we decided to invite her stepbrother, Jerry, to join us. Jerry showed clearly that he was eager to support Maureen, even if it meant facing hard things. With this cooperation on his part, Maureen was finally able to confront Jerry about the secret she'd carried with her so long. As it turned out, he had completely blocked out the memory of Maureen's fifteenth birthday (he was often blank following drinking binges). After some probing, a sad irony emerged: Jerry had actually felt protective of Maureen, because she was the only one in the family who had expressed any concern for him. He recalled how he'd wanted to show his appreciation in some way. Back then Maureen had told him how ugly she felt. So, he conjectured in a moment of painful candor, it was possible that he had deluded himself into thinking he actually *was* giving her a birthday gift. At this point in the session Maureen and Jerry both broke down sobbing.

Since Maureen had gone through so much with me, I took the risk of conducting this session. But after that powerful session I referred her and Jerry to separate counselors. As a pastoral counselor, my interventions tend to be short term. This is a complementary role to that played by many other helping professionals. Thus, I depend on an extended network of professionals and laypeople to help me in my own work, both personal and professional. And so it goes. The circles of care—like the wheels of the bus in the well-known children's song—go 'round and 'round all over town.

Transform Anger into Loving Change

Our social nature requires that we reach beyond ourselves to decrease the suffering and increase creativity in the world.

—FROM *EIGHT COMMITMENTS OF ETHICAL CULTURE*

Healing begins at home. But, happily, it doesn't end there. The natural course of repairing takes itself out into the world. Couples begin to help with the healing of the world by binding up each other's wounds. The luckiest of us realize that one of the most effective ways to heal ourselves is to heal someone else, to widen the sphere of repair.

Medical research shows the healing powers of volunteerism, of "making a difference." It is a form of letting it out and letting go. Even if all else fails in your own predicament, helping to ameliorate or prevent similar problems for others can be immensely gratifying.

So rally, volunteer, help a child who is in similar straits to yours. Whenever possible, do these things *together*. Invite your partner to be a part of your healing process. Share with each other the satisfactions of making a difference.

One of the most tragic things that can happen to anyone is the loss of a child. We never fully recover from such devastation. But we can go on, offering up the wisdom born of suffering to the larger community. Bernard and Catherine Brown, for example, lost their twelve-year-old son, Linc, to a drunk driver. Four hundred people showed up at the funeral, including Linc's skating instructor. The huge photo of the champion ice-skater Scott Hamilton that had hung over Linc's bed was taped to the podium. As the aching months went by and people stopped calling so much, the Browns sought a more continuing form of solace. They found this in part by starting a scholarship fund for talented young skaters from families with modest means. Five years after Linc's death several of these skaters sponsored an event in his name to raise money for programs aimed at reducing drunk driving.

Leticia, a woman who was brutally beaten by her ex-husband, had to live with her son on the street for over a month. A few years later she helped to found a local women's shelter. We stood in a corner of the library during a fund-raiser being held in our beautiful Ethical Society in Brooklyn and talked. "Every time I see a frightened woman come through the door," she told me, "I see my old self. Being able to help those women is so fulfilling for me." She smiled. "It's indescribable."

The book of Job in the Bible addresses human suffering in a challenging and profound way, posing this question: Why do good people suffer? People have given a broad variety of explanations, including that Job's suffering is a test of loyalty. There is also the argument that God's favor—or, to put it in terms more comfortable to the secular mind, goodness—cannot be achieved unless we persevere through adversity. Others have emphasized that life is a learning journey and that we have to get over the stones in the road to reach the final reward.

At the conclusion of Job is a passage in which *no* explanation is given. Instead we are lifted up into the poetry of the cosmos, shown the big picture, and told that the incomprehensible beauty of it all makes the experience worthwhile:

Who watched over the birth of the sea,
When it burst in flood from the womb?—
When I wrapped it in a blanket of cloud
And cradled it in fog?

—JOB 38: 8,9, THE NEW ENGLISH BIBLE

In the end, pain and joy alike remain mysteries, and we must strive to forgive life for the inevitable hurt it brings in order to reap its abundance.

Relationship Repair

You should propagate yourself not only forward, but upward! May the garden of marriage help you to do it.

—FRIEDRICH NIETZSCHE, *THUS SPAKE ZARATHUSTRA*

In this chapter we've looked at different ways to effect healing change as an integral part of building a spiritually fulfilling marriage. In fact, enacting the Eight Commitments in your partnership is really a large-scale form of repairing. Through them you are restoring the trust, connection, meaning, and enjoyment that make a marriage shine.

A person with deep damage cannot ultimately make significant recovery without the love that a spiritual partnership provides. As we move in the direction of fulfillment in marriage, let us not forget the healing power of the spiritual life itself. However it is that we as individuals feel comfortable increasing the spiritual dimension of our lives, there is a demonstrable restorative force to meditation, prayer, wonder, and a community's devotion to high ideals. With a restored peace of mind, we can enrich our ways of being together. Whatever lifts up our spirits, raising us out of our troubles and into good health, is precious in our busy lives, for it gets us past the nicks and squabbles of the day, past the dark shadows of more lasting pain, and back into each other's loving embrace.

Any repair within our relationship strengthens the whole relationship and the whole family. Sometimes the nature of the repair work is so imperative that if we do not attend to it, the partnership itself is at risk. If this is the case, you may be shaking a little in your shoes. But be brave. Good things come of mighty wrestling. In fact, a marriage is made better out of such marathons. In the process of tough struggles, we, and our partnership, are transformed.

Keys to Lasting Repair

- Say you messed up when you did.
- Write a letter to someone who hurt you and ask your partner to read it.

- Tell your partner about the little things that hurt you within a week of their happening.
- Call upon mutual respect as an aid to forgiveness.
- Stop an old bad pattern in its tracks.
- Accept that not all wounds can be fully mended.
- Picture your nemesis in a new light.
- Find healing power in repetition and in rituals of your choosing.
- Help yourself by helping others.

Repairing Questions to Ask Yourself

1. Where can you go where you feel safe enough to admit failure and pain?
2. Can you acknowledge any poor choices that contributed to present problems?
3. Can you honor your partner in the midst of pain—even when your partner is the one who hurt you?
4. If something that really matters to you has been violated, what can you do to restore and nurture it?
5. Where do you find the hope and determination it takes to recover from grave disappointment?
6. What steps can you see yourself taking in order to mend what is broken in your life?
7. Have you reached out appropriately to others for support in repairing?
8. Do you acknowledge small triumphs with others or positively mark the end of a struggle?

Binding Up Each Other's Wounds: A Repairing Exercise

The following is designed not to help *you* heal, which is much of the focus of this chapter, but to help you help your partner. Before beginning, remember that supporting each other includes being aware and accepting of when your spouse is ready to heal—and when he or she is not. Also, be sensitive to your partner's capacity to "bear" pity. When pain is raw, a really warm hug can send some people into convulsive sobs. For others, pitying compassion can come across as patronizing rather than supportive.

The most important part of this exercise is to make sure you know your companion's preferred ways of being nurtured when he or she is in pain. Prearrange to discover his or her best forms of solace—if you don't already know—so you'll be prepared when trouble hits or wounds appear. This may involve a formal conversation, or you can just be observant and reflective about behaviors from difficult times in the past. Here's a sample list of the kinds of active support that can help us demonstrate care when our partner is in need of repair:

- Stock the house with soft tissues, and be sure to put them in the bathroom if your hurting loved one feels the need to cry in private.
- Bring her flowers on the anniversary of a traumatic event.
- If he's miserable at work, tell him you'll cook his favorite meal on Monday nights so he has *something* to look forward to when he gets out of bed.
- On a bad day bring your spouse her favorite comfort food, be it chocolate, chow mein, pizza, or Ben & Jerry's.

- If he's shown a willingness to seek help but a lack of motivation, do some legwork—getting numbers and making appointments. (Just be sure not to pass judgment if he still doesn't follow through. Sometimes a lack of motivation is really a lack of readiness.)
- If a wound is fresh, make sure to check in with her, asking her if she's doing okay.
- Leave little notes around the house, in private spots (like a wallet) where he will come upon them by surprise: "I'm here for you" or "Your body is beautiful to me in sickness and health" or "Don't forget to call me at work if you feel upset" or, simply, "I love you."
- If, due to pride, she doesn't like to be coddled when the chips are down, find ways to secretly support her—stroke her face while she's asleep, light a candle for her at the cathedral, be extra careful to pick up after yourself, put the toilet seat down, or pretend her favorite TV show is what you're in the mood to watch.
- Walk the dog, do the dishes, or take on the groceries even though it's not your turn.

In the end you will be doing your husband or wife a great service if you can find creative, concrete actions to perform to help him or her in trying to heal.

Listening

🐝

I will stay open to new insight,
however unlikely the source.

It was the night before the wedding, and Maureen was a nervous wreck. She called me three times in one hour to check on details of this and that. I knew that the real reason she was calling, though, was to hear a calming voice. "Why am I acting like this?" she complained good-naturedly. "I should know better."

"Why should you know better?" I countered. "You've never been married before."

In a bow to tradition, Josh was out with his college buddies. The clock struck two as Maureen turned the light out in her old attic bedroom. As she curled up under a thick quilt that her grandmother had made, she listened to the sounds of tapping rain on the roof. She closed her eyes and counted loved ones as some might count sheep—those who would be in the wedding garden tomorrow, those who would not. . . . Soon her breathing grew heavy, and she drifted off to sleep.

She awakened at the sound of a slamming noise. She heard nothing now but the patient rain, felt nothing but a light breeze. The curtain was billowing gently, like a wedding gown . . . or . . . more like Nanna's white hair. "Did I leave the window open?" she wondered. Too sleepy to go check, she was just slipping back to sleep when another bang sounded. Was it wind? Tap! it went now. Tap. Tap. What was making that noise?

The following day Maureen recounted her late-night experience to me while we conferred in a corner of the crowded dressing room. She wasn't sure whether she'd dreamed what happened next or if it had happened for real.

Once she was really awake, Maureen told me, the room fell totally silent. Fearful of the dark since childhood, she noticed that she was not at all afraid. Then she felt what she could only call a presence—like a feather or a gentle hand, first on her shoulder, then on her cheek. All at once an image of her grandmother came vividly to Maureen's mind.

"Nanna?" she whispered. "Are you there?"

At that, Maureen told me, this feeling of a presence seemed to withdraw, and as it did so, her attention was drawn toward the old pine bureau. When Maureen was little, she had kept a diary in its top drawer, and now she thought she heard again a soft, insistent tapping coming from the drawer pull. That was the last thing Maureen remembered before falling headlong into dreamless sleep.

The next morning she jumped up barefoot and ran immediately to the drawer. It was empty. With her ally the sunlight streaming through the window, she laughed.

"But, Lois," Maureen said, as I waited, sensing that the story was not quite finished, "when I arrived here just an hour ago, Josh's mother was waiting for me at the door. She said she'd felt a strange urge to go through Erik's dresser drawers this morning. And look what she found buried underneath the handkerchiefs."

I unfolded a piece of loose-leaf paper and read the scrawled words. Erik couldn't have written this very long before his heart attack, I mused, recognizing it as the first draft of a wedding toast. "Dearest Maureen," it began, "I can't imagine anyone other than you as Josh's wife."

Open Communication

Most people see what is and never see what can be. —ALBERT EINSTEIN

I was open to Maureen's experience of a "visitation," although we might have differed some in our theories of what really happened. No matter, as long as we both admitted we didn't know it all—and received it gratefully as the timely gift it was. Although Erik hadn't lived to see his son marry Maureen, somehow he still managed to have the last word. If Erik had been present to give his toast, the bride and groom would have expected something ambivalent, since he had once voiced his disapproval to Josh so clearly. Instead, Erik's last word on the matter was much more direct and supportive. His last word was something like "love."

If we commit to listening openly and intently, as Maureen did on the eve of her wedding day, we can dramatically increase our interconnection with each other and the world around us. It is impossible to be completely isolated in life—from life. Synapse to synapse, thought to thought, we are all of us caught up in the exquisite puzzle of the universe. At memorable moments we catch a glimpse of where we belong and get the messages that we most need to hear. At such moments we are often reminded how little we actually understand. And yet at heart these messages tell us simply this: We are not alone. We are loved. We are already connected in more ways than we can ever know.

Listening is not just about using our ears but about opening our mind and taking in wise insight from likely as well as unlikely sources. It is about making way for new experiences as we ask ourselves, Why not? A rich resource for handling problems, listening is marvelous for finding fulfillment and understanding in our marriage. It helps to enhance our intimacy with one another, with nature, and with all that transcends our full understanding. But most important, it is joyful and has the potential to be great fun.

Think for a moment about the openness of communication in your partnership—about how you share with and hear each other. As you read this chapter, I will encourage you to listen between the lines, uncovering hidden desires, fears, and expectations. You will also discover the undreamed-of communicative force of the smallest gestures and words. A kind touch, a word of appreciation, an honest assessment of the other's painting—all are enfolded in something much larger, including the long conversation that families carry on across the generations. Valuable insight is to be found inside ourselves (through intuition and dreams, for example), in our interactions with each other (through unconscious as well as conscious signals), through family traditions, and everywhere within the universe spread out around us. In each of these areas of life, listening can be enjoyed and used effectively to improve your partnership and you in it.

Body Language

There's language in her eye, her cheek, her lip,
Nay, her foot speaks; her wanton spirits look out
At every joint and motive of her body.

—WILLIAM SHAKESPEARE, *TROILUS AND CRESSIDA*

In a way the first ethical act we can accomplish is listening. Being a listener is in fact a powerful and necessary role wherever communication is happening. Every artist needs an audience, every speaker someone to say, "I hear you." A classic Chinese folk tale tells of a lute player who, upon losing a friend who had listened to his playing for many years, broke his instrument in half and cast it into the river Po. He did this because he knew that it would be a meaningless pastime to play his lute without his friend there to listen. Musicians, artists, and speakers need listeners to bring their messages to life, to hear them—really hear them. With this simple connection community itself becomes possible.

Our engagement with the outside world necessarily involves the senses: touch, taste, smell, sound, sight. In communicating with each other, much more than words are involved—your mouth smiles or frowns; your hands gesture; your feet tap; your eyes water; your lungs sigh with exasperation. The human body and its many sensations are powerful tools for developing loving exchanges with your partner.

Whatever the form of our communication with each other, the language of love always takes the whole person, body and all, into consideration. As Nelly and Mike discovered, it's a full-body language: She knows that when his legs twitch, he's just slipped off into sleep. He can tell when she looks down at her lap in a certain way, that she's trying not to cry. When Nelly falls silent, Mike told me, he knows something's really wrong—whereas those same emotions will make him a chatterbox. Either way, they both know their cue to be concerned and extra nurturing if necessary. All marriages have this special kind of body language—a patient, observant, and, above all, loving form of communication.

Not surprisingly, there are countless creative approaches that utilize the body for enhancing relationships. Much body language is direct and pretty simple to understand. But learning how to use it as a vehicle for deeper communication with your partner takes just a little attention and practice.

One body-focused relationship exercise I enjoy teaching couples is called the "Anatomy of an Interaction." To begin, think of a small incident, either good or bad, that has happened recently. For example, perhaps your spouse missed or ignored something you said, as was the case with Crystal and Dan. To help them work on having more constructive conversations, I encouraged Crystal and Dan each to imagine that their whole body was communicating about what had happened. These are the steps I outlined, which you can use to process your own situation:

Start with your hands and body, and "mime" the incident, step by step scripting it out. Make sure every detail is in place, almost as though you were playing charades. For example, Dan entered the living room brushing his hair out of his face with frustration; he threw his jacket on the big chair and sat down to sort the mail that he'd picked up on his way in. Crystal's miming included opening the door to the bedroom, calling out with hands outstretched, "Boy do I need you right now!" and letting her arms fall limp at her sides when she received no response.

Next, feel how your body reacts. Call on the stomach, or whatever other part of your body—your clenched-up shoulders, your aching head, your stiff neck or pulsing jaw muscles—acts as an early-warning signal that something troubling is going on. A nervous tic may kick in—nail biting, knuckle cracking, head scratching. Or it may be a more general physical sensation, such as a wave of fatigue or nausea. In this case Crystal felt short of breath, and Dan felt slightly dizzy.

Now look to your heart to see what it was you were feeling. The stomach reacts. But the heart responds. Sometimes we confuse these two ways of processing experience and mistakenly put down our feelings as something primitive. But feelings are actually a sophisticated part of us and provide us with rich understanding of both ourselves and our partnership. In the current situation Crystal felt hurt and ignored, while Dan felt trapped and anxious. Their physical reactions were simply clues. Another time goose bumps may hint at fear, a hot blush may indicate shame, or pallor may signal rage.

Now use the head to obtain some distance from the heavy feelings (without discarding them) to give you room to explore many possible meanings. Discuss why you think this incident happened, from the mundane or immediate to the more intense and deep-rooted triggers. Try not to judge each other's contributions at this point. Just openly receive them, assuming that they come out of a desire for more closeness. Crystal remembered that she'd really been missing Dan and looked forward to an intimate evening after her tense working day. Dan remembered being distracted by an envelope marked "urgent" that turned out, when he opened it, to contain a collection notice. Digging deeper, Crystal remembered her father coming home from the city each night and disappearing into the silence of his (off-limits) den. Dan recalled his mother, often weepy and complaining, demanding he kiss and make a big fuss over her whenever he came home from school. He also remembered his family's being evicted after his father lost his job.

I suggested that Dan and Crystal use their physical reactions and emotional responses to this encounter to communicate to each other when other, similar scenes seemed to be happening between them. "There it is again!" Crystal or Dan would think when breath came short or dizziness set in. To help them disentangle themselves from the pain of loaded, symbolic situations, and to deal only with their present circumstances, I encouraged each of them to draw up personal "marching orders" and make commitments to one another based on them.

This speaking with your feet is a powerful form of communication. It conveys that you have firm intentions of moving beyond the barriers that separate you. For example, in response to this incident Crystal promised to give Dan a little space when he first came in and to read his body language to see if he needed extra support of a nonintrusive kind. Dan promised not to go to the mailbox until after dinner so that he wouldn't be tempted to bury himself in any hassling notices that came in the mail.

Important conversations need to end up with your asserting your commitment to one another. Below every exchange in marriage a critical question lingers: Am I, by my actions and attitudes, saying yes or no to our marriage? Answering this soundless question may be the most important statement you make each day.

If your marriage is under great strain, or if a scenario involves a particularly sensitive topic—sexual dysfunction or weight issues maybe—then the preceding exercise should be undertaken with great care. It can be tough to get through discussing your emotional reactions in the scene without reverting to defensiveness and hurt feelings. You might want to consider doing the exercise with a professional present. Alternatively, practice first with a positive memory: How did it feel in your body the last time you had a really great time together? In addition to increasing your understanding of how this exercise works, a positive first round also builds a foundation of appreciation and goodwill.

As soon as you begin to attend consciously to your communication signals, you become more connected to your spouse. Notice how your partner physically expresses it when behavioral patterns or past issues are triggered—she's bingeing on chocolate and sleeping in, he's cracking his knuckles and drinking a lot. In the end these observations will help you to be less hurt by, and more understanding about, emotional outbursts if they're disproportionate to the situation. This in turn will keep you from developing resentments and help you to be more supportive overall. Intentional discussions about these body signals will assist in strengthening the flow of care in a marriage. But simply paying attention to the signals is an excellent start.

Decoding and Translating

The essence of being a genius is to be able to talk and listen to listen while talking and talk while listening

—GERTRUDE STEIN, "WHAT ARE MASTERPIECES AND WHY ARE THERE SO FEW OF THEM"

There are many elements to the language of love, and to truly connect we need to attend to all of them. To really amplify our listening skills, we need to decode all the bits—the facial expressions, the physical tics, the tone of voice, the emphases and omissions, the pace and flow, not to mention the words themselves. If we can put it all together, we will become stronger (more understanding, more cooperative, and more connected) as a couple and more capable of bringing out the best in ourselves and each other.

A woman named Nadia, in response to an item in a workshop questionnaire, wrote, "I love to listen to people speaking languages

I don't understand. It's easier that way to hear the tunes." To enhance communication with your partner, attend specifically to each other's style or tone of voice—the "tunes" that you're "singing" beneath your words. If you sarcastically say, "I love it when you stick out your tongue," it will be interpreted one way, but in another way entirely if you say the same thing offhandedly, in a baby voice, or like a sultry sex kitten. In any given situation the style you use to communicate to your partner is as important as the content.

Paying attention to our tone of voice is important for many reasons, especially when we're trying to help. For one thing, we can become more aware of how confusing it is when we're speaking one thing and "singing" another. "I can't hear your good advice," my husband has said to me more than once. "Your words are meant to be soothing, but your tone of voice is attacking me."

As we communicate with one another, we slowly begin to listen beneath what our partner is saying, both verbally and nonverbally. Is she consciously saying what she means, or is she broadcasting an unconscious message as well? When he says, "My back is aching," is it just his back, or does it always ache when the closets need to be cleaned out? Often we'll hear what our partner cannot—motivations, perhaps, or hidden longings. Active listening entails a deeply respectful appreciation of messages that our partner may be incapable of uttering expressly.

We must help our partner, gently, to recognize hidden minefields in our relationship. When using our new skills in deciphering our partner's silent messages, it's not fair to do so antagonistically, saying, for example, "There you go again with that passive-aggressive junk!" Sometimes having a wise third person present for your discussions helps facilitate open listening. At other times just speaking directly from the heart and eliciting honesty in return is enough.

We might perhaps ask instead, "Why not just tell me you can't bear the thought of chores right now? I do need your help, but I'm here to help you, too."

Charlie, whom I had encouraged to attend a workshop with his partner, Kevin, in order to practice such active listening skills, learned to hear Kevin at this subterranean level after many mess-ups in which listening to Kevin's literal words backfired. Charlie began to understand that when Kevin said, "Go away," he actually meant, "I'm scared and angry. I want you to care about me, but that's impossible, because I'm an awful person." At first Charlie would respond simply by saying, "Okay. I'll go into the next room and give you some time. I'll be there when you need me, because I love you." Little by little, Kevin began to be able to speak truthfully to Charlie, saying, "I'm feeling down on myself and need to be alone."

Without knowing each other's language, it is impossible to work together. Consider the popular accounting from Islamic scripture, which tells the story of four men, each with a bit of money (a *diram*). They had to pool their resources in order to have enough to purchase something to eat. A fight broke out among them as to what to buy. The Persian said he wanted *angur*. The Arab disagreed, insisting they buy *inab*. The Turk clamored for *üzüm*. And the Greek would settle for nothing except *istafil*. They got into a bloody brawl, and all went hungry that night. The sad thing was, all four words meant "grapes."

Here's some good news: Decoding and translating signals are subtle arts that we already know how to do. Moreover, we do them all the time without even realizing it—and we do them more and more the better we come to know each other. Maureen knows the Larsens' family values and Josh's stance with regard to them—for example, his almost genetically progressive political views. She gets cued in by a certain blush that comes over Josh when his "politically correct" buttons are pushed, as they were the year before at a school reunion dinner. When someone made a derisive comment about "knee-jerk liberals," Maureen knew to tactfully steer the conversation in another direction. For his part, Josh knows to steer clear of Maureen immediately preceding gatherings with her family. He knows that her distrust of others in her family makes her irritable and defensive. Temporarily retreating into her shell makes her feel safest—so Josh gives her a kiss on the forehead and lets her go there for a while.

Josh and Maureen's understanding of one another came from a mutual sensitivity to the other's personality, past experience, and family backgrounds. The cultures of our ancestors, our nation, our social group, and so on invisibly but dramatically influence our communication styles. Assumptions about gender roles and ideas about the appropriateness of emotional expression are just two examples of issues that affect how we communicate with our spouse.

When Trevor, a man from Missouri, went with his new wife to visit her family in the Bronx, he was so amazed by the style of conversation around the dinner table that he sat in silence for almost an hour. Finally the family patriarch gave Trevor a nudge. "Cat got your tongue, kid?"

Trevor blushed and responded, "I guess I was waiting for someone to finish a sentence."

His father-in-law laughed loudly. "Well, jump right in, 'cause that don't happen around here," he said.

Over the years Trevor came to enjoy the stimulation of his New Yorker relatives' fastball conversations. In time he came to understand that the New Yorkers' style of communication, which some people from other regions considered rude, was simply their way of exchanging ideas with warmth and enthusiasm. His own family took care of themselves with equally as much love, just at a different tempo.

Because our respective backgrounds create a language or "dialect" that couples must translate, every marriage is on some level a mixed marriage. In order to better understand each other, many couples have found it useful to explore this area together intentionally. So, as you continue to improve your communication skills, go ahead and acknowledge such things as inherited religious or philosophical beliefs, family patterns and values. What different words do you and your partner use to mean the same thing? Make sure you know where important concepts are "translated" differently for the two of you—the golf course is his sanctuary (*not* a frivolous way to use up the whole day); her knitting is a deeply calming practice (*not* a symbol of docile domesticity).

I remember a wedding in which I could tell who was from which side of the family by the question they asked me at the door. "Is this the church?" the bride's side asked. "Is this the temple?" the groom's side inquired. Instead of getting into esoteric discussions about word usage, I simply nodded yes each time and shook their hands in welcome.

The Sacred Conversation

The generations of living things pass in a short time, and like runners hand on the torch of life. —LUCRETIUS, *DE RERUM NATURAE*

Without benefit of sight or hearing, Helen Keller discovered language while her teacher, Anne Sullivan, placed her hand under an open tap and signed the letters for "water." Suddenly a connection was made, and Helen was instantly propelled into the sacredness of the human conversation. When Helen grew up, she declared, "Imagination is the greatest nation."

Civilization is composed of a people who share a common memory. To *not* remember, to be disconnected, is perhaps more profound than any other loss. Memory is a weapon against the ruptures of death—the death of stages of our lives and the settings in which they transpired, the death of those we love, even our own anticipated death.

Each of us has something to add to the human conversation. I once asked a man who was dying what he wanted me to convey to his wife and son. Removing his oxygen mask to form one painful word at a time, he passed on a message which haunts me to this day: "Draw two points in your mind, one for the present, and one where you want to go. Make your life a straight line to it, and don't let anything stop you from going there." This was, in fact, an astounding, brief summary of what he had learned from his very interesting life. The time to exchange such messages with your partner is now, now, and now again—moment by moment—not just in the hour of death.

There is undreamed-of communicative power in even our smallest gestures and words. Be a witness to what you are expressing to your spouse, your children, and the people around you. If you've discovered areas of meaning that you don't tend to "broadcast," consider finding new ways to do so. This includes not just lessons you've learned during your own lifetime but also any lessons that you've received from previous generations. Share these by writing them down, telling them verbally, showing photographs, or in other, more creative ways.

Take one last look now at the stories in your family that get told again and again. All these jokes, parables, and ancestors' adventures carry a hidden message or two. Josh, for example, recalled how Great-grandpa Klaus escaped from a prisoner-of-war camp and walked hundreds of miles to get home. Klaus's message to his family was that survival was possible despite the direst of odds. Maureen told me she feels a burst of pride and longing whenever her mother talks about growing up pioneering a ranch in desolate country. They had all slept in a loft in winter, on the floor in summer, and they worked sixteen hours a day. Maureen's grandfather used to say that a family working together was the epitome of life at its fullest.

Do you take notice of vocal or physical hints of inherited expression? A grandfather's brogue, a niece's singsong, the Yiddish jokes, the Italian hand gestures? While considering all the wisdom that's been handed down, be open to other gifts that may come along: Write down what you recall of your father's best maxims and find solid advice there, relevant to a current problem. Take inspiration from a family story of triumph over adversity. Use family recipes to nourish your life in the present. And don't forget to collect great questions to really make you think ("Why is this night different from all other nights?" or "Whence cometh my help?").

Contemplate this treasure trove of inherited material. What amid all this collected data has been toxic, and what works for you? What do you want to pass on to future generations? Both sides of Josh Larsen's family were passionate about social justice, displaying a kind of integrity that Josh and Maureen told me they were eager to instill in their own children. In contrast, the Larsen family tradition of (in Josh's words) "moving around the country like vagabonds" in search of their ideals was something the young couple planned to avoid. "We'll sow the seeds of justice closer to home," Josh told me.

Those who came before us have passed on not only their splendid twists of DNA but also the spun wisdom of community recollection. In time we, too, will have something to contribute to the sacred conversation. What stories do you hope get told about you long after you're gone? Our endeavors as listeners and speakers last as long as we have thought and breath. But our impact lasts much longer.

Playing in the Fields of Our Lives

I seem to have been only like a boy playing on the seashore, and diverting myself in now and then finding a smoother pebble or a prettier shell than ordinary, whilst the great ocean of truth lay all undiscovered before me.
—ISAAC NEWTON, *MEMOIRS*

It's not only the elders who came before us who can teach us how to live well together. Children also can show us a thing or two. This is because they naturally have the playful style that listening requires. One day I was exiting my office at the Brooklyn Society for Ethical Culture along with a couple that had come to me for help in dealing with a dreaded move. At once we were struck by the sight of their precocious three-year-old, playing on the floor of the library amid a pile of toys. "And now," Juliet announced to the teddy bear, "we will help Mommy and Daddy pack for the move. They are very scared, and it makes them fight, but we will make it a game so they can have fun." Tears filled both parents' eyes as they realized that their youngest child had shown them the way. Why is it that play is thought of as frivolous, when it is one of the most helpful forms of human activity? Without playfulness—a spontaneous and original response to our circumstances—we can easily miss out on essential information.

Jesus of Nazareth put it powerfully: "You must be as a little child to enter the kingdom of heaven." As we saw in the chapter on abiding, being playfully childlike is wonderful for making us resilient. It can also open us up to new ways of dealing with problems and remove the walls of defensiveness that we tend to put up when we're distracted, stressed, or frustrated. A child learns constantly, but she's not trying new things for the sake of "growth"—she's doing it for joy, because she wants to play. In her world she is always listening without even realizing it. We, too, need to play—in order to be open and to *enjoy* communicating with each other more.

Maureen told me that her grandmother had taught her many lessons as a little girl, not by preaching rules but by joyful participation. The best mentors, like Nanna, don't assault their charges but instead create room for them to listen and absorb. Maureen and Nanna used to finger-paint on the floor of the old attic bedroom. They'd glob paint around, making rainbows and butterflies on long pieces of butcher paper. "With just these few colors all the possibilities of the world are in our hands," Nanna would tell her, as she taught Maureen to mix yellow and blue to make mottled green leaves.

The "business" of marriage can easily take over, as every married couple knows. When problems and responsibilities abound, it gets harder to hear each other out, to listen for subtle calls for support, or to connect. Still, I've seen partners recover freshness in their relationship in many ways. I've seen parents put love notes in their kids' lunch boxes or cartoon clippings into their partners' overfilled calendar. I've seen half-birthday parties and favorite holidays celebrated early because someone just couldn't wait. I've seen chores turned into silly contests (complete with prizes) and onerous duties made into memorable, laughter-filled afternoons.

Some people are tempted to suppress their sense of humor because they think they'll be more appreciated if they act more "grown-up." Murphy, for example, was afraid to act too silly around Vasili when she first met him. She thought he might think she was stupid or crazy or discover some other turn-off. Finally her best friend pointed out that if Vasili were truly turned off by Murphy's vivacity, then their breakup would be for the best anyway. "You can't keep yourself in a straitjacket with the guy you're going to spend your life with," her friend wisely advised. We need to display our full selves to our partner, both the responsible grown-up and the fun-loving child in us.

It's important not just to be playful ourselves but also to recognize the need or the call for play in our spouse. Burt was working so hard he couldn't remember the last time he'd really enjoyed himself. "When do I get my turn?" he complained when Ashley bought yet another doll for their four-year-old. Quick on her feet, Ashley read Burt's pout as a warning signal and replied, "This weekend. We're all going on a safari." Burt and his daughter both loved animals, and just two hours away was a wildlife preserve. Ashley packed safari hats for everyone. She also packed animal crackers, which were passed out liberally during the drive to whoever correctly made the sounds of the animal shapes Ashley took out of the box.

Burt and Ashley couldn't afford the time or the money for a real trip, but thanks to their very young daughter they felt freer to plan a safari anyhow. When looking for ways to lighten your lives with loving play, don't forget the great advantage of having kids. It gives you an excuse to make believe. Parents can surf the net with their kids, researching the history or attractions of faraway and exotic places. Then they can plan a meal at home or find a local restaurant. French cuisine? Brazilian? Or they can choose an imaginary destination—a planet, Hogwarts school, or a bygone era like the Renaissance or imperial China. They can go around town to museums and shows on a theme, make hands-on projects or video-taped sketches, and just have fun together.

Not only does the experience of play let us enjoy the world and people around us, it also helps us to hear them in new ways. Mel and Zoe had a blast when they reversed roles with their teens. While they were "Teen for a Day," they were allowed to behave in stereotypical ways—gossiping, chewing gum, being flirtatious, grooming themselves just so. And, of course, their teens could respond in stereotypical ways, too—making their parents eat their lima beans and grounding them for talking back. The family saw quite a few important messages exchanged, with laughter, in that one day of make-believe.

It should go without saying that all these activities can easily be adapted, with minimal embarrassment, for childless adults. Doesn't a day or a week of creative adventure sound like fun? Plus, privately, this same attitude of experimentation and playfulness can really help to make a married couple's sex life thrive.

As we pause to catch raindrops on our tongue and name the shapes in the clouds overhead, we can begin to understand why playfulness is considered by many traditions a sign of holiness. It is a joyful state of mind that opens up our eyes to new solutions and to each other. Too often we wait to have fun, and the moment never arrives. It's actually to our benefit to do it today.

Listening to the Still Voice

[Siddhartha] learned more from the river than Vasudeva could teach him. He learned from it continually. Above all, he learned from it how to listen, to listen with a still heart, with a waiting, open soul, without passion, without desire, without judgement, without opinions.

—HERMAN HESSE, *SIDDHARTHA*

The most creative levels of communication are achieved by drawing an ever-widening circle of receptivity to new ideas and new sources of insight. Listening involves not just hearing the telephone ring or even just having a good conversation. It's also using our mind and senses to attend to messages from deep within. Unexpected sources of understanding can take many forms: intuition, unorthodox solutions, visions, melodies, wishes, or epigrams—anything that feels truly significant to us or to our spouse. The still voice is that wise listener in us that knows which of these innumerable sources of insight carry a message of special importance.

Maureen and I could have had a long discussion about strange coincidences or about her grandmother's ghost versus her own unconscious. We put that aside, though, and looked instead to the underlying significance of her encounter with "Nanna." In so doing we got to something much more essential—the enduring power of love. The still voice told us both, *I don't know what happened, only that it was moving and meaningful.*

As you turn to inner sources of help with an open heart, pay heed to the hunches, the voices of rest, the rhythms of your body. A number of years ago I became painfully stiff and extremely exhausted. I was eventually diagnosed as having a weakened immune system. My exhaustion became so constant that I took a day off to go to a spa. There I swam in a saltwater pool, took a needle shower, and indulged in a seaweed wrap and a massage. Noting how listless I was even after deep tissue work, the massage therapist suggested I rest as long as I wished in a darkened adjoining room. After a while as I lay there, I felt myself crying out inside, "Why do I hurt so much?" To my surprise, after a time I felt a soft, motherly voice washing over my body, saying, "See how tired you are. Every cell in you aches. Can you feel it? You need to rest, my dear, really rest." When I got home, I planned a long stay at a campsite for the upcoming summer. That extended rest, not easy to procure in my overbusy life, may very well have saved me from becoming a chronic invalid at the time.

An openness to the still voice offers solutions to sticky problems that can't be fixed conventionally. How many writers have solved plot problems in their dreams? Though rules and guidelines are dependable, they're not effective every time. At tricky moments we need to look beyond (or beneath) the standard procedure and engage our creative minds, whose mouthpiece is the still voice.

Listening to the still voice can be an uplifting, lighthearted enterprise, but it is always more responsible than fuzzy, magical thinking. Any mother who has accurately "sensed" that her child was in danger will tell you that the still voice's messages have the potential to be disturbing. Perhaps because the still voice within doesn't always tell us what we want to hear, we sometimes resist the wisdom of our inner guide.

Dreams are nightly still-voice messengers for many of us, bringing messages both enlightening and uncomfortable if we care to listen for them. Many problems that plague us during the day can be delegated to the world of dreams. In this safe otherworld we can deeply respond to our problems in a restorative manner.

Once I went out to make copies of several drawings that I was particularly proud of. On returning home I realized that I had lost those cherished drawings (and the copies) somewhere along the road. I searched long and hard for my little portfolio throughout the neighborhood. Then one night I found my dream-self at a cemetery mourning their loss with a flood of tears. When I awoke, I resisted what predawn's discerning shadow had clearly told me. It wasn't until I told my husband my dream that he helped me to accept its message: Those drawings weren't coming back. Here, then, is another benefit of communicating openly with your spouse— sometimes it takes the two of us for listening's wisdom to sink in.

We catch glimpses of the still voice in each other when we ask, What did you dream about last night? What is your fantasy for life ten years from now? What songs, pictures, and memories speak most deeply to you, and why? In the first flush of love, couples have these conversations all the time. It is a way of asking, Who are you really? What's inside? Such discussions (or even the answering of a single question along such lines) help us to reconnect with the hidden parts of our partner—and of ourselves.

The still voice can pick up wisdom from *without* as well as within. World events, fearsome weather, and the kindly acts of strangers can all speak to us in a special way, giving us important messages of purpose, love, or encouragement. Once a woman came to me for help in dealing with her fear of public places. I referred her to a specialist, and a while later she called to tell me an inspiring story. That week she'd been standing by a crowded shopping mall escalator. She had worked for months to get that far. But she couldn't seem to muster up the courage to step onto the moving stairs. A diminutive elderly woman who must have noticed her apprehension came up, took this woman's hand in hers, and patted it without saying a thing. Matter-of-factly, she led the younger woman to the first step. Then, together, they made it up to the top. Not a word was spoken—they hardly even made eye contact—but the communication between them was both memorable and important.

The Open Zero

I used to believe that anything was better than nothing. Now I know that sometimes nothing is better. —GLENDA JACKSON

Mrs. Violet, my beloved sixth-grade teacher, understood well the value of "nothing." She used to tell our class that there were two kinds of spaces—full spaces and empty ones. But people, she'd explain, were always trying to fill up empty spaces. To help redress this cosmic imbalance—this too-human tendency not to leave room for new things and new ideas—Mrs. Violet announced that she was elevating the role of blackboard monitor to the highest position in class. For, as she proclaimed, there was nothing finer than a freshly cleaned slate board. Not to mention, the blackboard monitor got the coveted prize of her famous fresh-baked butter cookies.

As the proud student of the week made large sweeping motions with the thick felt eraser, Mrs. Violet would ask us all to close our eyes and imagine that our mind was a chalkboard. "Now erase all the marks until it's clear," she would guide us. She firmly believed in the power of open spaces to coax out new solutions to daily problems—from schoolyard scuffles to homework assignments.

It was during this same year that I had my breakthrough into higher mathematics. While Mrs. Violet drew a large zero at the center of the clean chalkboard, she told us that the space inside the zero was the most important part, a *portal* of entry ("spelling word for the day"), a gate to a brave new world. Negative numbers come from the other side of the zero, Mrs. Violet said. She encouraged us to think of them not as scary or hard but instead (since they'd been hiding right there this whole time) as maybe a little bit more special than the regular numbers, maybe a little bit more fun.

By clearing our mental and physical space, by making our own "open zero," we create a portal for new experience. If we peer beyond this new empty space, we can glimpse what's missing that could make the situation more fulfilling for us or for our partnership. So, take a good look at the empty spaces around you. There's that bare wall that could use a piece of artwork. There's also the empty rocking chair where Aunt June used to sit or the vase that calls you to remember the flowers that came with it—a gift of love from your wonderful spouse. What about the blank parts of your career? Where is the creative aspect? Or your marriage? Where is the relaxed enjoyment of each other's company? Each time you notice what's missing, a new avenue for enrichment opens up for you—appreciation, fond remembrance, room for growth, reminders to have fun. . . .

You can also review memories to retrieve lessons of the heart you may have lost along the way, or to see old scenes from a new perspective. Think about spiritual teachers in your early life. How did they help you to see the promise of sacred nothingness? Did a counselor at camp help you crouch so still and low that the little deer didn't even know you were there? Perhaps by putting out a few extra folding chairs for newcomers, a workshop leader signified that your learning circle was always incomplete. Or did an uncle sit you down on a park bench and encourage you to look at each person passing by, realizing that each one had strong feelings and a whole lifetime of experience you'll never know?

The open space, the zero of expectation that we draw on the chalkboard of our mind, is clear of old habits, set rules, preconceptions, and fears. Once this opening up has been achieved, we're ready to communicate and to let our loved ones in.

The Necessary Unknown

Who can tell us whence and how arose this universe? The gods are later than its beginning. . . . Only that god who sees in highest heaven: he only knows whence comes this universe, and whether it was made or uncreated. He only knows, or perhaps he knows not. —RIG VEDA X.129

There is something to be said for confidences and mysteries. Getting to feel okay about *not* knowing it all is a hallmark of growing up. Only seventeen-year-olds and tyrants are convinced they've got everything figured out. At heart, the lessons of listening show that the unexplainable aspects of life—dreams, coincidences, intuition, the unconscious—are not only useful tools but also gifts to be cherished, cherished precisely because we can never understand exactly how or why they work.

When I was younger, I strove passionately to discover the workings of the cosmos. I wanted to find out how and why things were the way they were. I quested for an explanation to the mystery of what my family called God. In time, finally, it dawned on me: If that mystery were no longer unknown to me, then it wouldn't quite be a mystery anymore, would it? Was it maybe better after all to have the mystery than to lose it?

We need the unknown. It is the seeding place of awe and wonder. It is the reason to stop and think, an enticement that keeps us guessing. At times I think that "mystery" is the best single word to describe the divine. Human beings were born to question. What would become of us if all the questions were answered?

Nature, of course, is the great womb of the unknown. As John Muir once said, "None of nature's landscapes is ugly, as long as it is wild." Whether it is the vista from a mountaintop or the sweep of oceanfront on a clear day, there is ample grace in nature. It is a splendid reminder that our lives are dependent on powers greater than ourselves and, also, that it doesn't all depend on us.

The natural world provides us with not just physical sustenance but beauty, inspiration, and endless possibilities for seeing our world with a fresh perspective. It is the metaphor of metaphors, because its meaning can never be fully captured or defined. It is a model of partnership, for we also go two by two into the ark of time, bound together by our covenant and yet also always unique and separate beings, mysteries even to each other.

Early on in their relationship Hans and Georgia took a vacation in Big Basin. The redwoods towered over their tent, and the pungent smell of eucalyptus was everywhere. On the first day, setting out with cheese sandwiches and bottled water, they wandered at will down this path and that. As shadows lengthened, they found themselves lost. Georgia, who had never gone camping before, clung to Hans's arm, making it difficult to navigate the uneven terrain. She couldn't take it and began to cry. Just at that moment they came upon a clearing with megalithic redwoods circling round, almost like Druidic stone sentries transported from another time. Instinctively they knelt down, listened to the wind in the branches far above, and allowed the powerful scene to hush their fears. "If we had died that day," Georgia related to me two years later, "it would have been okay. We didn't know where we were. But we felt the beauty of the place and knew that we belonged."

Listening takes us out of isolation. We are never really alone. Life speaks to us all the time, and we speak back. In the calm silences in between, we open to new possibilities, new ways of understanding ourselves, the world, and each other. It is not necessary to make perfect sense of what we hear, only to receive it with an open heart.

We may forget the names of the speakers and the intonations of their words. We may forget the words themselves and the patterns they form called a language. But as long as there are people, deep listening will continue. This wind of memory brushes us even as we sleep. It drifts in beneath our doorways and settles over the dinner table. Everyone yearns to be invited to the table. Everyone wants to share in the feast of silence and hope. And every new voice brings a universe of knowing.

Keys to Openly Communicating

- Ask not just "why?" but "why not?"
- Pay attention to body language.
- Tune in to your partner's unconscious motivations.
- Read between the lines.
- Translate family dialects into the common language of love.

- Allow yourself to be as playful and open as a little child.
- Receive the messages of the still voice—write down your dreams, listen to your intuition.
- Receive enlightenment from unlikely places.
- Don't try to conquer the unknown. Befriend it.

Listening Questions to Ask Yourself

1. What places can you go where your mind feels free to open up?
2. Have you and your partner committed to staying open to each other's input, respecting the differences in each other's perspectives?
3. When you feel reverence for your partner, do you keep it in or let him or her know?
4. Are you able to recognize and appreciate gifts of care and concern from your partner?
5. What untapped resources can you think of now that would make you stronger in future times of trouble?
6. What sorts of healing or repair would allow you as a couple to experience greater openness?
7. How has open communication brought you the joy of connection with your inner self and with your spouse?
8. Are you able to find new and unique ways to enjoy each other and your other loved ones?

Sound and Silences Walk: A Listening Exercise

Go on a walk and sit together in several different spaces of your choosing—a library, a mall, a cornfield, a railroad station, an ocean beach. Sit without speaking for at least ten minutes. Listen together closely to the noises all around. How many different melodies of the day can you hear? Listen to the rhythms of the rush of traffic, the birdsong, a businessman's cell phone patter, the crash of waves, tree leaves rustling like taffeta in the breeze. Listen to the silences, too: when the lights turn red or the waves draw back again.

Take several deep breaths once you've settled in, and slowly attune your breathing to the rhythms of the space you're in. Can you hear your breathing or the beating of your pulse? Concentrate by turns on simply breathing, opening up your awareness of the sounds around you, and relaxing.

Listen to whatever calls your attention. You may even hear or feel messages from inside your awareness. Some of this may be chatter, the useless "did I leave the back door unlocked?" kind of distractions. Don't fight these thoughts; just let them go by not concentrating on them. Other thoughts—and you'll know intuitively which ones—will have more meaning. This may be a word repeating, the image of a loved one's face, a bit of a melody, or a gently surging emotion. Notice these as well as the "real" sounds you hear around you.

Finally, think of your grandparents. What was happening in these spaces when they were your age? When your great-grandchildren take this walk, what sounds might they hear?

After at least ten minutes check in with each other about your experience. Ask yourselves what, among these sounds, do you hear all day but seldom notice? What sounds are special to this day or this place? Share with each other the particular sounds you noticed and see if they're the same as your partner's. You may not have noticed how the librarian's typing sounded like knitting needles, or you may find that you missed another sound entirely. Listen again now for a minute or two before going, enjoying the sounds from your new, enriched perspective.

Celebrating

🍒

I will celebrate spiritual values
with my partner and others.

Just after a bride and groom have publicly declared their abiding love, when they turn before me and embrace, I feel a rush of joy that has never faded over the years. I felt a special thrill on Josh and Maureen's warm spring wedding day. As they joined their lives together and the crowd rose clapping, nothing seemed impossible.

Fifteen minutes before the evening ceremony, during our final check-in, Josh had been struck with worry. "Who will Mom dance with at the end of the ceremony?" he wanted to know. They had decided to have the first dance, including the folding in of family, as the concluding part of the formal ritual.

"Your mother will dance with you, Josh," Maureen murmured with a smile. Then, after a moment, she knowingly added, "She will dance with the Erik in you."

Pondering this profound thought with a little smile, I left to put the final details in order in the rose-lined meadow where the ceremony was to take place. As I carried Erik's flute to the first row and placed it on an empty chair, I suddenly knew that Erik was right there. His presence was going to be palpable, if only because he would be on everyone's minds. But I suspected there was a lot more to it than that.

Toward sunset the ceremony began at last. The flower girl, in pink silk shoes and a matching dress, was first to steal the show. The night before she had practiced carefully dropping rose petals in the grass to the right and left as she waltzed down the improvised aisle. But no one had told Cindy that there would be a hundred people watching. As soon as she saw the sizable clan, she blushed crimson, dumped the basket upside down, and ran straight into her mother's arms.

Josh and his best man stood up front with me under an arbor, seeming in their formal garb much older than their years.

When Maureen made her appearance at the far side of the meadow, I could almost have mistaken her for the girl in the yellowed photo I'd seen, of her grandmother in a rented wedding gown. Maureen had worked with her great-aunts to create a fluted satin train just like Nanna's . . . and it was a knockout. Even without that dress she would have looked stunning. There's a glow in every bride, Maureen included, that transcends all makeup, hair spray, and trim. Gazing at her, Josh looked as if he could faint with pride.

Toward the middle of the ceremony the parents were happily surprised to receive flowers as a sign of gratitude. The ring exchange, brief and solemn, came next. The vows were stirring, a mix of carefully chosen personal touches and phrases from different traditions.

Why do we need these moments? I do know happily married couples who eloped. But the truth is, done right, a spiritually meaningful wedding ceremony, like a spiritually meaningful marriage, offers grounding. It is a chance to broadcast the core commitments that will get us all through good times and bad. It is a time for soliciting a circle of support and for celebrating important life passages together.

As friends and family danced their way back up the grassy aisle toward the indoor reception, I looked over and saw Josh and Maureen, wrists crossed, hands clasped, their arms extended as they twirled around beneath an aged maple. I noticed the loose ribbons around

Maureen's bouquet lacing around the couple's intertwined hands, and I was reminded of an old Celtic custom in which young lovers were married by handfasting—their hands lightly bound together as they stood beneath the trees. Did Josh and Maureen know the history of their motions? Did the history know them? No matter. It was the finale to a ceremony that, though brushed with late-day shadows, had all the promise of dawn.

Gatherings and Gifts

The universe is a spiraling Big Band in a polka-dotted speakeasy, effusively generating new light every one-night stand.

—ISHMAEL REED, CITED IN JIM HASKINS, *THE COTTON CLUB*

The difference between a mechanical marriage, where partners move by rote from stage to stage, and a resilient, fulfilling marriage, is eight seconds. See for yourself. Take a deep breath and hold it, silently counting to eight before letting it out. This technique is commonly used to teach meditation to beginners. In these self-aware moments when we separate out from our automatic responses, music and purpose and intelligence are born. It is this same calm attention that brings real meaning and sustenance to the occasions when we mark the major passages of our lives, as well as to the smaller celebrations that we are capable of enjoying every day.

The Commitment of celebrating is a joyful acknowledgment that we belong to one another, that we are fulfilled in loving relationships, and that we are deeply connected to the universe. This meaning-drenched form of celebration, like breathing, has two parts. We "inhale," *gathering* in energy that restores us and heightens our pleasure, and we "exhale," *giving* back happiness to our beloved and to others.

The "breath of life" is a theme that runs through many traditions and religions. Creating breathing room (call it safety, consciousness, order, or peace) is a common goal of all sacred traditions, whatever the particularities of theory and practice. The breath of life restores to our lives peace, balance, and belonging. Inhaling and exhaling, we marry up our coming in and our going out, our age-old traditions and our new growth, our togetherness and separateness—our resting and going forth once again, renewed.

In the rhythmic give-and-take of this dance of the spirit, each step has its own aspect. The *gathering* phase of celebrating suggests that we revel, in both senses of the word—to savor the gifts of life and to share those delights in the festive company of others. In the outflow phase the *giving* of celebrating allows us to enjoyably press back the boundary of self-engrossment. We give pleasure to others, through gifts both little and big, taking the joy that we've created in our home and spreading it out everywhere around us.

As we learn to cherish and revere the best in ourselves and in each other, we naturally develop a mirroring gratitude for this high potential in the world outside our home. Celebrating, the Eighth Commitment, is about pausing to express that gratitude—and in so expressing it, magnifying it yet again. Finally, after all the hard work that you've been through together, it is time to *commit to enjoying your marriage.* It's time for sitting back, relaxing, taking in, and making sure to have fun. In the end that glint of love, as on a twirling disco ball, showers back down on us in festive light, calling us to grab our loved ones close and do a little more dancing of our own.

Gratitude

My heart is like a singing bird
Whose nest is in a watered shoot;
My heart is like an apple-tree
Whose bows are bent with thickest fruit.

—CHRISTINA ROSSETTI, "A BIRTHDAY"

My parents, both writers, would never let me get away with just any old letters. They always made me write thank-you notes from the heart. At the time I grumbled, but in retrospect I'm grateful that they taught me this simple yet powerful form of acknowledgment. As I sat thinking about what to say, I'd find myself really noting what I appreciated so much about the gift I'd received. Saying thanks in as earnest a way as I could was, in turn, a little gift back to the giver. Teachers who get a whole class to write thank-you notes from the heart are magnifying the good feelings of each student, and of the notes' recipients. The fact is, the expression of gratitude (however seemingly insignificant) is the first seed of generosity. Conscious appreciation is strangely akin to the desire to give.

Be sure to express gratitude for each other, to each other. That is the first and simplest way to give back. Write a card or e-mail, leave a little note, give a tiny gift as a token of your thanks for something in particular. See if you can indicate in some way how it is linked to your larger relationship. Before my husband thanks me for something I've done, he often prefaces it with "Have I told you lately how glad I am you're my wife?"

One woman I know gave her husband, Angel, a gift one morning for breakfast. "What's this?" he asked Rochelle as she plunked down a square box in front of him on the breakfast table.

"Open it up," she said, giggling. Angel removed the lid, and there, nested in tissue, was a new hand-painted egg cup with a perfect two-minute egg inside (Angel's favorite breakfast).

"I saw the egg cup on sale and knew it wanted to be yours," Rochelle said, smiling. "I figured you'd enjoy it more if it was full."

Once, when I was out with my husband for an anniversary dinner at an elegant restaurant, I looked over to see what food was being delivered to the couple at the next table. Incongruous as it seemed in the cosmopolitan atmosphere, they joined hands and sat in silent prayer before eating. Saying grace before a meal is a wonderful and basic form of thanksgiving, though it's rarely done in public these days. One needn't necessarily thank a stylized deity (i.e., "God") for one's food or use typically religious language to derive a spiritual gift by spending a moment in gratitude. It helps simply to be aware of the unseen benign forces, human and otherwise, that brought this meal to its place before us. One of my favorite mealtime reflections is this: "We are grateful for all the hands that brought this food to our table, for the earth that held it, the sun that warmed it, and the life force in it that moves through everyone and everything." Any meal, especially any formal meal, can be made more meaningful if begun with conscious moments of thanks.

In fact, *any* activity can be enhanced by beginning it in brief but thankful contemplation. You might breathe in deeply after fastening your seat belt and perhaps think about the many places having a car allows you to go. Or maybe hold a ripe tomato in your hand and take a moment to think about how good it will taste. Watch your child gladly walk, bulging school bag bouncing, to the end of the block where the bus stops. Be glad for the firemen who regularly save people at the risk of life and limb—and perhaps even stop by the local firehouse to tell them so.

It's possible to consciously nurture this sort of gratitude—for each other and for the many other gifts in your life. Start your day, for instance, by sitting in a certain spot, surveying the space, and thinking how grateful you are for your body, as you stretch the muscles on your legs, torso, arms, and neck. Think of how glad you are to have this comfortable space to sit in. And think of your partner and how this space was created out of mutual vision and care. Little by little, imagine larger and larger segments of your world, pausing to feel grateful that you are in it, experiencing it, alive! This simple stance can intensify your spiritual life. A single moment spent in deep appreciation is really a universal form of prayer.

Romance

What is love? 'Tis not hereafter;
Present mirth hath present laughter. . . .
In delay there lies no plenty;
Then come kiss me, sweet and twenty.

—WILLIAM SHAKESPEARE, *TWELFTH NIGHT*

Within the privacy of our love relationship, celebrating takes the form of savoring one another, laughing together, and finding new ways to please each other with each passing day. Giving our partner what we know he or she wants, or what we know would give great pleasure, is in fact a workable definition of romance in marriage.

Romance isn't necessarily silk sheets, rose petals in the bathtub, champagne and strawberries. There is also the unexpected big bouquet of peonies (her favorite) the night of her big promotion. There is meeting each other for burgers in the middle of a regular weekday. When his favorite sports team makes the playoffs, you surprise him with tickets to the game. Or you run out and get the new Paul Simon CD the day it comes out, because you know your spouse is a lifelong fan.

Any unexpected gift for any reason will heighten the romance you share. This includes gifts that don't cost a dime—a few sweet nothings, a back rub, an extra chore, a phone call. Perhaps my favorite everyday gift of all is when Hal offers me his hand to put in mine. Simply holding hands is, to my mind, one of the most romantic things in the world to do.

People who stay in love laugh together, often. Many couples have inside jokes or silly voices; others tease each other or get the giggles. They sing along loudly to sappy love songs or disarm one another's bad moods with a well-timed joke. They make sure to do things for fun—racing each other to the car; going dancing; playing backgammon, Frisbee, gin rummy, or even make-believe. They celebrate with humor, in little ways, every day.

It was clear the first time I saw them together that Nelly and Mike were in love. There wasn't anything dramatic about it—just an easy tendency they had to make the other laugh, an enthusiasm in their conversation with each other, a smile ready to break at any moment. Three years into marriage Mike told me, "We don't really seek out romance. It just seems to follow if you take the chances you get to be spontaneous and have fun." Once, on the way home from a Saturday-morning visit to Nelly's mother's home along Central Park in New York City, they decided to walk a bit in the park. They wandered for a long time under the autumn-colored trees, until they found themselves just across from a certain giant toy store. "Want to go in?" Nelly asked. "Not really," Mike said, speeding up. "I'll race you to the door!" They spent the rest of their romantic afternoon amid the sports equipment, giant teddy bears, and chemistry sets.

Of course, not everything in marriage can or should be hilarious good times, especially if your fun comes at your partner's expense. For Kitty and Rashid the first year of marriage was one big, long blast. But when they bought a house together, tensions began to build. Kitty, an oldest child who'd had responsibilities since she was tiny, wanted to go out partying all the time. Rashid, loving her spirit, compensated by taking all the grunt work on himself. Only when his tenacious cold turned into bronchitis did Kitty realize how her excesses were hurting the man she loved. After that, she changed her tune but kept the fun, rethinking the challenge of fixing up their new house as a game, like a giant crossword puzzle. Making sure they enjoyed themselves equally not only reduced tension but also brought them closer to the contentment of their earliest married days.

Romance and laughter are closely related. They make quite a nice pair in themselves—one stimulating the playfulness of our mind, the other stimulating the playfulness of our heart. Try having a candlelit dinner and following it up with a comedy-club show. Celebrate your anniversary by surprising your spouse with an "I Love You" party, and invite all your friends. Commemorate your achievements, your favorite activities, your knowledge of each other, and your lasting love. Make sure that revelry has a part in your personal lives.

Dancing in the Dark

A merry heart is a good medicine.

—PROVERBS 17:22, MASORETIC SCRIPTURES

While celebrating is the fruit of marriage at its happiest, we must not wait until everything is perfect to begin. The obvious reason for this is that marriage is never perfect—or, shall we say, it's always perfect, but in a very real, very human, flawed and complicated way. The truth is, the more trouble we're having, the more important it is to create the pleasures of celebration. For example, making a conscious effort to express gratitude or say appreciative things (even if it seems awkward at first) often helps start getting our marriage back on track. When we're hungry, food tastes especially good, and so it is with appreciation and with play. If loving words seldom get exchanged between us, how much more gratifying will a small bit of praise be—not only to hear but to give?

Problem solving in marriage is indeed more an art than a task. As often as not, the art of finding solutions runs on improvisation, do-overs and blindman's buff. So find moments for playfulness—however you imagine it, feel it, or wish it to be—when the chips are down. Sit back, relax your defenses, and just try to enjoy the moment. You just might find yourself closer to solving a problem than you ever got by worrying.

For those long-lasting healing projects in life, we must make sure to set festive road markers. To let out built-up steam or to mark your passage on the road to repair, you can simply treat yourself to a massage, a movie, or an outing with friends. Or you may consider something more extraordinary. Monifa's thirtieth-birthday party was a celebratory event that reflected the repair work of generations. Her husband played the sax while she read several poems by Langston Hughes. Blown-up photos of ancestors filled the walls, including one who had been a slave. "All African-American children celebrate twice on their birthday," she said in a little improvised speech just before the cake was served. "First, that they were born. And second, that they were born free."

Whatever form it takes, celebration is a natural, socially acceptable way to get out of the formal, drab garb of tough living and to kick up our heels and have fun. David and Ming-Fang say that in a way every day is Chinese New Year for them. They carry the colorful memories of this festival with them into the gray halls of their jobs, recalling the joy and rich tradition of their ancestors before them. The golden thread of festivity, braided up with the silver thread of fond remembrance, brightens the fabric of their lives.

Celebrating calls us to nurture faith, to cultivate optimism, and to play in the shadows as well as the light. Easter Sunday for the Wilsons was especially important in the years when both grandmothers required intensive family care. Easter became a time for them to refocus on values to which these two brave matriarchs had consistently borne witness over their long lives. And it reminded everyone to think of the triumph of renewal as something real. Celebrations like these can be a great source of sustenance. And they don't have to be solemn or dour to carry us through challenge and change.

When trouble hangs especially heavy, it's good to close the doors to the outside world for a short time, pull down the shades, turn off the television, and make a simple meal. Give thanks for what you have and find some small absurdity to laugh about in the midst of sorrow and pain. Then tenderly take in the precious presence of every person gathered around the table.

In hard times it is twice as necessary to celebrate together. When developments in the world outside our union become disturbing, it's critical to increase our efforts to make our married life full of warmth and ordinary miracles. At such times the togetherness of humanity takes on its most dignified, poignant expression: the spontaneous candlelight vigils in the park, the flowers piled up in memory of a beloved public figure, the crowds cheering on our bravest civil servants. If there is something the two of us can do to help, we should arrange to do it. Leaping into meaningful action provides a potent form of personal deliverance. There is no better way to celebrate humanity and our place in it than to extend helping hands.

Community

The sun brings forth the beginning; the moon holds it in darkness. As above, so below. For there is no greater magic in all the world than that of people joined together in love. —WICCAN BLESSING

For many years my husband and I have celebrated milestones and birthdays with the simple ritual of joining up with a few friends at our favorite restaurant. Sometime during the event the birthday person or honoree is asked to "check in" on dreams—dashed, fulfilled, deep underground, or pie in the sky. The chance to reflect on our lives amid caring listeners reminds us that our dreams are worthy to be heard out. Our friends give us feedback and reality testing, as well as support. We note together the old dark clouds that were lined with silver, the hardships we endured, the fact that we have prevailed so far and that surely the best is yet to come. Over the years the idea of "best" has changed in all our minds. Still, we all know, as we share the warmth of fellowship, that the best is right in front of us.

Community is as community does, and it happens anytime people actively and consistently care for one another. We as couples, just as surely as individuals, need circles of support to celebrate the power of caring, to keep us smiling when times are tight, and to share our triumph when all is well.

Carol and Olivier, two photographers who supplemented their incomes by developing a Web page that sells photography supplies, discovered and then nurtured a growing community of friends in the process. As they shared the trials and triumphs of Web-page work with other developers, they found many companions. In time they formed a chat circle of these online friends and made plans to meet up occasionally in different regions of the country.

Carol and Olivier were especially fond of Malcolm and Vita, a couple that cowrote a Web page on weaving and whose life experiences closely paralleled their own. When Carol and Olivier returned from giving birth to their first son (all ten pounds of him!), the joyful, exhausted new parents found a note taped to their front door from Malcolm and Vita, who lived a thousand miles away. Malcolm and Vita had rented a nearby motel room for a few days. Since Carol and Olivier's folks were too frail to help, Malcolm and Vita figured that the best gift they could give was their loving presence and willingness to pitch in with the dirty work. In the days to come, gifts poured in from other Web-page friends, including a couple of promissory notes to help update the couple's Web page.

Their *virtual* community of friends during this period actually provided more sustenance than most of their actual neighbors did.

After major events such as having children, our relationship as a couple in the world inevitably changes. Our life may become smaller, more private, as we nestle into our new routine. Or we may end up having *more* contact with others, as friends and family fall over each other to help us out. Obviously, in the strongest of marriages we find balance between community and privacy. One of the keys to Malcolm and Vita's welcome gift was that they had rented a motel room, so as not to infringe upon Carol and Olivier's privacy. Sensing the readiness or special needs of our friends is part of the art of real generosity.

If you ever feel crowded by the loved ones in your life, remind yourself that they're trying to help because they want the best for you. As soon as possible, it's important to tell them that while you appreciate their concern, you need some more space. Reminding yourself of their good intentions will make it easier to be compassionately truthful in the situation; not putting it off will prevent your anxiety from building beyond proportion.

Ironically, our community can actually serve as a support for our privacy, as Santo and Vivien discovered. Vivien's parents had recently retired and couldn't get enough of their two young grandchildren. Their delight made it hard for Santo and Vivien to turn them away, even when quiet time with the kids became rare and time for just the two of them was almost nonexistent. Finally Vivien broke down and asked her mother to help them find a way out.

"Darling," her mother replied without hesitation, "I'm so glad you told me—and nicely, too! I have the perfect idea: Go on a trip for a week, just the two of you. We'll watch the little pumpkins, and," she added with a wink, "you'll get that spice back in no time."

When Santo and Vivien got home from their romantic getaway to Vermont, they set up one "night of romance" every week that was to be exclusively theirs, while Grandma and Grandpa played with the kids all evening long. In addition, they set aside a time for the inner family, when Grandma and Grandpa knew to let Santo and Vivien have the kids to themselves.

We Gather Together

Now we must either learn to live together as brothers or we are all going to perish together as fools.
—MARTIN LUTHER KING, JR., SPEECH IN ST. LOUIS, 1964

The old English word for worship, *weorthscipe,* translates literally as "worth-ship"—a vessel to hold what is most worthy of praise. This poetically captures the spirit of an intense, symbolic form of celebration that aims to sustain a community by pointing it toward its most revered values. Such celebration provides a forum for a whole community to gather and express gratitude for what makes life and families and love possible. Effective worship experiences inspire all those participating to live up to their full potential while at the same time being free of overcontrolling strictures, scapegoating, shame, or idolatry (by this last term I mean the confusion of words and things with the larger realities they represent).

Worship, as I use it here, involves the high side of what contemporary religious institutions have to offer. In its most mature form worship always includes some sort of reaching out to repair the world. As such, worship can sow the seeds of both love and righteousness, reminding us that whole cultures (not just private lives) need transformation. The Reverend Martin Luther King, Jr., understood this well and used the powerful African-American worship practices to help create a joyous throng of committed social healers who would not let go of their shared dream.

You and your partner may want to seek out an institution that invites you to receive deeply and give generously, an organization that impresses upon you that you are connected not just to each other but also to a larger community of concern and delight. Of course, many people today have had poor experiences—or none at all—with formal religion and they feel uncomfortable in traditional churches, temples, mosques, or shrines. If this is the case for you, you may find the next section of particular help in developing resources for group celebration. But it is also worthwhile to visit the "old places" and to try to see them through new eyes.

My pastoring used to include involvement with the Ethical Society Children's Assembly. Every fall the children visited sister religious communities: They dipped fingers into holy water at the baptismal font at a local cathedral; they poured an offering of yogurt on a statue at a Hindu shrine; they sang gospel songs while swaying and clapping hands. These adventures became cherished memories and directly exemplified the vast variety of celebratory traditions available in any modern metropolitan area. (They also sparked thoughtful dialogue: "At exactly what second did this become holy water?" a nine-year-old budding scientist once asked me.) From pilgrimages like these adults as well as children can learn much about what works for them (and what doesn't). Then they can translate this new knowledge into effective celebratory habits of their own.

Homemade Holidays

*Piglet thought that they ought to have a Reason for going to see everybody,
like looking for Small or Organizing an Expotition, if Pooh could think of
something. Pooh Could. "We'll go because it's Thursday," he said, "and
we'll go to wish everybody a Very Happy Thursday. Come on, Piglet."*

—A. A. MILNE, QUOTED IN BENJAMIN HOFF'S *THE TAO OF POOH*

To add meaning and impact to our celebrating, we can ritualize our
thanksgiving, gift giving, volunteering, and gathering by *repeating*
these events. Homemade holidays can help us cycle joyously
through the seasons, while building in time for reflection, family
togetherness, and recommitment to our most central values. Someone once gave me this jocular definition of tradition: "Anything
done twice." Certainly by the third time through, any children involved will treat our improvised celebratory event as an "always" occurrence—as in "We *always* have the Brave Bears and Prickly Pears
Fest the weekend before school starts."

What kind of homemade holidays do you already celebrate?
What traditions does your family follow every time around? The
World's Greatest Stuffing on Thanksgiving? A badminton tourna-
ment each Memorial Day? A palm-weaving contest for the kids
every year on Palm Sunday? Some traditions are so subtle you
hardly realize they're there—a new dress every New Year's, watching
the Boston Marathon each year on television, even treating yourself
to a new book whenever you're feeling especially low. All of these
practices help you to make sense of things, to mark the time as it
goes by, to put your personal stamp on your experience, and to
share it with your loved ones.

We can start with this base of preexisting customs and deepen their impact by personalizing special days even further. We might celebrate, for example, our "Meeting Anniversary"—by throwing a party featuring elements of the day we met. Polly and Omar, who met as counselors at a camp for children with special needs, now volunteer every summer to run the Special Olympics Parents' Weekend at the camp. Their two teenage daughters go with them, too—and only the nuclear family knows about the added "Meeting Anniversary" meaning of the celebration. It is a time of great cheer that they prepare for all year, gathering fun prizes and new ideas for the opening parade and halftime antics. Not only is the festivity great fun, but it also nourishes and bonds the whole family, leading them out as well into an extended "family" of caregivers.

Like Polly and Omar, we can make up holidays that aren't normally celebrated. We can decide, say, to have a back-to-school blowout to offset the sadness of summer's end—or an "April Shower" in the spring, where everyone takes home a tulip. Or we could throw a half-birthday party, with half a cake and half-cut paper plates, for a friend whose real birthday in late December is always overshadowed. Make sure, too, that you have a full-fledged celebration in each of the four seasons. Everyone in your close family circle should have his or her own special moment sometime during the year.

Every first week in December for the feast of St. Lucia, the Jones family gathers on Cape Cod in a house built for a sea captain's daughter. One year I tagged along. With seashells and glue we crafted a skirt for an angel and trimmed a tree with little paper fish strung on threads. After dinner everyone gathered to sing carols from a songbook designed online by teens across three states. Nobody got gifts. Instead we chipped in to buy one present for charity. There were lots of candles, and everyone took one home as a memento.

One of the most common forms of personalized celebratory gatherings is the festive dinner. These meals can be done in honor of a person, a new season, an accomplishment, or any holiday, whether traditional or homemade. I recall one such dinner vividly— a Thanksgiving gathering with the added element of a twenty-year reaffirmation ceremony. It was a cooler fall than usual, and the sudden drop in temperature had caught the leaves in bright red and gold. Although I wasn't scheduled to do the ceremony until after dinner, Joan and Larry had invited Hal and me to come early. I watched Joan hang a clutch of dried corncobs on the front door and run inside to the welcoming warmth of the kitchen. She peered into the oven. The sweet potatoes were bubbling with tasty things you only dared use once a year if you valued your waistline. Joan appeared radiant as she stirred the peas and baby onions around and around with the slow persistence of a Buddhist monk turning the Wheel of Life.

This was the first time Joan and Larry were having folks over to their home for Thanksgiving. In other years they'd been at his relatives' houses, and one year they'd gone away on vacation all alone. Although they had eaten at a world-class restaurant that year, Joan told me the spirit of the holiday had been missing. Now Joan peeked out the window as a car pulled up in the driveway. The Weermantry family was joining them, and their two little boys in white pants and shirts were first up the flight of steps. Larry came down the steps and flung the door wide open to let in the stream of arriving guests. "Close the door!" Uncle Louie bellowed as the wind picked up.

"No, no, not yet." Joan countered. "I want to get a good look at those beautiful trees." Turning to me, she remarked, "It's funny, isn't it?"

"What's funny?" I asked.

"A house with an open door seems somehow more complete."

Love and togetherness underlie all celebratory gatherings, which may feature formal reflection, expressions of gratitude, a ritualistic "rebirth," a celebration of triumph, or the spirit of joyful play. Homemade holidays support couples, their close friends, and their kin by telling them to breathe in and out, to connect to each other and their loved ones, and to remind them of what is below the surface—and above the clouds. In such moments we come to know that whatever is out there is "in here" as well—in ourselves and in each other.

Four Qualities of Spiritual Gatherings

If we practice religion properly or genuinely, religion is not something outside but in our hearts. The essence of any religion is a good heart. Sometimes I call love and compassion a universal religion. This is my religion.

—DALAI LAMA, "SPIRITUALITY AND NATURE"

The most fulfilling celebratory gatherings feature four elements that are commonly included in traditional rituals. The spiritual benefits we receive from rituals can be greatly magnified when shared in community—whether that community is made up of Tibetan monks, close friends, fellow pilgrims, or country parishioners. At the very least, understanding the four common qualities of spiritual gatherings helps to add depth and meaning to a couple's experiences within existing faith communities. If we wish to create our own unique, personalized spiritual celebration—call it worship, group prayer, family time, a drum circle, or what we will—these four categories will help us to cover the (holy) ground most universally traversed in the practices of established traditions.

Succor: A place of sanctuary and renewal. Pat was a neighbor of mine who'd had children late in life with her younger husband, Manny. Until she was fifty-three Pat could always count on getting away to Ma's house for a brief respite from her hectic life. Pat would heave a big sigh of relief as she turned off the Long Island Expressway and pulled onto the north road, still dotted with farms and open fields. The bed at Ma's had been Pat's bed as a teenager, with a thick chenille cover and feather pillows. After sleeping as late as she wanted, Pat would be treated to a breakfast of oatmeal with brown sugar and raisins, freshly squeezed orange juice, and licorice tea.

Most of us don't have the extraordinary luxury of Ma in our lives (even Pat, in time, had to make do without Ma). We all need safe places to regress, to seek out nurturing for the spirit, and to be held. Pat found later in life that she enjoyed lighting candles in a local church and sitting in silent solidarity with other petitioners. Her husband, Manny, raised Catholic, joined her during these occasions, and this deepened their feeling of interconnection. Some churches keep their doors open all week for this purpose and welcome in wayfarers whatever their faith tradition.

As with centering, the First Commitment, an important by-product of sanctuary is renewal. A good ceremony will renew its participants, whether that "cleansing" goes by the name of clearing the mind, forgiveness of sins, repentance, or simply setting aside for a while the trials of the regular world. When we've had some time to escape to loving community, we return to the world refreshed in spirit. Even when we enter a sanctuary all alone, we are sharing the succor of that place with the countless others who have retreated there in the past, as well as with those who will turn to it in the future.

Reverence: An expansion of the spirit. The great twentieth-century thinker Alfred North Whitehead said that all education is at the heart "religious" and has the same purpose: to teach us attitudes of reverence and responsibility toward life. We can seek out communities dedicated to this concept of learning by taking workshops at religious institutions, by joining continuing-education organizations, or by going away on annual retreats. We might go to lectures on history, culture, or science and let them get us to ruminating long and hard on what an incredible world we're in.

Also, engage with others from time to time—or, even better, on a regular basis—in an activity that raises up your awareness of spirituality, of the "interrelatedness of all things." Every synagogue, church, mosque, Shinto temple, and sweat lodge inspires this kind of attitude the moment you enter. The rituals undergone there extend this feeling with music, incense, language, symbolic motions, sacred tokens, and scriptures. Among the many purposes of these practices, the inspiration of wonder and the appreciation of mystery are universally intended.

Whatever makes us aware that we are not alone, that love sustains us, and that life is worthy of respect is further reinforcement of the religious sentiment of reverence. We may prefer the Quakers' starkness or "smells and bells." But whatever it looks like, if we are designing our own celebratory ceremonies, reverence should in some way be a part of it.

Gratitude: A forum for expression of thankfulness. We need access to those people and groups who are in the habit of seeing the glass half full (this is especially true when we need a little uplifting). One minister I know has a poster that features a gigantic YES made up of an equal number of little yeses and noes. People like her, who show us how to emphasize the positive in the middle of mixed experience, should be especially cherished. They seem to live in a state of continual gratitude.

We've already seen the power of expressing appreciation in our home lives. When it comes to services and ceremonies, time spent in gratitude is also important. Vespers, songfests, award ceremonies, roasts and toasts are all occasions for gratitude. Every day I try to begin in thankfulness, finding some small thing to focus on, if only for a moment. There is a wonderful Apache song that expresses this gratitude, praising the sunbeams of a new day: "Dawn boys, with shimmering shoes of yellow." Take this full-hearted attitude with you into your spiritual gatherings.

Hope: An inspiring message that elicits positive expectation. Certainly we make sure we get regular meals. But feeding the human spirit intentionally and regularly is just as important. So many experiences touch us with life's promise: a magnificent sunset, the anthem at a ball game, a baby's sudden smile. But why leave such inspiration to occasional encounters or to chance?

The spirit of truly joyful events lingers on, continuing to reverberate in you and your partner and all those affected by the celebration's outcome. In the history of the Jews every fiftieth year was a jubilee year, commemorating their deliverance from Egypt and offering an opportunity to express generosity and to rest from sweat and toil. Catholic and African-American traditions in turn have their own meanings for the term "jubilee"—signifying, respectively, a time of special solemnity in which works of repentance are undertaken and a song about the future happiness of the people. Taking all these meanings into account, you can see that real jubilation will *both* inspire celebration *and* offer a chance for us to hope for a better future.

In a broad sense any celebratory event that renews us, inspires us, and reminds us there are others in the world is a jubilee. The extra punch is that not just our immediate needs but also our long-term needs get met. A jubilant gathering creates safe ways to let go of tensions and discouragement, while also allowing room for personal or social rejuvenation. A reading marathon to raise support for a struggling theater group. A jokefest at lunch between rounds of a work crew's labors. A basket left out in which Thanksgiving guests may deposit canned goods for the hungry. A birthday party where guests make a get-well collage out of the cards received and send it to a friend who was too sick to come. Such activities inspire authentic hope because they contribute not just to personal support but also to the common good.

Different communities have created their own regular activities for the purpose of restoring a sense of hopefulness to all participants. You yourself can benefit from studying how others have succeeded, by visiting various religious institutions and personal celebrations. See what resonates for you.

The Order of Ceremonies

I am the Way, and the Master who watches in silence; thy friend and thy shelter and thy abode of peace. I am the beginning and the middle and the end of all things: their seed of Eternity, their Treasure supreme.

—THE BHAGAVAD GITA

Because I've worked with couples from so many walks of life, I've thought long and hard about spiritual gatherings we design to mark our sacred time. Beyond the four common *qualities* of such occasions, there is also a common *progression* toward a common *goal*. The overall intention, it seems to me, is always the same: to turn a ragged bunch of individuals into an orderly community gathered to affirm an important purpose, such as the remembrance of a life well lived, the affirmation of abiding beliefs, the worship of the group's conception of God, or the celebration of a marriage.

I always begin a ceremony with the obvious: a declaration of the intention of the gathering. Like a bugle sounding, it is a wake-up call, an alert to all gathered that we are about to form a very special, intense, celebratory period in community. The goal of a ceremony can be made clear, too, through a title on printed programs: "A Celebration of . . ." (a virtue, a holiday, a life passage, or other milestone event). Invitations can also clarify and prepare friends and family, giving us the added opportunity for personalizing the tone and style of the gathering.

Opening activities should help participants experience themselves as part of the whole. In Jewish congregations this is done by solemnly parading the Torah before the entire community. To begin their Sunday gatherings Methodists sing a familiar hymn from a bound hymnal. Muslims prostrate themselves, chanting in unison at the opening call to prayer. Quakers begin with a shared silence charged with potent expectation.

Somewhere toward the middle of a ceremony, many groups include personal expressions (petitions or affirmations, for example), to bring warmth and intimacy to the gathering. Unitarians may invite congregants to come forward and place a flower in a large vase, saying something about their week before returning to their seats. Toward the climax of a ceremony there may be a brief presentation (such as a homily) by a group leader or inspired speaker. If there is no public speaker in your circle, a scriptural or inspirational reading can serve the same purpose.

At the end an affirmation of commitment is especially helpful for carrying regained hope back out into the world. At a baby-welcoming ceremony, for example, there may be vows to raise the child in love. Regularly repeated celebrations may include, instead, a poetic statement of purpose or a recitation of the major commitments on which a community is founded—a credo or creed, for example. Finally, a closing musical piece, a blessing of the community, or some kind of formalized farewell, sends people forth with energy and focus. Those who had entered separately leave together, united and inspired.

Darrell and Fiona designed an annual celebration using the four qualities of succor, reverence, gratitude, and hope, and following the general sequence of more typical ceremonies. All their grandparents had passed on by the time their kids were born. They wanted their children to have a way of keeping these treasured elders alive in the collective family memory. Out of this desire was born the Great Grand Picnic. Each June they went to the same park where Darrell and Fiona had both played with their grandparents when they were young. Sitting in a circle on a large blanket, they lit a candle in a hurricane lamp and placed it on a large flat stone. Darrell or Fiona would speak first, saying, "We've gathered here to witness and celebrate the love we carry for family members who are gone." They would say each one of the grandparents' names out loud, along with the dates they were born and died. Then it was time for stories, and over the years the children told the ones they had heard from their parents. The ceremony concluded with an affirmation to continue to remember all those commemorated and a vow to "carry their love like a flame in our hearts." Everyone was then invited to come around the candle and blow it out together. The rest of the day would be spent with old-fashioned games and refreshments, like burlap sack races and homemade lemonade.

Giving More, Getting More

Giving is the only flight in space permitted to human beings.
—ANAÏS NIN

There is a wonderful song that I learned at an Ethical Society Children's Assembly. This song, "The Magic Penny," begins, "Love is something if you give it away . . . you end up having more." Don't be afraid that by widening the circle of each other's arms to include others you will be depleting a scarce resource, for just the opposite is true. In the wider space that you've created, there will be more room for the feeling of plenty to seep in. Just as giving to one nourishes the other, so giving beyond yourselves nourishes your love life.

Acting in tandem to give to your community, you will simultaneously be nourishing your own union.

Deep contentment begins with the right attitude. So to make your celebrating truly enjoyable, adopt this simple assumption: *The more you give, the more you receive.* The life of the spirit is bountiful. When you have truly internalized this fact, a natural generosity follows almost directly and spreads. And as you and your partner express it, so will others express it, and it will become a living reality benefiting all. This is an everyday-sacred concept, as plain and available as the good soil of a kitchen garden and just as nourishing.

Giving begins by seizing these small opportunities at home and by creating moments of pleasure for those outside your household as well. During a time when Hal and I were going through a tough phase, my brother and his wife invited us over every weekend to watch rented movies. It was a gift of care on a hard sea. Looking back, I don't know how we could have gotten through without this small generosity of theirs. Giving doesn't have to be big or stretch you dangerously thin. Little things can make all the difference. The sanctuary of just a few hours can last a whole week, a month, a year.

Jeanne and Sanjay volunteer regularly for a program that collects unused food from restaurants and distributes it to those in need. They told me what had inspired their avocation: During the lean years they were running along the rainy streets of the city when a stooped, rumpled man suddenly jumped out of an alley. Before Jeanne could even scream, the man spoke: "Here. Found it in the junk pile, but works pretty good." It was a red umbrella. They never forgot this act of generosity from one himself in need.

I remember the uplifting effect of a simple phone call from a new acquaintance. I was feeling down about something that had recently gone wrong. This new friend's call, her earnest inquiries about how I was doing, and her calm listening were gifts greater than any store-bought item. They helped immeasurably to turn my head around and get me back on my feet.

We are the good strangers and angels in one another's lives. We never know when something that seems insignificant to us can have a profound effect on someone else. This means that we stand the chance of *real* helpfulness and generosity by the slightest acts of consideration. How easy it can be to start making a difference in the world!

There are lots of opportunities to offer help beyond the four walls of the place we call home. We can derive the same pleasure reaching out to strangers as we can helping our friends, family, and neighbors. You'll find rich opportunities to make a difference together through projects listed on bulletin boards, in neighborhood newspapers, and at community-service centers. You can tutor, paint murals, clean up a park, teach someone to read, or take at-risk children to a baseball game or to the circus or bowling. You can and should give money. But you should also engage in the especially gratifying hands-on work that allows you to see when you've made a real difference. These are the experiences that stick in your memory, warming your heart like a flowering in the chest.

The highs of celebration spill over from event to event, as each new thoughtful act triggers memories of other times you made a difference. Joel and Lena, a couple on a local service project in which my community participated, once threw a mitten party for kids on the ward where Lena worked. They had so much fun that they decided to do it annually, buying up dozens of different-colored mittens at end-of-winter sales in anticipation of the next year's fun. They save one pair each year, pin a date on it, and hang it with the growing collection—which they've dubbed "The Kissing Arch"—in their hallway. Just a glance at this evidence of their fulfilling little tradition is enough to bring a smile even on a gloomy day. This spillover effect is one of the special extra punches we can expect as we simultaneously give and get.

For people like you and me, giving is a way of *enacting* our connection to the world. Generosity says, "We are not alone." It speaks in the powerful language of deeds. However we enact it, the Commitment of celebrating reminds us and our partner that we are both continuously connected to life. Whenever we give to a neighbor, we are giving to ourselves. Whenever we give to our community, we are giving to ourselves. Whenever we affirm the voices of nature or culture, of endangered resources or suffering people, we are giving to ourselves. The spiritual life, and the marital fulfillment it inspires, is a celebration not only of our own well-being but also of the greater good.

A Luscious Cycle

And the end of all our exploring
Will be to arrive where we started.

—T. S. ELIOT, "LITTLE GIDDING," *FOUR QUARTETS*

A spiritually fulfilling life together is one in which we find joy in the journey. Because our learning never really ends, every exploration delivers fresh understandings about how to be better people and partners. Every moment is a new moment, another chance to be renewed.

In such a union, heartfelt commitments—not absolute convictions—provide the sturdy stuff of which a strong marriage is made. We can easily celebrate the Eight Commitments every day: creating holy ground in our home, making life-directing choices little and big, lifting ourselves up in deep respect, affirming our values despite conflict, keeping the faith. We can celebrate milestones on the road to recovery and rejoice in the daily things we receive. At last, we can, as a united front, embrace the world at large.

The next time you lean on your lover's chest, you might take a moment to listen, really listen, as Laura Larsen listened to her conch shell. Beneath the breathing in and out, the beating sound, is a deeper something, a holy silence, ripe with aspiration. It is yours.

Keys to Celebrating Your Spiritual Marriage

- Be actively open to joy in your partnership.
- Inhale, gathering in gratitude. Exhale, giving back in return.
- Spend a moment in thanks before eating, sleeping, or starting the day.
- Keep romance alive with laughter and play.
- Play in the shadows as well as the light.
- Connect to others by responding generously to their needs.
- Gather with others to affirm reverence for the source of your deepest values.
- Make holidays wholly yours.
- Get more by giving. Love accumulates fast when we give it away for free.

Celebrating Questions to Ask Yourself

1. Is your home set up so it is easy to have fun and fellowship?
2. Have you made a commitment to enjoy your marriage?
3. Do you celebrate in ways that feel comfortable for both of you?
4. Do you reinforce values that you both cherish through regular enjoyable activities?
5. When times are good, do you have a community or practice to replenish your reserves of faith for harder times in the future?
6. Do you reach out together to help repair the world?
7. Are you open to finding new and unique paths for celebrating your partnership?
8. Do you commemorate life's passages together in deep and meaningful ways?

The Party of Your Dreams: A Celebrating Exercise

Imagine that you and your partner have rented a summer bungalow. You decide to have a party, and since it is imaginary, anything goes.

Whom do you invite, living and dead? Make up a guest list. (Are there any invitees still around that you haven't seen in a while?) Is there an occasion you'd like to celebrate? The start of summer? Your son's great help with his new baby sister? The renewal of your vows? What can you do to make the place in which you are meeting warm and welcoming? Maybe candles in brown paper bags—with sand in the bottom—along the walkway? Is there a special concept you feel would be particularly festive? Green tulle, pearls, and martini glasses to celebrate the era in which your parents got married? What happens when everyone is assembled? Is there dancing or a sing-along, parlor games or beef stew? Have you asked people to give toasts from the heart? Imagine this as the most complete celebration you've ever had, and don't hold back.

It helps to write out your plans in a stream-of-consciousness style. If you're a detail person, you might even want to design an invitation, assemble any recipes or special drink instructions, or plan the order of ceremony. Finally, imagine the guests leaving and picture how they've been changed for the better by this event.

Afterward, if you wish, have a *real* celebration! It doesn't, of course, have to be as fantastical as your dreamed-up version. But you can include echoes and elements of it.

Alternatively—or additionally—bring elements of your dream festivities into your everyday life. For instance, you may be inclined to track down a long-lost friend or two who made their way to your guest list. Or simply tie a ribbon of green tulle around the handle of the vacuum cleaner as a reminder to whistle while you work.

Infuse everyday tasks with the spirit of your imagined party. Find a way to celebrate each day—with a bit of music, a cherished recipe, or any other hint of whimsy that strikes your fancy. Life is not just full of celebrations. It *is* a celebration, every single day.

Postlude

From joy all beings have come, by joy they all live, and unto joy they all return. —FROM THE HINDU TAITTIRIYA UPANISHAD

I stood with Laura Larsen on the balcony overlooking a ballroom. We were in a small jewel of a mansion abutting the rose garden where Josh and Maureen had just exchanged vows. Laura's hand on the rail trembled slightly, and I placed my own hand over hers, noticing the pulse there. Laura turned toward me and smiled with watery eyes. Then, in silence, we watched the unfolding dance below.

The sounds of the live band reverberated off the carved oak ceiling as couples and singles, children and adults pirouetted, jived, and whirled about. At a distance, with the two of us looking down like two unlikely goddesses upon this assortment of folks, all the random motions coalesced, taking on the appearance of an exploding supernova. Before us was the manifestation of many very particular dreams—for a better way to love . . . for a better world to love in.

Laura's brother Sherman, the civil rights activist who had marched with their grandfather in 1964, danced with his beloved Maya. The different colors of their arms were repeated in several couples coming to the center of the circle now: Sue Lin, whose family had survived a per-

ilous boat trip from Vietnam, danced with Chad from London. Miriam and Malik swayed while they held between them their baby daughter. In the center Ron and Ralph were doing the lindy. Gavin was dancing with his first wife, Charlotte, while his present wife, Lana, danced with Charlotte's new husband (the four of them had a date for dinner the next week). A circle of single women spun and twisted together while a dozen children raced about and others jumped in place for joy. A few brave ballroom dancers thrust themselves into a free space nearby. And later they were all going to dance the hora together.

You might say the dance floor I'm describing exists only in my mind. But if you did, you would be wrong. I've looked upon many such a scene, and each year the mixtures become more amazing. I'm glad for the gift of living through so much good change, even with all the uncertainties and new paradoxes that modern life brings. On this day, the last day I was to see the Larsen family all together, Erik's father, Laars, who had flown all the way from Oslo, came and joined Laura and me on the balcony. I told him how much I was enjoying the sight of the dancers. "Lucky for you," he said. "Cataracts," he added, pointing to both eyes. He was a man of few words.

As we looked down at the swiveling patterns far below, I wondered if the blurred and milky patterns Laars no doubt was seeing reminded him of the conch shell he had given to Erik back in Norway when he was a boy. And I wondered also if Laars knew the story of Josh's conch shell, which was prominently displayed on the wedding table.

Now, looking down, I saw that the crowd had formed a conga line, with Maureen at the front, Josh holding on to her waist, and Cindy the flower girl holding his. They snaked around the ballroom, picking up more and more people as they went. As the long curving line made its way around the hall, I closed my eyes, thinking on breaking waves, spi-

ral galaxies, on coils of genetic information full of promise as in the beginning.

I wondered about the great-great-grandchildren of this exuberant clan. How would they continue in the traditions of their ancestors, once our tomorrows became their yesterdays? I imagined stardust falling to earth, small pattering feet in sand, and the spiraling circle below me spinning back out into the wide world. When I opened my eyes, confetti was falling from the ceiling, courtesy of some giggling children in the upper balcony. The crowd roared, and the energy of their swirling bodies and loving lives rose up like a great song. I didn't know the words, and I didn't know the tune, but it had been playing for a long time—forever, perhaps—and it was beautiful.

Leaders. Thanks to all loving family and encouraging friends, especially Jimmie and Michael Ritchie, Mignon Rittenhouse, Horace Albro Woodmansee, Bill and Deborah Bly, Susan Rittenhouse, Samuel Neiman, Peter Schlachet, Dick and Bobbie Corson, Jeanne and Joel Arougheti, Rebecca Ryan, Liz Randolph Rappaport, Laura Fink, Diana Rubin, and David Kellerman.

Finally, boundless gratitude to Hal Kellerman and Mike Arougheti, spouses par excellence, for their input, endless patience, and undying support, and for so fully living out the commitments that this book is all about.

Acknowledgments

Heartfelt thanks are due to the many couples who by the witness of their lives created the substance for this book. Their identities and circumstances have been rigorously protected (indeed, it was for the purpose of preserving their privacy that the anecdotes in this book are fictionalized). Still, the true spirit of their experience, both inspiring and instructive, lives on in these pages.

Words cannot convey enough gratitude to Janet Goldstein, whose ingenious editing and energetic support helped immeasurably from start to finish. Thanks, too, to Susan Hans O'Connor for her commitment and enthusiasm and to all the Viking Penguin staff who work so diligently behind the scenes. A special and sustained thanks to the very dedicated Judith Ehrlich, as well as to her colleagues at Linda Chester and Associates, including Meredith Phelan, Joanna Pulcini, Laurie Fox, and of course Linda Chester herself. Thanks to movers and shakers Judith Eckerson, Jone Johnson Lewis, and Joy McConnell. And special gratitude is due to Pat and Chuck Debrovner for their loving sustenance. Grateful thanks to readers Jenny Mayer, Lisel Burns, Patrick Miller, and Curt Collier; to the lay leadership of the American Ethical Union, the Brooklyn Society for Ethical Culture, and the National Council of